D1458670

18-550-32

Students Without Teachers

Harold Taylor

STUDENTS WITHOUT TEACHERS

The Crisis in the University

McGraw-Hill Book Company

New York   Toronto   London   Sydney

Contents

v

"We are students without teachers. . . . We study, but we are not taught. . . . No one will admit that we are the real foundation of the university."

Homage to Ortega y Gasset from Spanish students, spoken at his graveside, February, 1956

Introduction

I intended writing this book ten years ago, but circumstances intervened. I wanted to show how the experience of the experimental colleges could be used for the radical reform of mass education and the big university, and to urge that education be given back to the students in order to liberate their minds and lives from the grip of educators. The ideas I meant to present were an amalgam of what I had learned as a young man teaching philosophy to undergraduates at the University of Wisconsin, and from working with the students and faculty at Sarah Lawrence College, where we had an open curriculum, with no system of required courses, lectures, examinations, grades, credits, formal departments, faculty hierarchy, or other educational impediments, and a student body whose members were thoroughly involved in making college policy and in running their own lives. There was an integrity of purpose in what the students were doing, whether they were dancers, writers, teachers, scientists, social reformers, or generalists. There was an immediacy of relation between their lives and their education. I believed there was a way of transposing into the big university the free and open environment in which they flourished, and I wanted to show how it could be done.

As the years went by, I put off the writing in favor of social action, and worked with educators and others here and abroad, and with students across the country who, I discovered, were beginning to do on their own many of the things the book would have advocated, and who had begun to take responsibility for their own

x   *Introduction*

education without waiting for others to show them how. By 1964,
the Berkeley students had acted out the local history of an incipient
national and international movement I had hoped to predict; by
1968, Columbia University was shut down by students at nearly
the same time as the Sorbonne, while student revolts were in
progress in Europe and elsewhere around the world. Reality had
overtaken my intention.

But with the new reality came a resting point, the end of an
era and the beginning of a new one, bringing together in one place
everything that needed to be written about. So much had been
said, so much had been done, so many fallacies and complacencies
exposed, so many issues had found a visibility to match their
urgency, that the subject of students and university reform had
entered the public domain with a kind of explosion which cleared
away all past assumptions and irrelevancies and left an open space
in which the students were now moving, talking, and acting. There
had been, after all, no need to introduce the subject earlier. It had
introduced itself. Since there is no greater force than reality to
communicate truth, no author could have so inadvertently acquired
a more formidable or helpful ally.

The reality beneath the appearance was simply this: the students
were without teachers to whom they could give their loyalty, respect, and trust; they had turned to each other for the intellectual
and moral leadership they failed to find in their elders. The universities were entangled in a crisis of their own making, the crisis of
neglect.

In the 1950s and the first half of the 1960s, it was almost impossible to convince those responsible for the control and advancement of higher education that in the flush of their economic, social,
and political triumphs, the universities were becoming educationally bankrupt. There were those who commented, some of them
continuously, with a flow of witticisms, on the dehumanization of
higher education, its loss of purpose, its links with the military,
with industry, business, corporate capitalism, and the American
white middle class, but without showing either passion or example,
for ideas and action to bring about change. The comment and
criticism were more often in a style of genteel cynicism, or of
latter-day Veblenism, with the Captains of Erudition replacing the
robber barons. We witnessed the irony of Clark Kerr's position as

author and educator in the fact that while he was writing so perceptively and acceptingly about the external conditions responsible for the present state of the universities and the neglect of students in them, the total set of conditions President Kerr described and for which he had provided no cure were conspiring to create a cure by the actions of neglected students on his own campus.

The failure in the 1950s and 1960s was not only that the universities and colleges busied themselves so thoroughly with the problems of money, power, research, public influence, expansion, and organization that they had no time for education or students. The failure lay in not recognizing the complex of factors which made the students the living energy through which the university could recreate itself, and that the major political, social, and cultural forces of the country revolved around their lives.

One of the tragedies of the McCarthy period of the 1950s, among a series of tragedies, was that the universities and their surrounding intellectual community were so out of touch with their role in defending and advancing the intellect against the control of political systems that they accepted an anticommunist ideology and a Cold War posture. In so doing they helped to sustain McCarthyism long past its possible breaking point, by agreeing with McCarthy that the test of a man, a scholar, or a citizen lay in his attitude to communism, not in his attitude to life. It was the university community and its affiliated intellectuals which so severely damaged one of the greatest creative minds in the twentieth century by what it did in just this way to Robert Oppenheimer. Here, in the clearest of manifestations, was an extraordinary man, a visionary scientist, in touch with the mysteries, secure in his faith in the power of the intellect and of man, faithful to his calling, of exquisite sensibility, capable of a range of imaginative thought beyond most others, aware in intricate detail of the character and quality of the age, a true citizen of the world of the mind. He was shot down in full flight by the artillery of the academy, by the use of its cruelly calibrated instruments of ideological warfare.

It was left to a handful of defenders, inside and outside the academy, and to the electronic journalists, led by Edward R. Murrow, to take the steps necessary to break the control of an unscrupulous politician and his aides over the political and intellectual health of a troubled society. The educators in that era had so little confidence in the institutions of the mind that they failed to create the conditions among themselves which could more promptly have destroyed the power of the enemies of intellect. They did not clearly recognize the face of the enemy. They had so little faith in the intelligence of students and their capacity to judge the qualities of teachers that they took it upon themselves to screen out of the faculty of the American university those who might, by political affiliation, not by private or public statement, influence the thinking of the American student body in a radical direction.

I had not realized until then how vulnerable was this society to its internal forces, how slender was the thread on which its political freedom hung, how crucial were the colleges and their students to the sustenance of freedom itself. I learned at Sarah Lawrence that a student body entrusted with responsibility for an equal share in reaching decisions about educational and political policy was the strongest antidote in existence against falsity and hypocrisy of all kinds, including that to be found among Communists, Democrats, Republicans, Socialists, faculty members, administrators, parents, or the human race in general. What students need is not protection, but freedom and responsibility, and the chance to show what they can do when they come to grips with the issues confronting their generation and ours. History accords its honors without regard to age, and alters its course in response to those who act within it. We could do history no greater honor than to recognize that fact and to realize that the younger generation must have equal opportunity to act in the world while they are learning about it.

In any case, the facts about the universities are now out in the open. It is not necessary to repeat again that the big universities have become huge bureaucracies with an academic mind and no heart, careless and ignorant about students and their intellectual needs, organized by managers and managerial professors absorbed in their own pursuits, giving service to the existing social order and dispensing its conventional wisdom, bereft of a philosophy and the social imagination to create a new and compelling conception of their own future. The literature of education and social criticism has dealt with that, events have affirmed it, the students have found their voice to proclaim it. What is now necessary is to seize the situation and to grapple with it.

The grappling is necessary because we do not have as much time as we used to, and it is clear that the forward motion and astonishing speed of a multiple social revolution already under way must find a direction through the instruments of education or go blindly into a future which has the dual characteristics of a mine field and an ambush. I am not arguing that only the universities can save us, that the students and their mentors are the saviors. I am arguing that unless the universities take the leadership in giving a sense of direction and of unity of purpose to the social order, we are unlikely to be saved.

For it has also been fully asserted and generally recognized that the universities are the central pivot around which a modern post-industrial society turns, the central resource for the development of all the talents, skills, technologies, plans, ideas, and forms of knowledge which can give content and motive force to the progress of a mass society. That means world society. What is less recognized is that the colleges and universities have within them a set of extraordinary resources for the transformation of human lives, and for the creation of new models of human community which can change the quality and character of life in that society.

It is in the colleges and universities and what they do in the community that the confrontations between nation-states, between blacks and whites, between man and man, can find new ways of mutual accommodation, new sources of talent and social intelligence for infusion into the culture at large. It is from the combined efforts of universities in the world community of scholars and scientists, with their students, that plans and educational programs for the peaceful resolution of world conflicts can be brought into the stream of political and social action. It is in the colleges and universities that the arts may flourish and the inventions and attitudes of the creative mind can find a central point of diffusion, where boys and girls, men and women of all ages and conditions can find their way to poetry and to all those forms of experience which open up the senses and liberate the intellect.

It is here that the nerve of moral intelligence may be touched, the sensitivity to political values induced, the opening up of persons to each other may be accomplished. It is from the university as its center that students may go into their society to teach what they are learning, and have learned, to others in the community who have not learned that much. It is to the university that the community may turn for help, while refreshing the store of academic knowledge there with facts and experience drawn from the reality of its own life.

The university can be the teacher of the world. Of all the institutions in society, it holds within its grasp the possibility of bringing a sense of humane purpose and international unity into a fragmented collection of separate units of power and interest. Its graduates run the mass media, tell us what we are doing, tell us our faults, correct our mistakes, confirm our errors, support our follies, run our society, and give us our teachers, our ministers, lawyers, artists, scientists, healers, political leaders, and democratic citizens. On the quality of their acts and the level of their humanity rests the character of our society and the quality of its purposes. On the quality of their education rests the possibility of our achievement. These are simply students who have graduated into the center of society, with or without the qualities essential to its welfare.

New York City
January, 1969

PART ONE

The University
and Its Students

1: Students and Society

Somewhere in the middle of the 1960s the students and American society together reached the end of an era. At a certain point it became clear that the texture and quality of the national life had altered within itself, and in such a way that the institutions designed to support it—the universities, the government, the economic structure, the social agencies, the political system itself—had become incapable of responding to the deepest needs of its citizens. Before that point it was possible for the old ways of life to continue while an American war went on and a social revolution gathered strength. America made continual proclamations and admonitions to herself as the bodies piled up and the violence grew. Reports were written, speeches were made, political leaders were murdered, analyses and literature of every kind told the story of a disintegrating society while the country entertained itself with filmed, televised, and written versions of the violence and social disorder it claimed to abhor.

Then something started to happen. The students and those whom they admired entered into a common perception of the size of the national failure and the enormity of possible disaster. The enemy was seen to be within: it was a moral complacency in the use of national power, a turning away from a reality which had lost its true meaning. It was then no longer possible simply to proclaim, to point, to denounce, to deplore, to stand slack-jawed while the evils multiplied. There had to be action of a large-minded and generous kind, and it began to be seen that if the field of action were not taken by those within the present institutions of a democratic society, the institutions could be swept away, or altered in such degree as to become unrecognizable in a democracy.

The content of that common perception came to national consciousness through the influence, insight, and social action centered in a younger generation which sought and found its own allies, and the center of that influence toward national self-understanding and national change has been and will continue to be in the student body of the American colleges and universities. The history of social change is a complex affair, and I do not mean in this to reduce the American change to a crusade of children. In every major social change within the succession of eras, it is possible to identify the locus of ideas and focal point of action without which the rest of the complex of factors would have remained inert, unable to coalesce.

In this case, the relation between the student movement and the historical process is not one of simple cause and effect. It has been an effort, hopeful in its outlook, by the members of the younger generation to join history before they were officially permitted to do so, to act in and on events by adopting a role in which individual acts took on a wider meaning. The opposition within the younger generation to a present war and the unjust treatment of the American underclasses gained strength from the moral legitimacy of opposition to all wars and all injustices. The young acted on a campus, in a city, on a street, but they belonged to a world movement whose character they came to recognize and with which they could identify.

Yet what force they had in the United States could not have been exerted without the surrounding conditions and energies of the black revolution and without the spread of mass education and the mass media in a society controlled by the institutions of the white middle class. That was where the students came from, and that was what made their political and social activism possible. They were freed from obedience to the norms of the system by their favored economic and social circumstance and by having been part of a society tolerant of its youth. As their number and variety increased within the universities and as the scope of their action broadened through the intensity of their concerns, they reached a point at which a critical mass was formed among the active minority.

I am not speaking here of the concept of "student power" as the term has been used by the students and their spokesmen in the mass media, but of the actual social power of students, as yet not wholly recognized within their own ranks and within the academic society. Students are formed into a separate class, supported by the society for its own good. In another sense the students are classless, transmission agents of whatever ideas and values they have adopted as their own from the sector of the society which produced them. They are protected inside the social system, and therefore have a greater possibility than others to be of independent and forceful mind if they care to, or if they are taught to exercise their minds independently and forcefully.

The protection comes from their parents, who want them to be educated, are willing to pay for it, and are proud of their accomplishments. It comes from the Federal government, which provides one in four of them with loans and scholarships and defers their military service, and from state governments, which subsidize their tuition. It comes from the colleges and universities themselves, who officers and teachers have as their occupational duty to nurture their growth in whatever ways seem appropriate. They are protected to a large extent, except in the Southern Negro colleges, from harassment by the police, unless they choose to move outside the university framework and take their chances in direct action against the university and the law-enforcement agencies. Even here, if they are white, they receive a degree of preferential treatment over the poor, the uneducated, and the black.

They also benefit from the over-all protection of a national attitude to college students which accepts their separateness and their value. I am a college student, the young say as they wait on tables, distinguishing themselves from the real world of waiters, identifying themselves as young people of a certain kind in a transitional stage to something else. By reason of their protected position, they have more privileges and therefore more power. Although they are held responsible for what they do and do not do, they have help in exercising their responsibility. Not having taken a full place in the society, their actions may be judged by reference to their present status. Everything is potential, nothing has been finished. They are inventing a new culture just by existing in it.

They are also continuing an old culture by accepting it. They form a mass of 30 million in the high schools and more than 6½ million in the colleges and universities; they are the clients of an educational system designed to develop them into Americans according to explicit and implicit values of American capitalist democracy. By the age of approximately twelve years they have been inducted into the American mass culture and taught to accept it loyally, complete with the idea of the superiority over any other of the American form of government, its economic system, its education, its national purpose. There are 10 million of the new young, between twenty-one and twenty-four years of age, 10 per cent of the electorate, who were eligible to vote in 1968 in their first presidential election; the percentage will increase in the 1970s as we reach a point at which more than half the population will be under the age of twenty-five. More than any other nation-state, with the possible exception of the Soviet Union, the United States has produced an educational system so intimately connected with the going values of the society and so powerful in its effects as a socializing instrument that it creates a nationalism strong enough to support the basic policies of whatever government is in power.

[ii]

That is to say, it has until recently. Among those who have been properly inducted into the mass culture, there has appeared a sufficient number of the young who are creating new forms, new attitudes, new conceptions of what it means to be American and what life in the United States can be, to make a difference in the mass attitude. To speak of a younger generation and to characterize it is to speak of those in it who go against the norms of their own generation and give the information to the society about what exists in the developing consciousness of the next phase of America.

The student movement of the 1960s, activist, politically conscious, sensitive to personal values, critical of the social lie, is a minority which expresses the hope of liberal democracy that if the society can be kept open to fresh political insight and new kinds of democratic political action, the new generation will furnish the social energy for the progressive reform of democratic institutions. If the response of the society is to repress those actions and to refuse the gifts of the new young, it faces a continuation and a deepening of the disintegration of national purpose and national unity which has been the characteristic of the United States in the 1960s.

In the interim, it is important to remember that the large majority of the students in the United States continue to be among its most tractable citizens and to furnish the major link between the colleges and the conventional American value system. The student radicals and militants are more publicly celebrated but few in numbers. One hundred thousand is a rough approximation of the number of activists in the 6½ million total of college and university students.[1] By radicals and militants are meant those who hold radical views about changes necessary in the American social and educational system and are willing to act on them, as well as a very small group among them, perhaps 15,000, who actively seek the overthrow of the present system of government and of the university as its educational instrument. Seymour Martin Lipset and others have documented the relative conservatism of the rest, most of whom stay out of political and social involvement of any kind, most of whom accept the idea of education as an instrument of social mobility and personal advancement.

On the other hand, among the approximately 750,000 college students who, in one degree or another, have demonstrated an interest in social change and political action, a main body of liberal and progressive students have supported the radical impulse of the minority in a variety of ways, from unconventional dress and forms of behavior to cultural invention and political action. They act as the major resource for individual and collective social action in the present and future.

For example, as the years have gone by since 1964, the National Student Association, organized from a base in the conventional student governments in nearly four hundred colleges and universities, has felt the influence of the more radical student movements in educational and social change, and in turn has influenced the American student body as a whole in a liberal and activist direction. The proven competence of the students in the Association to carry out educational projects on their own, involving more than

200,000 students working in tutorial programs for children in the slums, and the development of educational reform projects for the colleges, has meant recognition by the government, the private foundations, and the general public for the validity and maturity of the student movement in education. The student section of the National Education Association, traditionally the least activist and most adult-dominated organization in the American student body, has now begun to take its own initiatives and to organize its own ideas and programs for the education of teachers throughout its 1,000 branches and 110,000 members.

The rest of the students, those who are attending rather than influencing one or another of the 2,300 American colleges and universities, divide themselves into the largest section, from 60 to 70 per cent, who have simply gone on to college after graduation from high school and who take what is given to them, as do the members of another large group within them who attend the community colleges with the explicit intention of learning an employable skill. The professional and academically inclined students are among the remaining 30 to 40 per cent, and see a clear line of professional development ahead of them, while the lost and undiscovered ones attach themselves to colleges for a year or so without knowing what lies around them or ahead of them.[2] In all of these cases, what is needed is not more pressure to push them at a faster pace and a higher level through the academic curriculum, but a new curriculum in a college environment which increases their capacity to respond to ideas and to learn how and what to learn. They need a life-space to move around in, a place where they are welcomed and cherished, where they can move toward the realization of purposes as yet undiscovered or only dimly perceived.

[III]

There are many ways of teaching students and many ways in which they are now taught. The most common way is to take them as they are and leave them that way. That is, to take them as intellectually unmotivated products of a socially oriented high school environment, give them more of the kind of education which left them unmotivated there, and then categorize them as one-dimen-

sional students who do not know enough about education to have
a part in making it. There is a huge circular effect at work in the
system, by which the boy or girl who is going to be a teacher,
and thus be in a position to break the cycle of intellectual and
political apathy, is taught to accept the competitive academic and
social system through twelve years of schooling, then given another four years of the same kind of thing in college, a little practice in teaching at the same kind of school the student attended
for twelve years, and is fed back into the machine at the age of
twenty-two to keep it going as before.

Yet nearly all these young aspirants are perfectly willing to do
what is asked of them. They are a young generation of good will.
If they were asked to do important things, they would try to do
them. They show a kind of trust that what is being done in their
present education is proper and right, and that the goals their
society has given them are good ones—achievement, success, popularity, a start in the society by which they can compete with
others to improve their position in it—without knowing why and
without doubts about the system. If they are captured by the
football–basketball–hot-dog–television culture and they find their
deepest satisfaction in the continuing festival of youth and its
weekly spectacles, that is because they have been taught to accept
what they have and not go beyond it. Edgar Friedenberg and
others have documented the process in education by which that is
done.

The tacit acceptance of the educational and social system as a
beneficent and profitable instrument for personal advancement is
especially characteristic of the first-generation college students,
now the source of the largest expansion of the college-going population, whose parents had little formal education themselves and
who believe in it for their children. These students are usually
looked upon by the educators as the ones with the least amount of
talent for liberal education and serious intellectual effort. They
have, most of them, a strong vocational interest and do not think
of the community college or the state college or the university as
an institution of the liberal arts, but as a place where you can
learn a skill which will be employable. That is the way most of
them look at the teacher-education programs in the state colleges
and universities.

But again, they could hardly be expected not to, since that is the way they are taught. They are simply being asked to do the wrong things; and what could be, and in some colleges is, a college education which stirs new currents of thinking and feeling within their lives is corrupted into a mechanical system to assure certain kinds of automatic American behavior.

In a minority of institutions where entry is difficult and the atmosphere is congenial to the intellect, a high quality of teaching and the freedom to learn exist together. In most of the rest, which have taken their educational ideas from the prestigious minority, there are occasional provisions for independent study, honors work, advanced placement, the encouragement of the academically gifted, and some talk about the importance of the individual. But it is assumed that the student must already have shown that he is gifted, and that whatever special ways there may be for better teaching and more educational freedom, they should be reserved for those who are already better student-scholars than the rest. This, in spite of the fact that one can become a better student in this sense without having deepened and strengthened one's personal character and sensibility, surely the most important educational aim of all. The student, talented or otherwise, needs above everything else to come to terms with himself and his talent, and the college must find ways of helping him to do so. Otherwise he develops a character which never becomes complete. Having been successful in the terms he has been taught to accept, he leaves himself in the condition in which he finds himself.

Leonard Woolf says something about this in describing his school and college years in England:

> ... The character which I invented to face the world with originated to a very large extent in fear, in mental, moral, or physical cowardice. It was the fear of ridicule or disapproval if one revealed one's real thoughts or feelings, and sometimes the fear of revealing one's fears, that prompted one to invent that kind of second-hand version of oneself which might provide for one's original self the safety of a permanent alibi. When I said that I was half-conscious of doing this, I did not mean that I did it deliberately; I did it instinctively, but being introspective, was half-conscious that a mask was forming over my face. . . .[3]

The effect of the present academic system is to teach the student to conceal his real self, or to leave it undiscovered, and, as Woolf says, to invent a second-hand version which can either serve as a permanent alibi or as a permanent instrument of social success. Or it can serve as a shield to protect the owner from the psychic danger of exposure of the real self to the world. To admit ignorance of an answer to the questions raised in the classroom, to question the question, to be spontaneous in the exposure of ignorance, to ask one's own honest questions, not to know what it is customary to do, not to have one's own place in the system of popularity, not to be able to perform the conventional academic tasks—these are personal defects to be covered over if possible, and to be overcome by learning the skills of evasion and social patter, and the skills of answering the educators' questions. In this way it is possible for young people to conceal the real self even from themselves.

The skills of evasion, or, to put it the other way around, the lack of a commitment to seek out the center of learning in oneself, are the easiest to learn and, under the present educational methods, the easiest to teach. This is especially true in the case of students whose experience in society and in education has been conditioned by the standard American high school with its emotional and social connections to the white middle-class community, and who are now moving into the colleges in such large numbers.

The major national problem, now that we have expanded higher education into a mass enterprise, is with these new entrants into the system. The academically talented and culturally well-to-do are already being provided for, and are ushered through a different system which produces the same kind of behavior at a higher level —that is, acceptance of the competitive, achievement-oriented values, and the role of education as a means of personal advancement through vocational and professional skills. The same kinds of reform are as necessary for the academically talented as for the "ordinary" student.

The reform must begin with a shift in educational attitude away from the static concept of judging students and the kind of education they should have by the particular set of scholastic achievements they can present at the moment of their entry into the system. The shift must be toward the deeper question of their full range of possibility and the plenitude of their hidden talents. The fact that nearly all of them will have to make a living and that they want to learn how should not be held against them. There is no intrinsic illiberalism in learning how to do something useful. Education becomes illiberal when it aims at the use of the self for commercial purposes and leaves the developing self and its spiritual possibilities untouched.

[IV]

The way to begin the reform of the culture through its educational institutions is therefore not simply to mount a defense against the frontal attacks now being made by students on the structure and the role of the big university, but to reform mass education in the community colleges, the state colleges, the former teachers colleges, the liberal arts colleges, and the urban universities. It is in these institutions that the main body of American students is being educated, and it is from these sources that the teachers, the graduate students, the scholars, the social activists, the scientists, the writers, the artists, the educated voters are coming in a steadily growing stream. That is where the members of the widest sector of educated America has its beginning, where the decisions of the young about what they are going to do with their lives are in the process of being made, where the connection between the mass society and its educated representatives is most direct. As of now, the tendency for all these schools and colleges has been to link their fortunes to those of the institutions ahead of them in the hierarchy, from high schools to the community colleges, from community colleges to the state colleges, and on to the universities and the postdoctoral research institutes, with the undergraduate colleges considered as farm clubs for the major league.

It has been proposed, for example, by President James Perkins of Cornell University, and by others, that the farm-club concept be made into official national university policy, since to carry out the mission of the university—teaching, research, and public service—the simplest and best thing to do is to recognize the fact that to achieve all three successfully the universities should have their own kind of undergraduate colleges to do what they want done. What they want done is to get the students ready for their professors to teach them the things the professors know, just as soon as possible, without the intervention of liberal education.

That can be done elsewhere, preferably in the high school, or "by a special program that includes liberal along with professional studies—or a combination of both. . . . Those who need the sense of security which comes from being a member of a smaller, tighter community should not come to the university. For when they do, they keep looking for a kind of faculty-student relationship that can best be found in an independent liberal arts college, a fruitless search that adds to the problem of internal cohesion in the university." Although this might cut down the numbers of undergraduates coming to the university, it would be good for the university, says Mr. Perkins, because it would "tend to bring teaching and research together and so help make our university communities coherent again." [4]

It would certainly do that, at the expense of destroying another kind of coherence—the coherence between the quality of a man's life and the quality of his professional skill. Everything is sacrificed to internal coherence, or, more accurately, to administrative efficiency.

The undergraduate colleges are the last best place we have in America for letting the young mind and spirit roam free, and as the years have gone by since the beginning of the century, it has been the first place to which the universities have turned to capture young minds for professional use. It would be honest in this case for the universities, in view of the actual role they are playing in the culture, to organize the undergraduate colleges directly and quite specifically to do better what so many of them are doing badly, that is, preparing students for doing academic research.

I say honest, in the sense that it would do directly what is now being done indirectly, just as the "channelling" philosophy of selective service has taken a social instrument designed for one purpose, to procure men for the military, and has put it to use for another purpose. It has been made into an instrument for controlling the flow of manpower into occupations, roles, and professions whose social value has been decided, not by sensitive analysis of the social organism and its needs, but by bureaucrats, military men, social engineers, and politicians.

Liberal education has to do with the enquiry into human values and what man can know and do, not with preparation to enter a predetermined social role. The universities have taken charge and have organized the liberal arts curriculum into a huge testing program for academic aptitude, thus converting it into their own device for channelling.

But liberal education in its true sense is not an education which you get over with in order to go on to an adult preoccupation with professional academic studies. It is the source of the ideas and attitudes which infuse the professional studies with their meaning for society and mankind. It turns the doctor toward the healing arts in a spirit of humanity, the lawyer toward the protection of human rights, the architect toward the beauty and function of form in creating the human environment, the teacher toward his students, and defines the uses to which knowledge should be put. Unless these liberal values in education occupy the central place within the university in the lives of the undergraduates, and from there move into the stream of life in the full university community, what is left is something a good deal worse than what now exists—an institution for producing clever young professionals. It becomes a much more efficient instrument for creating the intellectual component of an élitist society in which the university heads the social hierarchy.

[v]

Another way of driving deeper into the culture the concept of channelling and of educational hierarchy is through the extension of the idea of the master plan for systems of higher education in the states. Obviously, plans have to be made, master or otherwise, if educational expansion is not to be chaotic and mindless. But when the plans are made on the basis of a hierarchy, with academic scores and percentile ranking determining student assignment to one kind of institution or another, each institution and its student body becomes educationally subservient to the policies of the institution above it in the hierarchy. Once more, all roads lead up to the university and its graduate schools, not outwards into the society. The result is that each institution is again compelled to emulate the educational patterns of the major university, no matter what the character and needs of its own student body.

Not only that, but the institution lower in the hierarchy is stripped of much of its capacity for creative thought and action in the invention of new kinds of education, since master plans demand a standard set of courses for all in order to make administratively efficient the movement of students from one part of the system to the next. The best student is defined not by intellectual or even cultural standards, but by standards laid down by the academic profession—the student is best who can best do the work of the academic profession and move upward in *its* hierarchies.

At this point we have invented the concept of the professional student, who, like the college athlete, is sought nationally by the universities and paid by scholarships and subsidy to perform his work and to act as an additional incentive to recruit and satisfy professors who want to teach only highly professional students. This means that the educational system as a whole is built for the best, that is, the most professionally qualified student with the greatest aptitude for academic work. The rest—the average, the ordinary, the slower ones, the culturally deprived, the intuitives, the artists, among others—are thrown into a system which works against them, and, in the long run, against the system. Against the system because, having been designed for the education of the best, with the best defined so narrowly, the system pays little attention to the fact that the ordinary student constitutes 95 to 98 per cent of the student body.

Under his label, the "ordinary" student conceals a wide variety of potential talents, interests, and personal qualities ready to be liberated by an education sensitive to his condition. What is true of the "ordinary" student is even truer of those who have not yet learned how to become even ordinary, but whose background and previous educational experience would be rich in possibility if the educational system were flexible enough to accommodate the possibilities instead of the existing reality.

Once a pattern of admission has been adopted which classifies the entrant as one in the top percentile—as some institutions boast, the top tested 5 per cent of all American students—the curriculum is automatically frozen into one designed for those with scholastic aptitudes, since that is assumed to be the character of the student body. This automatically eliminates most black students, along with the poor whites. But then too, in view of the variety in the quality of the schools from which the tested students come and the inherent ambiguity of test scores and percentile ranking, a curriculum designed for a student body assumed to be of high-level academic ability turns out to be ineffective for an entire section of students whose test scores belie their lack of intellectual interests and capability. The university can then point with pride to the fact that its undergraduate curriculum is so good that 40 to 50 per cent of the freshmen are eliminated after the first year. From this it could be argued that the best institution is one so good that very few could be admitted and no one at all could graduate.

The way to break the grip of the universities on the rest of the system is to think of the undergraduate college as the central core of the entire system, the breeding ground for intellectual and social talents of all kinds, and to build the colleges around the students, not around the interests of the university and the admissions policies of the graduate schools. Colleges must have a life of their own. So must the high schools, the elementary schools, the kindergartens, the nursery schools. They must not be presented with a life predetermined by educational rules made by the bureaucrats of education.

When students come from the schools and colleges where they have gained a robust set of personal talents, including the ability to develop their own interests and to make decisions about their lives, the universities and graduate schools will have to shift their attitudes and policies in order to accommodate them. That is part of what has already happened—a new kind of student with a freer mind has confronted the university with the necessity to change. That is what happened to the colleges and universities when 11 million new students came into the system following World War II, subsidized under the GI Bill, bringing with them interests and attitudes which changed the social content of the institutions of higher education while releasing a new body of talent into the society.

If the community colleges, the state colleges, and all the various forms of liberal arts colleges and universities take as their mission the liberation of student talent into the stream of society, not merely into the system of university education, the entire society will benefit. So will the universities. There will be an immense range of new kinds of talent available for further development, ranging from newly recruited members of the black community with skills in the arts, the sciences, and social organization, to the white poor and the undiscovered ones of all kinds whose image of themselves now prevents them even from considering the possibility of further education. In turning their attention to their own students and deliberately setting out to teach them how to live a vigorous and rewarding intellectual life, and how to use the knowledge they acquire in a contribution of some kind to their society, the colleges will return to their true mission.

2: A World Generation

From all the varieties of high school and college students of the United States in the 1960s have come the activists, the self-selected ones, who have found their own motivation and commitment for entering the field of social change and social controversy. Since 1958 they have steadily grown in number, combining forces with other members of their generation, black and white, in individual and collective intervention against social injustice, in situations of their own choosing—lunch-counter demonstrations in North Carolina, freedom rides in Alabama, voter-registration in Mississippi, freedom schools in Georgia, peace rallies in Washington, tutoring in the slums, protests in Berkeley, civil disobedience in Chicago, draft-card burning in New York, teach-ins in Michigan, organizing in Newark, boycotts in Detroit.

These were the thrusts of new entrants into the field of social action. Behind the new entrants were the traditions, beliefs, and support of the older generation of parents, liberals, and democratic citizens who had set the stage and provided the theater of society, one large part of which was occupied by audiences in the university, with overflow audiences among the general public, serviced across the country by television and the mass media.

The members of the new generation then saw before their eyes the actions of their own members, young blacks beaten with clubs, shot with guns, assaulted with cattle-prods, chased by dogs, brutalized by police, and became the first generation to have the opportunity to gain a sense of national identity in pursuit of com-

18

mon goals. The students became the chosen instruments of social and educational change because the society had arranged itself to make this possible, and, by its own default, necessary. The war in Asia, if it were to be fought at all, had to be fought by young American men conscripted to kill Asian boys with whom they had no quarrel. It was therefore inevitable, in view of the actions of their government and the moral intelligence of the students, that a confrontation between government policies and student beliefs should rise to the level of national crisis, and that the anti-war students should gain the support of the older generation of liberals and moderates. Until the youth action raised the moral issue starkly, many of the older generation had not been involved in this kind of social or political controversy. As the students said, they were radicalized by the situation.

The individual acts of youth were then no longer isolated instances of local and personal impulse. The youth found that they were in a movement, whether or not they had consciously joined it, and that it was national and international in scope. The acts they committed—civil disobedience against the war, civil rights demonstrations, marches or the signing of petitions—made the students conscious of belonging to the stream of history, the history of the global village. Committing the acts themselves gave witness to their own belief and was the beginning of a new understanding on their part of what was happening in the world.

Before acting, they had to choose to act, and before choosing, they had to know why they were making the choice. The act of choosing set in motion a new kind of self-knowledge and self-education, partly because they had thrown in their lot with others more sophisticated than themselves about the situations in which they acted, but mainly because they had injected themselves into the world, and, having done so, unavoidably learned more about it. They had defined their beliefs by the action they had taken.

The simplest and most direct historical fact they learned was that there were specific reasons why we were at war and why the Negro and white poor were in the situation they were in, and that the two sets of reasons were in some way connected. The student activists learned to look at their country from the outside, and to see its problems in the same light as those of the world as a whole —racism, poverty, ideological conflict, the struggle between the haves and the have-nots. They saw a genuine world revolution in progress by the have-nots, with their country acting as a conservative counterrevolutionary force.

When their political education had gone this far, that is, far enough to provide a reinterpretation of the agreed-upon way for Americans to look at America, many of them went further and entered the radical movement. There they formed the core of radical action and radical thought which has affected the thinking of students of all kinds who had never been in the student activist movement, but who had been stirred into new thinking about the problem of America and world society by their awareness of the Negro revolution and by the effect of the draft on their daily lives. These students began to notice things they had never noticed before, and whether or not they became politically active, they accepted the general proposition that the American war policy had destroyed the integrity of the national purpose while alienating most of the world community.

[II]

There is therefore a necessary connection between the ideas and actions of the younger generation around the world and the ideas and actions of the American student protest movement. The most obvious, important, and available institution against which, and in which, to protest is the college and university, where the students have their own accredited place, and where the nerve center of the entire educational system of any country is located. The platform of radicalism in the world's younger generation is anti-war, anti-imperialist, anti-authoritarian, anti-institutional, and the foreign policy of the American government has provided fuel for the engines of revolt in the student movement here and abroad. In attacking America for acts against international peace and for failure to solve the internal problems of a mass democracy, the younger world generation is attacking the inadequacy of the political and social institutions of the older generation in every society. The anti-Americanism of American student radicals is not so much a denial of their country as the rejection of an America which now exists in favor of an America they want. Their country in their eyes and in the eyes of world youth has come to stand for the power of the haves to control the lives of the have-nots by military and economic force. Watts and Saigon are the same city. America in their eyes became a symbol of defeated hope.

It is harder to see that a kind of pro-Americanism is concealed within the revolt, and that the kind of society America *could* be is in many ways the kind now sought by American, Czech, Polish, Spanish, Italian, Japanese, French, and Soviet youth within their own borders. If we are the most powerful country in the world, and at the same time the most open, with a fresh and invigorating youth culture, and if we have in our possession the economic and social means to create a mass democracy responsible to the needs and rights of all citizens, then it follows that those of humanitarian sentiment and revolutionary commitment in other parts of the world and in other kinds of political systems look at the United States in anger and frustration for our having thrown away the leadership in thought and humanitarian action of which we are actually capable. We damage their cause by not pursuing our own.

It is as if the President of the United States were everybody's president, as if America were everybody's country, and the failures of the President and of America to use the extraordinary power of the organized American intellect in the service of all mankind were failures to be judged by a world electorate. One consequence is that a sense of identity has arisen, as yet without having found its means or mode of expression, between world youth and the student activists in the United States, who hold the respect of young activists in other countries, in part because of a shared anti-Americanism and anti-Johnsonism, in part because the American students have spoken and acted forcefully, and with some success, against the same ideologies and the same figures of authority which arouse the antagonisms of students in their own societies. A new set of allies of America has been developed within the world generation of youth on the basis of a common concept of anti-Americanism, anti-bureaucracy, and anti-authoritarianism.

But anti-Americanism is also a name for what any intelligent critic, American or otherwise, would condemn in the quality of life in the big post-industrial societies—the pollution of air and water, the destruction of natural resources, the ghettoizing of cities, the domination of human lives by technological devices, the poisoning of the channels of human discourse, the dehumanizing of persons, the collective callousness of anonymous crowds, government by mutual deterrence between citizens and leaders. Anti-Americanism then becomes a symbol for the attack on a kind of life which has developed in a certain kind of advanced society of which at this point the United States is the leading example. Like the situation of the airports, the dense traffic flow of problems induced by the advance of technology has become too great for the instruments of administrative control, and it is not possible by a series of continuing votes by pilots and passengers to decide in each case who will be the first to receive the benefits of the landing field.

In the search for priorities and solutions, the universities are the greatest hope and the greatest possibility for a new kind of national and international unity among peoples. The universities have the power to withhold or to give the things the controllers of society must have in order to stay in control. The universities can yield to those who want to buy them or they can decide whose aims of what kind they wish to support. The entire scientific community of the world could, if it wished, refuse to work on any projects which advance the cause of world weaponry. The social scientists could say that their own commitments to the cause of learning and human betterment make it impossible to work at tasks which do not further that goal. Scholars and scientists together could decide that the security and well-being of their society rested on the quality of teaching in the schools and universities, and that the fruits of their research belonged not only to themselves, to the buyers, and to the scholarly community, but should be used to nourish the intelligence and capability of students and, through them, the intelligence and capability of the human community at large.

Since the organized intellect is the source of power for constructing the future, and the universities are the locus of that power, the question then becomes: How can the university so constitute itself that its resources can be put to the fullest possible use in the service of mankind?

[III]

When the question is asked in these terms, it becomes clear that the nineteenth-century European model of the university as a privileged sanctuary for a separate class of intelligentsia and youth, over whom the scholars have intellectual and social control, has been rendered obsolete. A post-industrial revolution brewing since the nineteenth century has finally swept into the sanctuary. The representatives of revolution in Europe are not the workers, the peasants, the technological intellectuals and planners, the Communists, or the educators—these are the conservatives. The representatives of revolutionary social change are the students, who are the only members of the entire society who confront self-consciously in their daily lives both the philosophical and the practical issues of the constrictions the society imposes on all but the controlling élites. It is the students who have raised the fundamental social questions, not the faculty, not the older generation of European intellectuals.

The French students, more than any others in Europe, represent the modern sensibility of a world generation which not only rejects the politics of the old regimes and the banalities of official views of life, but presents a conception of revolution which is total. Their conception begins with a radical perception of revolution itself, one which calls for the subjective revaluation of all values. It goes on from there to the affirmation of new values alien to the old regime—the exercise of personal will, the politics of desire, spontaneity, depth in personal relations, participation, personal action, the importance of fantasy, imagination, art, expression. "Everything which is not strange is false," say the French student slogans. "Consider your desires the reality." "Forbid all forbidding."

That subjective revaluation is the meaning of the span of educational and social history running from the 1964 revolts in Berkeley to the almost simultaneous closing of Columbia University and the Sorbonne in 1968 in the midst of student revolts across Europe. As long ago as 1956, a thousand Spanish students of the University of Madrid made an eloquent statement of the situation of university youth in the world, when they went to the grave of Ortega y Gasset to pay tribute to his memory.

"It is the homage," said their spokesman, "of a university youth without a university, compelled to seek knowledge outside of classes, from books which are not textbooks, and in languages which are not Spanish. We are students without teachers. Every day we face the realization that we need someone to teach us as we should be taught. We study, but we are not taught. We feel that the university is not serving its purpose, and that many changes are needed. But no one tells us how to achieve this. No one will admit that we students are the real foundation of the university." [1]

The truth of what was said that day remains, although the tone of voice and the militancy of Spanish and European students has changed, as has the American. Their voices and those of others like them have been raised in Poland, in Czechoslovakia, in Italy, West Germany, England, Mexico, Indonesia, South Korea, Japan, India, Egypt, and they have been heard around the world. While the educators and political leaders went about their business of governing and controlling, protected from the reality of the ideas and feelings of youth by their position in the society and their support of its dominant values, an international community of world youth was forming itself deep within the collective unconscious of a new world culture.

Without communication among themselves, the world's students have formed the expression of a new age. In their separate societies, they have expressed in action what they shared in common without knowing it, and the place for their expression was the place where they were assembled in large numbers by those who hoped to induct them into the present society—in the universities.

Carlos P. Romulo put the case clearly in his address to the United Nations General Assembly at the twentieth-anniversary celebration of the Universal Declaration of Human Rights in December of 1968. General Romulo referred to the "clamor and agitation of disaffected youth everywhere" as having "dramatized the basic democratic right of dissent."

"By challenging the traditional values," said General Romulo, "it has compelled society and the State to accept, albeit with reluctance, the principle of the inevitable transformation of society. By invoking violence as a necessary tool or weapon in given situations, it seeks to speed up the pace of change through the adventurous spirit of innovation. The phenomenon of youth in rebellion is universal, respecting neither national nor ideological frontiers. Aggressive and defiant, fired by a raging discontent with things as they are, this young, brash, and impatient generation is our best ally in the effort to fulfill the great promise of the Universal Declaration of Human Rights. But we must try to discover the real sources of its discontent, for only then can society hope to harness its militant idealism to the goals of the common good. ...." [2]

Across the world, the ideas and feelings of youth have gathered around three focal points:

A refusal to accept any longer the social and intellectual control of those in the society who give them no part in making decisions about what that society should be.

A demand that the obsolete university curriculum, controlled by the academic faculty and made in the interests of the faculty, be subject to drastic reform.

An assertion that freedom to think, to speak, to act, to learn, to invest oneself in a new kind of life which opens up the future, is the right of youth and the central value which must animate social and political change.

The world's political leaders could echo President Johnson's remark to an aide in the midst of one of his own troubled episodes, "These are the best generation of young people we have ever had, and they are all against us." The reasons are clear. They have been stated and acted out by the youth themselves, who have simply made evident through their actions the existence of the underlying sociological and political fact of Western society—that the changes in post-industrial society have vastly outrun the capacity of its institutions to adapt to the changes. The university has acted both as symbol and point of reference for the static quality of institutional bureaucracy and the sterility of official culture. For the younger generation, the university also supplies the natural target for intellectual, social, and physical attack. An attack on the university is an attack on the values and structure of the society.

Daniel Cohn-Bendit, the twenty-three-year-old sociology student at the University of Nanterre who led the Paris revolution of 1968, is as startling a manifestation of the new power in youth to think, to act, and to lead in the spontaneous situation of an unplanned revolution as was Mario Savio in Berkeley in 1964. Both emerged into full power of action, with effects on a national scale, with the same unpremeditated suddenness and the same clarity of thought in stating the essential issues.

The student in the post-industrial world speaks not merely for students, but for the necessities of social change at precisely the points at which the changes are necessary. As Cohn-Bendit put it in conversation with Jean-Paul Sartre, the immediate question at Nanterre and the Sorbonne of student rights and student privileges in the life of the university was only the occasion on which the bigger questions were raised. "The defense of students' interests," said Cohn-Bendit, "is, in any case, very problematic. What are their so-called interests? The students don't constitute a class. The workers, the peasants form a social class and have objective interests. Their demands are clear and are addressed to the owner hierarchy—to the representatives of the bourgeoisie. But the students? Who are their 'oppressors,' if not the entire system . . . of French society today?" [3]

In the case of France, which in many ways is the case of the majority of the Western European countries where student revolts have occurred, the objective situation of the society made the student action almost inevitable. The post-industrial European generation has had the benefit of a very great increase in the availability of social, political, and cultural information and insight through the spread of serious writing in the mass magazines, through films, television, and journals. This generation has been released into the culture with higher expectations for itself and a relatively higher standard of living, making it possible for a sharp increase in the number of students with the ambition and the means to go to the university. The pressure on the museumlike system of French education thus came from every quarter. In sheer physical terms, it burst the space of the university lecture halls and exhausted the meager supply of faculty members. In emotional and intellectual terms, it applied the force of a modern sensibility among students and a vastly increased intensity of political intelligence to the banalities of the curriculum and the obsolete system of instruction and administration of the French university. The tensions among these forces were bound to produce the conditions for revolt.

But more than that, it had become clear to the French and European student that the intellectual interests which were intensely important to him—the issues in the social sciences and the humanities—could not find means of fulfillment in future employment after graduation from the university. Since the antagonism of the young radical toward the qualities of life in a technological society give him a built-in aversion to having anything to do with technical training or employment in the technologies, he therefore puts himself by his own interests and efforts into a situation of unemployment. In the United States, graduates with these interests return to posts in an expanding system of colleges and universities, in a situation not available to young Europeans.

[IV]

The arguments, built into the set of demands made by the French student groups at Nanterre after their committees had put them together in the early summer of 1968, were that there must be full financial support by the state for all students who wish to go to the universities, that the universities should give to students full opportunities and facilities for every kind of political action, that the university grounds should be inviolate from all outside interference by officials of the law or government, that there should be no qualifying standards for admission to the university, since this would exclude lower-income students, that there should be no allocation of students to any of the occupations or professions crucial to maintaining the society and its economy, and that the universities should be administered by the method of direct democracy, with general assemblies at which the faculty and students all voted together.

The appointment of Edgar Fauré as Minister of Education, the direct and open way in which Fauré admitted the faults of the French educational system and set to work to correct as many of them as seemed politically feasible at that point in the history of France, was an indication that the student activists had in fact rendered a great service to their country. The French would not have changed the educational system by one inch had the students not forced the issue through revolutionary action.

The French and the European universities now have a task new to them and of the utmost urgency—the education of their students in the terms raised at Nanterre. The questions in philosophy, the arts, literature, and society as raised by the students are the real questions of contemporary life and of world society. If a radical subjectivism is to be seen in the approach the students are taking to the consideration of all human values, this is the place where they are living intellectually. This is therefore the place that philosophy begins and the place where the university curriculum must take hold. Otherwise the curriculum and philosophy *are* irrelevant, not only to the interests and commitments of the students but to the role of philosophy in the world. If the philosophical issue for young intellectuals lies in the supremacy of will and desire in a new metaphysics, this is the place of intellectual confrontation by the university and its philosophers, educators, social scientists, and speculative psychologists.

But the practical questions are also philosophical questions having to do with the aims of life and education. When the students demand the removal of examinations, when the art students demand the removal of the *patron* system, which can and does restrict the flow of ideas from the artist into the aesthetic environment of the art school, these are practical matters which go to the heart of questions in social and educational philosophy. If evidence of this were needed, it can be seen in the outpouring of ideas and poetry in the wall slogans of the French students and in the poster art spawned by their revolution. The latent and actual talent of a generation of artists, intellectuals, and poets can find few outlets to the world in the existing economic and social structure, where poster art is commercialized, gallery and museum art is circumscribed by fashion and the control of entrepreneurs, poetry is a series of private communications among a few private persons. The arts of the younger generation, along with their philosophy and their politics, have broken out of their cultural prison and gone on the rampage.

There is here no need for examinations to establish the worth of ideas, aesthetic insight, and the quality of social thought. The university examination system on a world-scale is a form of political, social, and cultural control, not a test of intellectual competence. Strikes by students against the Japanese universities hit the Japanese educational system at its most vulnerable and authoritarian point. When looked at in broad perspective, the strikes can be seen to possess a legitimacy obscured by the physical action of the strikers themselves.

There is an absolute control in Japan over the whole society by an endless and impossible examination system from elementary school to the end of university and beyond it, reaching to the qualifications for appointments to government and business posts. The possibility of reforming that system by conventional means is remote, in view of the attitude of the Japanese government and its educational authorities. If, by the examination system, the life of the young in Japan is paralyzed, and failure to pass the intricate and in many ways socially and intellectually useless examinations results in the elimination of the Japanese boy or girl from any possibility of advance in the society, then, literally, the only path open to youth in changing the society is to strike against the examinations.

The attitude of government and educational officials, since the two are so intimately linked as to form a united front, in France, in Japan, and elsewhere, has been to deplore the violence of the strike actions and to mark them down as a movement toward the destruction of all intellectual and educational standards. But if the universities were true to their mission as centers of creative thought, they would already have stopped deploring and turned with a sense of urgency to study the question of examinations and their role in world society, and would have made some plans for the radical reform of the system. It is not enough to leave everything to tradition, to chance, or to the students.

For example, when the French student demands are analyzed, it becomes clear that while they call for a massive increase in financial support for an expanded university system and a much larger student body, they make no allowance for the fact that if the economy of France is to give that support, it will have to rely on its educational institutions to supply a generous amount of technological manpower. The economy will not run on the arguments of philosophy students or the indignation of poets, no matter how talented they all are. But it also becomes clear that the failure in social imagination lies in the university, not in the students. The failure consists in not having come to grips with the fact that the kind of education the university is giving to its students *is* irrelevant to their lives and to the social and economic needs of the country.

While the professors have been busy with metaphysical, literary, linguistic, and aesthetic problems of little consequence to the world as it exists, mumbling over their notes in the classrooms of the world, the social, economic, and political problems have been boiling up in the consciousness of students. These are the real problems, having to do with the reconstruction of world society. If the curriculum and the system of instruction do not deal with the actual social questions, the social questions will be raised by the students in other contexts, sometimes in the context of violence. The lines will be drawn according to ideological doctrines, not in the cooperative solution of practical and urgent problems.

Why would it not be possible to build an entire curriculum for the beginning year of social science and philosophy on the questions raised in the Nanterre demands? Those of us who have been active in pressing for the formation of world universities and for intellectual cooperation among the universities of the world have found that whenever international congresses are suggested or arranged, or plans for united world action are made, the idea of bringing students and the problems of the new generation into the discussion has been almost universally rejected. The universities prefer scholarly studies of the world's political and social systems, or the preparation of exhortations to the intellectual community.

What could come closer to the heart of the world's problems would be a series of cooperative action-research projects started by the universities on a world scale, similar to the projects developed by the oceanographers for the study of the future uses of the seas, or the development of arid lands. In this instance, they could be action-research studies of the world's educational system and its direct links to the social order, with students involved in the analysis of their own situation and in the development of plans to reconstruct the university on a world scale.

One of the most disheartening facts about the present mood of the United States Congress is that the possibilities of taking the initiative in doing exactly this have been destroyed by the refusal of the Congress to appropriate the funds for putting the International Education Act of 1966 into operation. The original and compelling idea at the center of that legislation is that each national system of education is part of a world system, and that at this stage in world history, the United States, alone among the present powers, has the money, the intellectual and economic resources, and the network of possible relationships in the world's intellectual community to set in motion the idea of a world educational system.

In the absence of government funds, there remain the resources of the American universities and the private foundations. These could be used, if American educators saw the American problem of student protest in world terms, to build into international programs already in effect, as well as into new programs which could be developed, a curriculum for the world community of students.[4]

[v]

If the French situation can be set down as an example of what has happened in Europe and elsewhere, it can also be used as a counterpart to the situation in the United States. The similarity lies in the fact that the underlying motive for student revolt is a deep antagonism to the social system and the values of a capitalist technological society, and that the university was both a natural target and symbolic organization representing the qualities of the society. The same factors of rapid expansion in numbers of students without adequate provision for teaching or reform of the curriculum, without access of students to decisions in educational policy, the same resentment of the interlocking of the universities with the political and economic system in a common front to sustain the social order, the same gap between the younger generation and the political leadership of the old regimes—all these are common to the American and European situation.

Where the situations differ is in the greater flexibility and openness of American society and its educational institutions. The American universities are much more concerned about their students, and they about it, than are their European and Third World counterparts. There is an internal organization of student life on the campuses of America, and American students already have many of the rights the European students are fighting for. We also have the powerful tradition of the land-grant university and the concept of "useful knowledge" to stem the inherent snobbery and class bias of the European and Third World institutions.

Although there is some of it, there is in the United States no great inclination by the students to assume that graduation from college entitles the student to think of himself as a member of a special class to whom the society owes a living and a kind of awed respect. The main tendency is in the direction of voluntary effort to correct social ills. One of the most troubling things about the present dissension and antagonisms developed by the American student rebellions is that the political aims and take-over tactics of the militant student movement are identified as the main thrust of all student reformers. They *are* in one sense. The militants are the front-runners, and what they do in most cases prepares the ground for the rest.

But there is a fundamental element of good will, readiness to trust, willingness to work things out which is characteristic of Americans at their best and of American students, once they are accepted in the fullness of their own sense of responsibility and are taken seriously as educational reformers. In many ways, the actions of the most militant students commit them to further actions, in the manner of athletes who must protect their lead. But in most of the American militants and most of the protestants, there is a better spirit than in the European activists, less dogma, less ideology, less rigidity, more sense of the humane.

These inherent qualities in American society, its students, and its educational system could be corrupted by infusions of hate once the issues are joined. The antagonisms of race, of personal gain, of group interest, of material benefit, of competition for public attention may begin to supplant the personal idealism which has brought so many young people into touch with the political issues. It is now the time of the universities to respond and to appreciate fully the positive use to be made of situations which seem so full of negatives, to take on responsibilities they have for so long evaded, to correct the defects exposed by student action.

When looked at from a large perspective, the struggles between students and the educational system symbolized by Berkeley, Columbia, the Sorbonne, to single out only three such symbols, are evidence of the last gasp of an obsolete system in which the universities are fighting a rear-guard action against the future of mass democracy. This too is the end of an era, and of the entire conception of the university as an enterprise run by the elders of the society to serve purposes of their own devising. It is the beginning of the end of the hand-me-down curriculum, the governess in residence, the mechanical production of manufactured intelligence.

It can now more readily be seen that all the knowledge in the world crammed into the greatest curriculum on earth will rest there, inert and unused, until quickened into life and projected into the future by the minds and energies of the students who come to it.

What we must now do is to invent educational forms which can raise the level of intensity with which students deal with ideas, a level at which it will then become natural for ideas to be fused into knowledge, knowledge into humane action, action into new forms of knowledge. In the crucible of dispute that intensity has been found by the students involved in it. It remains to find other means to keep the intensity without the necessity of a continuing crisis.

3: The Beginning of Revolt

It is not possible to create for students an educational environment out of which can come a sense of joy and the exhilaration of being caught up in the stream of intellectual history, unless the students have responsibility in their own terms for creating the conditions which give their environment its meaning. Otherwise their university is a place owned by others where they are allowed to stay for a while. In crisis situations, uprisings, and rebellions, the exhilaration lies partly in the sheer existence of an atmosphere of crisis, in which everything familiar has suddenly become new and strange. But above everything else, the exhilaration lies in the sudden release of feeling into actions of one's own, without the sanction of any authority, on behalf of a new community which has begun to create its own shape from the will and effort of all, and has begun to make a true community out of what was before a mere collection of persons.

That break with authority and the search for a new community has been long in the making. It has depended not only on the external conditions of American society through which the university came to represent to students the authority figure for the society as a whole, but on the connection in consciousness between earlier generations of students in the 1940s and 1950s and the present generation of activists. In the early 1950s I began to see among the students at Sarah Lawrence and among others across the country the stirring of a new consciousness and a degree of self-understanding which belied the labels assigned to that generation by journalists and commentators of an older generation which was out of touch with the private world of the young.

It was not that the young in those years were silent. It was simply that they were silent in public; they were talking with each other. The articulate minority among them, the predecessors and contemporaries of Holden Caulfield and Franny Glass, having seen McCarthyism at work, having taken note of the social lie and the destruction of the possibility of honest political discourse, withdrew politically from the older generation, escaping its controls by rejecting its communications. It was assumed that because the students were publicly quiet they were acquiescent. They were not. They simply did not care to speak publicly of what they knew. To those who were in touch with them and aware of their sensibility, it was clear that there was in the making a new generation of informed youth, nurtured by their own culture and the mass media, politically educated by the nuclear threat and the politics of McCarthyism, a generation which had begun to live its own private life. As one student then put it, "We are the generation of the third eye, the eye of self-consciousness. . . ."

They were the beginning of a new youth movement, not the silent generation. They were the first to become conscious of the gap between the generations and the size and nature of the world and its politics. They grew up in a world which mixed security and danger in so clever a way that at every step they were counselled by the older generation to rally to the security of their country in its defense of world society against the hegemony of the Communists, while within their own consciousness they knew that this kind of defense entailed the possible annihilation of the entire civilized world.

They were the first college generation of the "understood child," whose parents assumed that schools and colleges were places in which the young should be insulated from political and social controversy, and that the home was a shelter against psychic shock, a center of warmth, understanding, and togetherness, that relations between persons should be free of tensions, that children and parents must always understand each other. As a result, it was almost impossible for the child to rebel. He was understood, not repressed; he had only feather pillows to fight, and he grew up knowing how his parents should be treating him, even at times instructing them in their child-rearing practices. He knew that there was little his parents could do to assert an authority to which he was unwilling to give assent. He became emotionally independent of his parents and the older generation at an early age, and came to rely on himself and his friends for decisions, tastes, ideas, and styles of action. Since he had freed himself psychologically from reliance on authority, he was free to look with a cool eye at what was said and done by those who possessed it.

It was then in the mid-1950s that Jack Kerouac, Allen Ginsberg, Gregory Corso, John Holmes, Lawrence Ferlinghetti, Gary Snyder, and the others found a voice for the silent ones and an expression of a new generation's style of thought and sensibility. In their poetry, novels, and mode of life, they were the common man's J. D. Salinger. In another sense they were the successors to Thomas Wolfe and Walt Whitman. They broke with the culture and with the society, and demonstrated, publicly and privately, that there were other ways to live than those recommended by the older generation. As the forerunners of the hippy movement, they lived inside a society whose values they rejected, and, through their poetry and proclamations of rejection, gave strength and sanction to those younger than themselves who wanted to break out of the cultural prisons in which they had grown up.

These were among the necessary preconditions of the new forms of rebellion which are the mark of the present generation. The scorn of the generation of the 1950s for hypocrisy has become the social protest of the 1960s. The internal values have been externalized in action.

[II]

There were also political antecedents, not only in the union of white and black youth at the beginning of the 1960s in the civil rights movement, but in the form of spontaneous decisions for action made in the Eastern, Midwestern, and Western campuses by students who were unaware of each other when they made them. At Yale University in 1959 and 1960, students formed a new organization called Challenge, to carry out what they said was the necessity of bringing the issues of the outside world to the student community, since the campus had too long been isolated both from the issues and from the world. In that year at the University of California in Berkeley, the students had formed SLATE to bring together those who held political ideas contrary to the prevailing American mood, especially contrary to those of the Un-American Activities Committee. They made links with the issues in society on which they wished to act and around which they wished to build educational programs. At the University of Michigan, in those years, a branch of Challenge was established, and with the cooperation of the editor of the student newspaper, the *Daily Michigan,* a junior named Tom Hayden, a program of social action and educational reform was set in motion which reached to every part of the university's life.

In the spring of 1962, students at Swarthmore College organized an intercollegiate conference on disarmament, arms control, and American foreign policy to which 600 students and faculty members from 60 colleges came. Others at Northwestern University held a university symposium on "Personal Commitment in an Age of Anxiety." The Student Peace Union with the help of other organizations in that year mobilized a national student protest in Washington against the war in Vietnam to which 5,000 students came from everywhere in the country. The Northern Student Movement, a counterpart to the Student Nonviolent Coordinating Committee in the South, was organized to work on problems of discrimination in the cities of the North.

I knew at first hand what the students in these movements were doing, and recognized in them the educational allies of Sarah Lawrence students who already held the rights and responsibilities in educational policy and political action for which the students on other campuses were beginning to struggle. I had met some of the others at Sarah Lawrence, where the style of education and my own interests made it natural for the president to work more closely with the faculty and the students on educational questions than is usual at other institutions. There were formal and informal meetings with the student council, student committees, classes, student organizations, the editors of the student newspaper, individual students, and with visitors who were either friends of Sarah Lawrence students or others interested in the college's educational program as a possible model for reforms in their own. From the early 1950s on, there were intercollegiate conferences at Sarah Lawrence and elsewhere, on issues in education, politics, the arts, world affairs, and contemporary culture to which students from other colleges sent delegates, dance groups, theater groups, writers, and other representatives. Simply by staying still and listening I learned a great deal about what was happening in the universities, and what was happening in the younger generation.

It was not generally known at that time that a national network of students had already begun to assemble itself, not so much by formal organization as by personal friendships and common interests. Students thought nothing of getting a group of six into a car and driving for two days and nights to attend meetings they had heard about through a tattered piece of mimeographing or a note from a friend. An increase in energy could be seen in those years in the National Student Association, which began to collect members and ideas from the informal network of activists, student editors, and reformers previously out of touch with any national organization, some of whom in 1961 and 1962 were beginning to organize the Students for a Democratic Society and were preparing a manifesto for youth and America.

I had come to know Tom Hayden from his student days at the University of Michigan, and to admire his single-mindedness in dealing with the social and political issues which bothered other people, among them the liberal intellectuals, but which did not move them into action. Hayden had a quiet way of doing whatever was necessary to produce some action, and had endless patience with other people, not pushing them to agree with what he said, but persuading them by his own behavior that what he believed in and what he was doing was important and necessary. I have known few students who had as natural and easy a way of coming to grips with ideas and of putting them into effect, whether it was a matter of rearranging a dean's office to improve its operation or examining the operation of American foreign policy.

In 1961, Hayden and some of his friends prepared the draft of a policy statement to serve as a basis for discussion and action among a scattered group of activist students in the Midwest and around the country. They were loosely affiliated with a beginning organization whose name was an accurate description of what they intended to do, Students for a Democratic Society. After reading

Hayden's draft of the manifesto, and listening to the discussion of the issues it raised, at the first national meeting of the new organization in June of 1962 in Port Huron, Michigan, it became clear to me that the next phase in a national student movement toward political action had begun, even though the exact character of a program of action remained undecided and largely unpredictable. Whatever the outcome might be, it was also clear that it would depend entirely on the initiatives taken by students themselves, with little support from the older generation of radicals, trade unionists, liberals, or educators. It was up to the students to find their own political style and their own set of unifying principles.

The SDS manifesto, as I discussed it with the students (there were seldom more than forty or fifty of us together in Port Huron), did not seem to me to be an unusually radical document, but a clear and strong statement of the situation of American society— its racial, educational, social, economic, and moral failures and the assumptions on which they rested. It contained a description of the extent to which an interconnected system of government, business and industry, the military, and the universities controlled the social and political direction of the country, and called for a reconstructed society in which the individual had a chance to exert his right "to share in those social decisions determining the quality and direction of his life."

[III]

The manifesto was radical in another sense, and it was in this sense that it served as a rallying point for a new generation of activists to work together to achieve their aims. Its radicalism lay in three points. First, it rejected the ideology of anticommunism as a false and pernicious doctrine, false to the historical situation, and pernicious in its negative effects on the ideals both of liberal democracy and of democratic socialism. Second, it linked the universities to the economic and social system as instruments of their purposes. Third, it defined a role for students in the political system as a whole, raising them to a level of equality with all other concerned citizens whose lives were affected by national and international decisions over which they had no control. "Do not wish to be a student in contrast to being a man," said Hayden. "Do not study as a student, but as a man who is alive and who cares. . . ."

The rehearsal of the battle of the generations which has since developed into one kind of war was immediately begun. It took the form of a rejection, by the parent organization of SDS, of both the Port Huron document and the plan of organization of its proponents. Students for a Democratic Society was a continuation of the earlier Student League for Industrial Democracy. Its parent organization, the League for Industrial Democracy, had been founded more than forty years before as a coalition of intellectuals and the left wing of the Labor movement, a part of which at that time was located in the International Ladies Garment Workers' Union.

Within the board of directors of the parent group, of which Norman Thomas and I were members, there were enough persons whose memory of the internal battles against Communist infiltration of the organization was still fresh enough to produce a strong set of objections to the free and open way in which the students had dealt with the question of communism and of membership in SDS. The students, in rejecting anticommunism as an appropriate response to the doctrines and programs of communism, had enough confidence in their ideal of participatory democracy and decentralization of leadership to make no political conditions for membership in their organization. Anyone who wished to infiltrate would have to do his work by pressing his ideas upon the others, not by seizing control of the organization, since it had so little organization built into it that there was nothing much to seize.

In the debates and difficulties which ensued, involving at one point a decision by the board to dismiss the elected officers of the new organization, I was impressed not only by the intelligence and forcefulness with which these young men of twenty-two made arguments which were essentially my own, but by the fact that they showed more faith in the power of democracy and in what they could do with it in political action than did their elders in the parent organization. Two of the students, Tom Hayden and Paul Potter (the latter was responsible for organizing the Swarthmore Disarmament Conference), had already had the experience of working in the South on voter-registration and education projects, had been threatened, beaten, and jailed by white citizens, and knew what it meant to be a contemporary political activist, at least in the Southern part of the United States.

The position which Norman Thomas and I took, that the student group had a right to its own ideas and its own style of organization whether or not their elders agreed with it, finally prevailed, although two years later the students were completely on their own. That marked a turning point in American political history, the point at which a coalition of student movements had become possible and a radical student movement had been formed. It also marked the coming of age of the new generation, one which had formed its ideas and political programs as a direct result of its college education.

That is what is so often overlooked by those who condemn all radical students without looking either at their accomplishments or their intellectual character. Potter had learned his way to political clarity at Swarthmore. Hayden had learned about the politics, character, and commitments of the big university by studying at the University of Michigan and editing its student newspaper. His practical experience in social and educational reform came from there, and gave him the basis for the views he has since expressed about the university and society, just as his four years in the slums of Newark were the source of his knowledge of how the police and politics work in the American ghetto.

It is the absence of that first-hand experience of American society at work in the lives of the underclasses which prevents most American students and all but a fraction of the faculty and administration of the universities from understanding the nature of student radicalism or the problems to which it is addressing itself. Hayden's views, like those of so many of his fellow students and co-workers in the radical movement, have become more extreme as the years since 1960 have gone by, until they are prepared to accept the evidence provided by the Chicago police riot of August, 1968, that in given circumstances, violent response to violent attack is the only tactic available to those who oppose the policies and institutions of the American government.

In the case of present and future students concerned with political action, it is necessary to build on their strength and political courage, not work against it, to examine the nature of their intent, not assume what it does not say. If students want to change society, that is enormously to their credit. The society needs changing. If the older generation has no great plan, can summon up no great sources of energy and strength to match the size of the problems which haunt us all, why not grant at least the legitimacy of the beginning a new generation is trying to make?

If the colleges and universities are to act as educating communities rather than as public utilities without a point of view, they must come to terms with the contemporary world, and come to terms intellectually with the student left and the black-power movement, and not act as if both were populated entirely by opportunistic manipulators and strong-arm organizers. The universities and their trustees and faculty members will simply have to know more than they now know about both movements and work toward a more imaginative set of *educational* policies in dealing with them than has been in evidence so far. Within a very short time there will be thousands and thousands more black students in the colleges and universities than have ever been enrolled before, and they will not be the highly selected, middle-class blacks of previous years. They will be from the lower-income groups, and will hold social and political views closer to those of the black-power movement than to the conservative norms of the black middle class or to the norms of the academic faculty, the administrators, and the majority of the white students and their parents.

Each new generation of future freshmen, white and black, men and women, will contain a higher proportion of socially sensitive, activist, and articulate youth who in high school have already begun to follow in the steps of those recent high school graduates who have now become college activists. Already a new generation of activists has been bred in the suburban and urban high schools, and has begun to develop tactics and strategies in educational and social reform which parallel the actions of those immediately ahead of them in college. With the introduction of more ghetto youth into the stream of pre-college education, through Upward Bound and similar programs, public and private, it will not be long before the joint and separate efforts of black and white youth in high school and college will produce a much more radical point of view about the character and necessity of social change than any we have seen in the present generation.

If, in the meantime, the colleges and universities continue the present pace of their slow adaptation to the legitimate educational demands of the disadvantaged, black *and* white, they will find themselves outrun by events and changes over which they have no control. There are now forces within the mass democracy, below the level of public visibility in the past, which have begun to coalesce and to become highly visible through the instruments of the mass media. By the very act of organizing the black-power movement and using it to take political action for themselves, the members of the black community have created their own educational environment with its own intellectual and cultural style—a style of direct action and confrontation politics. Having been blocked from the regular educational system, and having found that large parts of that system are in any case irrelevant to their needs, the black activists have educated themselves through their life in the streets, through their rallies, demonstrations, speeches, churches, community groups, rent strikes, television watching, and the transistor radio.

The example of Malcolm X's life and what he has written about it, the life of Martin Luther King and his speeches and television appearances, the speeches of Stokely Carmichael, the actions of Eldridge Cleaver and the Black Panther Party, the manifestos and demands of the black student movement, the black comics, from Mabs Mobley to Flip Wilson and Dick Gregory—these are the teachers in an over-all educational environment in which black speakers at parents' meetings and protest rallies have replaced the role of white teachers and university professors. The classroom is the street. The curriculum is the whole culture; the arts of jazz, folk music, spirituals, church services inject themselves into life and replace the banality of art-appreciation classes in schools and colleges with live performances of public arts which are saturated with political, social, and spiritual meaning.

Direct action and political organization provide for the black community and its growing number of young activists the content of a new kind of social knowledge drawn from experience, and a new political style springing from the oral tradition of those who never learned to read. If you can remember what the preacher said, you don't need to read it; if you can remember what was done to you and your ancestors who have told you their stories, you can create your own literature by saying it, singing it, acting it while

others write it down. The others, both black and white, will put it
into their magazines and research reports, into their television and
radio programs, into their musical comedies, rock records, inter-
view programs, and films.

In this way, the black community has talked, acted, and organized around issues and demands rising from its own culture, creating its own intellectuals who start with a belief in themselves,
without the handicap of having been educated through the stereo-
types from the textbooks to explain the Negro to himself. Without
formal education, the black community is free to make its own demands in its own terms, and if it has not learned to follow white
rules of political and social behavior, it has learned instead how
to teach the whites about the blacks, and how to teach the educators what the black community wants from its schools and
colleges. The social science and humanities curriculum is thereby
being reformed, mainly because the black students, their parents,
and the black community have demanded the reform. They have
insisted on a reinterpretation of the historical past and contemporary history to take account of the reality of Afro-American culture. In doing so, the black activists and their surrounding constituency have become catalysts for educational and social change
while rallying to their cause a younger generation of whites who
see white society through their eyes and who find that they see
more clearly that way.

[IV]

It would be a great service to American education and to the
American public if educators would consider the current militancy
of whites and blacks among the students in the light of these causes
rather than their immediate effects. It would also be helpful to the
progressive reform of education if educators made distinctions
among the variety of persons and groups active in the student reform movement in general and SDS in particular. For every SDS
member there are hundreds of others outside it whose political and
educational interests have been aroused by the issues which SDS
has raised to public visibility. On many campuses, there would
be no political or social action by students if it were not for SDS,
and on many other campuses, Berkeley, for example, the main

thrust of activism is coming from groups which have nothing to do with SDS.

There are also some important distinctions to be made within the variety of groups which make up the SDS chapters. There are generation gaps here, as elsewhere; the generations in the radical movement at large are now about two years apart. There are also ideological gaps, between those closer to the anarchists and the Yippies and those of Progressive Labor Youth who follow the regular conservative Communist Party line, between the Maoists and the Castroites, most of whom missed the deep-going experience of the founders of SDS in the civil rights movement of the early 1960s and in the SDS community projects with the poor. A larger number of the new SDS generation is more likely to prefer a hard ideological anti-American posture, and to consider the university as an instrument of capitalist society which should be used either to change the society by revolutionary action or be destroyed in its present form.

In any case, students who are militant are, after all, students, in need of education, and they, as much as any others—moderate, conservative, or apathetic—should have the full advantage of intellectual and social challenge at a level that meets their seriousness without imitating their militancy. The younger radicals, as well as the others, need further education in their radicalism and in their methods of social change. They are often encapsulated in the emotional and intellectual environment of fellow students whose experience in political and social action is as limited as their own. They are seldom challenged by minds sympathetic to their activism and better informed than they about the issues which engage their attention.

That the new breed of militant blacks and whites among the students is difficult to educate and is often disruptive is not in question. Among other things, many of them are intolerant of all views contrary to their own, contemptuous of democratic process when it is applied to their place in the society or in the university. But until some better procedures than those presently in existence are made for students to take part in the decisions of university policy, whether in matters of curriculum, social action, or political freedom, it is impossible to arrange an educational program which can accommodate itself to their militancy while providing for their

education. The test of the worth of radical ideas, outside or inside
the university, lies ultimately in their power to generate change. If
university policy is made through a series of unilateral acts by the
faculty and administrative officers, or by boards of trustees and
regents, either as a way of placating militants or as a way of re-
pressing their efforts to effect change, the ideas themselves have
little chance to be considered on their merits. Instead, the entire
apparatus of education becomes a struggle for power between students who make non-negotiable demands backed by threats of
strikes and disruption, and a university which eventually finds itself
calling for the police.

[v]

All students who lay claim to the title of radical, either by their
acts or by their image of themselves, reap the benefit of a period
in left-wing politics when the prestige of the negative is at its height.
As in the case of measuring radicalism by the degree of one's anti-
Americanism, radical negativeness, not to say nihilism, is often
taken to be a sign of moral and intellectual superiority. Those who
start with a vision of America as a country so rotten that the only
thing to do with it is to tear it up or burn it down have a slight edge
over the rest, since it is possible to say such things in anger without
having a program to accomplish the recommended result. The difficult thing to do is to maintain the radical criticism and to work out
ways in which the problems can be overcome through collective
or individual action, and to find a vocabulary of radicalism which
preserves its own vigor while accepting its responsibility for action.

The effect of the prestige of the negative is to make many of the
young liberals feel that if they say a good word for programs of social
change under way, express the possibility of hope, or begin to work
inside the social system to improve the conditions they deplore,
they will be told by the radicals that they are either naive or that
they are selling out. Direct statements about the accomplishments
of the Eighty-eighth and Eighty-ninth Congress in social legislation, or about the accomplishments of the Peace Corps, or about
reforms in education that are already under way put those who
make them under a cloud. It is customary in many student activist
circles to denounce the Peace Corps as an arm of imperialism, in

spite of the fact that returned Peace Corps volunteers among the activists have their own experience to verify the fact that their service to other countries was designed to help those countries do whatever the country of invitation thought would be most helpful.

President Johnson has been a factor in establishing this mood by providing so personal an administration that to work for or against government policy or government programs gave the young the impression that they were working for or against Mr. Johnson himself. Most of the liberals and all of the radicals preferred to work against. They had something of the same attitude as North Vietnamese peasants who call the bombing planes over their country "Johnsons."

This is especially true now that the links between Mayor Daley of Chicago, Mr. Johnson, Hubert Humphrey, the Democratic Party, the old politics, and the use of repressive police action have all been made clear by the Democratic party convention of 1968. The younger generation could find reason to blame Mr. Johnson and Mr. Humphrey for the fact that their opportunity and those of their elders to elect a President with humane and enlightened views about foreign policy and the national purpose has been shattered, and that they are now asked to vote for and support candidates who in nearly every sense are out of touch with the needs and aspirations of liberal youth.

In the case of the student radical movement, Mr. Johnson, Mr. Humphrey, Mr. Nixon, and Governor Wallace in their role in the presidential elections represented so fully the materialism and ideology of the political system the radicals denounce, that they provided the students with exactly the symbols they needed to support their intellectual position. In some cases, this has encouraged student radicals to carry their argument so far that it defeats itself by becoming circular. You cannot reform this society because it has already become too decadent to be reformed. Therefore, do everything you can to break it up. But since the society is too highly organized and too powerful, both in the rewards it gives to those who support it and the punishments it can inflict on those who want to overthrow it, then all you can do is to wait for it to fall apart by itself, and in the meantime harass it in every way possible.

In the matter of the university, a similar circularity of argument occurs. Since the university is not a center for social change and merely supports the existing society, the university deserves to be destroyed; it can't be reformed because it is so integral a part of the society under attack. It follows that nothing will work, and that anyone who thinks it will is a middle-class fool.

The blunt truth is that for some student radicals, the revolution they support is one which, if successful, would install a centralized government allowing no "bourgeois" civil liberties and behaving very much like the governments of the Soviet Union and Communist China. But around the circular argument go the thoughts of those who deny the need for a program, and affirm the need for destruction.

The real questions for the revolutionary are two in number: If the system must be overthrown, how is it to be done? If by force, then the radicals should begin the conspiracy, buy arms, hide them, form a national network of secret training programs, avoid the FBI and the local police, and get ready for the *putsch*. If by non-violence, the movement should form coalitions with those who see life and politics as the radicals do, and begin the work of making a national movement. Political action will then have to take place on the basis of a commitment to replace the present system with one which can at least be described and which can capture the imagination of those who are to make up the movement.

In this situation, the universities have their own role to play. They are by definition committed to a philosophy of nonviolence and to the solution of educational and social questions by the use of reason, imagination, and sympathetic concern for human rights. Their role lies in the education of those who are on the attack, and in the use of creative intelligence to attack the problems, not the attackers. Unless by their actions they can convince their critics in the younger generation that the universities and colleges are as concerned as the critics to find solutions to the economic and social injustices which lie beneath the present incipient civil war, their only recourse is to the use of police force for maintaining their educational programs. In the long run, this means the continuation of violence and disruption on the campuses. It also means a continuing increase in the alienation of the blacks and the white militants from the purposes and programs of the educational institutions themselves.

It is therefore the obligation of the educators to find the ways in which the students, the militants, and the general public can learn to understand that the university must, by reason of its fundamental mission to mankind, take a constructive part in the solution of social and political questions. That means giving to students the responsibility for direct confrontation and experience with the issues now tearing the country apart, educating them to understand the issues and to work at their resolution, and bringing them into a position of responsibility for making decisions about how the university community of students and scholars can govern itself. Otherwise the students, radical or moderate, will constitute themselves as a permanent opposition movement to the university as a social institution.

4: Students and
Their Commitments

Those presently alarmed at the vehemence and militancy of American student action should be reminded that the history of American higher education is the history of students who came into it and transformed it by what they did there. The faculty came into the system because the students were there to be taught. College presidents and trustees were in it because the faculty had to be assembled to teach, and buildings, grounds, and equipment had to be bought, money had to be raised. The character of the curriculum and how it was planned depended partly on the available knowledge and its division into appropriate patterns, partly on the purpose for which the college had been started, but mainly on the purposes and character of the student body attracted to it.

In the nineteenth century, changes in education came about when it became impossible to continue with the old ways of teaching and with the old curriculum, because the older ways had lost their power to educate the people for whom they were intended. The educators therefore lost control of student lives. The purposes of the students were not linked to the content of the curriculum, no matter what the purposes of the college as stated by its authorities. The students either could not or would not learn what they were told to; they would not behave according to plan. They rioted, demonstrated, signed petitions, threw rocks and tomatoes, or simply put up with it and retaliated by not learning. Or even worse, they went elsewhere.

For it is also true that the history of American education is not so much the story of institutions as the story of a particular breed of men and women who started institutions for students, for a variety of motives, to do a variety of things. Sometimes it was simply a question of finding a job by starting up an educational business of one's own. At others, it was to teach a religious faith, to advance the cause of science, or industry, a vocation or a profession. Whatever the motive, the colleges could not have begun if there had not been a sufficient number of students who were attracted to the purposes of the institution as advertised, and the institutions could not have continued if the students found no purpose in staying there.

Another way of saying this is to point out that students act as instruments which register automatically the character and needs of their society, and act as the testing point for the relevance of one or another kind of education to the society. The change in the middle years of the nineteenth century from the classical curriculum to the introduction of the sciences and other subjects was not merely a sign that the curriculum had fallen behind the available knowledge of the nineteenth century, but that the curriculum had become irrelevant to what the students intended to do with their education. The students would not learn it because they could not use it.

If colleges continued to offer only those subjects sanctified by cultural habit and tradition, they would either lose their students or create a crisis in morale among the ones they already had. If colleges continued to demand particular standards of conduct in the students' personal, political, or social life in a society which was more open and free than the society inside the college or university, they inevitably found themselves confronted with direct challenges to their authority to establish and maintain controls. The changes came from the challenges.

In the structure of American higher education—the earlier academies which became colleges, the land-grant universities, the colleges for women, the Negro colleges, the Catholic and Protestant colleges, the community colleges, the teachers colleges—the forms and patterns and the curriculum itself have been shaped more by the constituencies which the institutions have attracted than by a philosophy of education to which the institutions and their adherents gave institutional and cultural expression. By constituencies

I mean not only the students. They are the center of an entire cluster of constituencies which revolve around them. These consist of their parents, the taxpayers, the legislators, the faculty, the administration, the employing agencies, the donors, the alumni, and, in a large sense, the public, which gives its tacit assent to a system in which public and private funds are encouraged to flow into the stream of education for the generations. The philosophy of education is formed by the demands of a democratic, pluralistic society, and by the tension between these demands and the response made to them by the educating community in the schools, colleges, and universities.

This is in fact the source of the enormous strength of the American system of higher education. It has kept the system in touch with its own society, again, through the necessity of dealing with the students who are its representatives. When education is planned from the top down, as it is in the European and English universities to which so many American university planners have given intellectual obeisance, it is bound to lose touch with the reality of the students' lives and what those lives contain, and is then unable to connect its own purposes with the needs of the students it teaches. The centralized system of European higher education and its colonial counterparts in Asia, Africa, and Latin America give expression to the political and cultural system of a class society, not to the life-needs of new sections of the society among the middle and underclasses.

[II]

Something of this attitude toward a centralized intellectual and cultural, and therefore political, authority has entered the American system. It has come through the rise to power of the universities as autonomous social institutions, whose autonomy is compromised by the very source of their strength, that is, the direct connection between them and the existing centers of power in government, industry, and the technological community. The academic profession with its administrative apparatus not only controls the sources of manpower for operating the society, it controls the curriculum and the institutions through which the manpower is developed, and dictates the terms in which education is conducted, with an influence spreading downward as far as the kindergarten and elementary schools.

That is how the universities lost touch with their students. In rising to their present degree of power, the academic profession and the universities were not carrying out a plan of centralization consciously developed by their members to gain control of the society and its educational system. They were simply carrying out the task society had assigned to them—to create and distribute the knowledge needed by the social organism to make it function. Their method of creating, assembling, and distributing the knowledge was to band themselves together inside the universities in groups of experts in each of the departments and divisions of knowledge, and to hand on what they knew by lectures, textbooks, works of scholarship and research. As far as students were concerned, the faculty assumed that they came to the university to receive knowledge from the experts, and that if they did not come for that, they had no business being there. Whatever might be the students' political, social, cultural, or personal interests or commitments, these were considered irrelevant to the primary reason for their attendance, which was to learn what was taught in the curriculum.

The reason the American universities, colleges, and schools have not had serious trouble with their students until the recent past lies in the fact that they have been class institutions, including the public universities and even the public schools, which have now been caught in the act of subverting the lives of an entire sector of the underclasses. While controlling the flow of entrants into the privileges of the society, the colleges and universities have benefited from the fact that until now the underclasses have submitted unwittingly to that control, without knowledge enough to understand the nature and possibilities of their own situation. The children and the families of the poor and the black, lacking the educational, political, or even psychological means to mount a revolt, have submitted in the past to the controls of a society whose educational system has screened out the have-nots in favor of the haves.

This is not because a band of class-conscious white racists have built a national system of education designed to hold down the underprivileged. There are sections of the country, more than is commonly recognized, where this is the case. If it were not for the law, there would be more. Other sections, mainly in the suburbs, develop their own educational enclaves which are in fact private schools to which tuition is paid and called local taxes, and have nothing to do with have-nots of any kind. But this is not the national intent nor is it claimed as national policy. In fact, the main struggle to achieve a democratic educational system is between the Federal government and those in the separate communities and states who oppose it.

The American educational system has gradually evolved over the years from the intentions of a democratic society whose members have not faced the consequences of their own intentions, and whose educators have seldom thought of the intimate connection between education and social change. The universities and schools have simply grown to their present size and power by adapting to the needs of those with a political and economic constituency, and as new constituencies have arisen and the numbers within them have increased to an overwhelming size, the older patterns of educational and social thought have persisted until blown out of their place by social or economic dynamite.

It was Horace Mann who went to the center of that problem. "Education, then," he said, in his classic American statement, "beyond all other devices of human origin, is the great equalizer of the condition of men—the balance-wheel of the social machinery. I do not here mean that it so elevates the moral nature as to make men disdain and abhor the oppression of their fellow-men. This idea pertains to another of its attributes. But I mean it gives each man the independence and the means, by which he can resist the selfishness of other men. It does better than to disarm the poor of their hostility towards the rich; it prevents being poor." [1]

[III]

There is now a very large population of college students; the 6½ million of them compose 40 per cent of all college-age American youth. Except for a half million, they are all middle- and upper-class whites, many of whose parents at one time were poor, and they have confirmed Horace Mann's prophecy. They have the independence and the means to resist the selfishness of other men;

a minority among them have created the conditions under which a humanitarian movement has been set in motion. The concerned students, whether radical, liberal, moderate, or conservative, are seeking commitments which can give direction to their lives and meaning to their education. I can recall Hannah Arendt in a flight of controlled eloquence before students at Northwestern University in 1962 saying what it was to be committed, and reaching very close to the center of the student sensibility. Miss Arendt read from Malraux, from *Man's Fate:*

> We who wanted to make the Revolution for the others, for the downtrodden, for the wretched ones, in order to liberate them and in order to help them—the first who are saved by this revolution made for the others are we ourselves.

Miss Arendt then went on to tell the students, "If we now say, What is the meaningfulness?, I would say that the moment you begin to act . . . you begin, you start a story. And the meaningfulness of which all these people speak [writers in the French resistance movement] is actually that all of a sudden their lives are filled with stories which they can tell, and they will be able to tell to their sons, and even to their grandsons. That the stories are the real results of actions, so to speak, the products of action, just as objects are the products of luck, is, I think, important for you to remember, because you can have such stories only if you refuse to forget. You will not be able to have meaningful lives if you cannot remember what you did and what was done to you. Only all of this together will finally end up in something like the meaning of your lives. Nobody is born with a meaning, so to speak, 'smack on the palm of his hand' and can say, 'This is the meaning of life.'. . . All action really demands interaction with many people, or we throw our act into a vat of relationships. By acting we already enter a group. . . ." [2] Miss Arendt was talking in 1962 to white middle-class students in a privileged institution where few had ever acted out of a sense of social commitment, and where few had ever heard the story of commitment as it was told by Miss Arendt, Norman Thomas, Saul Bellow, and the others whom the students had invited to address them. These students *wanted* to act, but didn't know how and didn't know what to act about. They were not radicals. The reason they had organized their symposium in the first place was precisely that there was nothing in their formal education which gave them clues to action or meaning in their lives.

In the case of the newest generation of students, they too seek to act, and they have hit upon those acts which can give them stories and a sense of identity with the poor, the wretched, the victimized. As they read Fanon, Che, Marcuse, and the others, they find justification for their acts in the important stories they can tell, not to their sons and grandsons but, in the short half-life of the present college radical, to themselves and to the freshmen and sophomores in the next class behind them.

It seems to me that the educators need to understand both the necessity of the young to act and the content of the action in each case—its exploratory quality. In testing themselves through action, the young are beginning to attach meaning to a commitment they wish to make. My concern is that the issues be made clear, that there be an understanding of the *reality* of the acts, in the sense in which Hannah Arendt's message to the students refers to that word. Educators must look at the issues in educational terms, and thus shift their attention away from the conventional counterinsurgent posture of the university to one more in keeping with the university's true function as the educator of society.

There is simply more to it than the overt behavior of the hard core of militant student activists, black or white. Once attention is drawn away from the immediate crisis of campus disruption, and away from the fact that there are those among the dissidents whose tactics one may decry and whose motives one may honestly suspect, it is clear that a mood of alarm and anger among the educators and the public does not exhaust the possible range of emotions one may feel about the movement as a whole.

The mistake is to think of the disruptive as the only one who counts, or that in the long run it is with the relentlessly anti-American student who says that he abhors his country and its institutions that we must all contend. It is possible that, in educational terms, little can be done with him at the moment he is in full cry. But the radical student movement has strength, idealism, and a growing social energy. It also has many close links with the informed moderates whose thinking moves in parallel channels. We are dealing here with a significant body of political and social thought which already starts to the left of the American center, and which has already pushed the center of gravity of the politics of youth to the left of where it stood before the student movement sprang into life. Some of the evidence is to be found in the new constituency which Senator Robert Kennedy was forming in response to the new coalition of the young, the black, and the disenchanted. Had he lived, it is clear that Senator Kennedy would have come to terms with the serious radicals within the student movement, just as he came to terms with those in the black community.

Other evidence comes from the work of the student movement on behalf of Senator McCarthy in New Hampshire and elsewhere, and those nonradicals who now announce themselves as having been abandoned by the political system after Senator Kennedy's life was taken. There is a very serious question to be faced by the country and its universities together in considering what is going to happen during the coming four years when the polarization of political thought and action between left and right becomes even more extreme by the disenfranchisement and disenchantment of so many of the young. Under certain circumstances, this could bring about such a gap between the generations and the races in each that it could lead to the kind of civil disobedience and civil disorder which is another name for civil war.

[IV]

Considered from this point of view, the universities and colleges can be seen to lack an entire sector of educational insight and educational resources. They have too few facilities for dealing with the commitments of those with radical views and the actions of students who hold them. There is no radical tradition within their academic communities, and very few people there who are capable of teaching radicals except by denying their premises and thereby denying out-of-hand their interpretations of history and contemporary politics. Because the colleges and universities have been operating a system of cultural and social paternalism, they have appointed to their faculties and administrative staff the experts in academic studies and administration whose talents and values are those of the academic profession and the managerial class. The conception of the objectivity of the academic mind conceals within itself a particular set of assumptions about the correctness of the premises on which one or another kind of objectivity rests. Objectivity in scholarship consists in the accommodation of one's conclusions to the immense variety of existing facts from which one draws the salient items. But only those innocent of the content of historiography would argue that the selection of fact does not depend on premises and hypotheses around which the facts select themselves. The result of the conception of objectivity most often found in the academic profession is that the conclusions expressed are conservative, and a confusion develops which identifies objectivity with conservatism.

That is to say, the radical tradition among intellectuals within the history of social thought has seldom been represented in the college and university at large, and on those rare occasions when a professor of radical political or social views has been appointed, it has usually been an appointment made inadvertently of a scholar whose deeper convictions were unknown at the time of appointment or one whose thinking became embarrassingly radical after he began his faculty career. As result, whatever intellectual excitement has arisen on the campuses over political and social issues has usually come from the students, whose political views before admission are not assessed with the same degree of care as are those of the faculty. At other times the political excitement comes from outsiders invited by the students, with the faculty serving as a solid gray background for the political lightning flashes.

Academic freedom itself has been defined in defensive terms— the protection of the scholar from the economic and social effects of his own beliefs, public statements, and political acts. Freedom of the academy is construed as the formulation of professional standards and safeguards to protect the scholar's professional position. But that concept does not go to the root of intellectual freedom itself. Freedom lies in the positive act to make man free, not merely in the protection of professors who deviate from established norms of belief and public expression.

The policy among educational administrators who make faculty appointments in the humanities and social sciences contrasts sharply with appointments made in the field of the natural sciences, where high prices and the lure of facilities for research await those who have distinguished themselves by coming to radical conclusions on basic questions in the physical and biological sciences. Although the rigor of method of the natural scientists in addressing them-selves to phenomena and theory is of a kind which can take more complete command of the complex of variables, scientific enquiry into the material and natural world is of essentially the same charac-ter as that into the social environment. The enquiry starts with existing premises, established and accredited by scientists, and moves to forms of reinterpretation by shifting the premises and rethinking the distribution of facts which support them.

A case in point might be drawn from the experience of the scientists and intellectuals of the socialist republics, where the premises for social thought are pre-established by the doctrine of dialectical materialism and its link with the theory and practice of a centralized government. Among other things, this means that an entire sector of social thought is eliminated from serious treatment among university professors in the socialist countries. Radical views in the arts and in social philosophy, disallowed in the academic community, find their public expression in the actual works of art or in the actual operation of the mechanisms of production and distribution of goods, or in the practical work of controlling the society, including its intellectuals and artists. The artists—film-makers, playwrights, poets, novelists, actors, painters—in touch with an aesthetic consciousness below the level of doctrine, create works which challenge the official view of life and society presented by the professionals of the university.

Through their work, the commitments and ideas of the artists and intellectuals reach the younger generation, and the problem for the socialist universities is identical with that of the government. The problem is to square what is taught in the universities with what the students already know, and at the same time to maintain a control over what is known without betraying the function of the university as the home of truth. The living experience of stu-dents, not only with the arts and literature but with each other and with their communities, informs them that their intellectual and political lives are being controlled to a degree which stifles their own forms of knowledge, which denies validity to what they know. Theirs is a form of knowledge and communication which does not depend on the academic culture; they are therefore in a position to criticize it and, if the occasion demands, to protest forcibly against it.

The solution, theoretically impossible in the socialist state, is to allow full play to the radical tradition, in this case the heresies of the Western post-industrial society, in the curriculum and student community of the universities. The socialist universities are now fighting their own rear-guard action against the advance of democratic socialism, handicapped by economic and social policies which are perceived as reactionary by their own younger generation. In the United States, although theoretically we have no such doctrinal handicap, in practice we do. What the socialist republics do by social doctrine, we do by conservative educational and social custom.

The difference is that the American university has become so involved in the operation of the social system itself that the ideas of a wider sector of the intellectual community are being carried directly into the campuses by students and by outside intellectuals whose views and social attitudes deviate sharply from the norms of the academic profession. Nor have the colleges and universities taken account of the fact that the tensions produced by this very confrontation have made radicals or, at the very least, concerned activists of many students who were formerly apolitical.

[v]

We are therefore seeing the effects in the universities of the presence of students with commitments to social action and social change, who bring their commitments with them to the campuses only to find an academic community which not only does not care to teach students, but does not share their commitments. Among the 23,000 young people who have returned from Peace Corps service abroad, and among the 10,000 who will be returning each year in the future are some of the most politically informed and intellectually able members of the present generation, whose social philosophy and political insight are developed more fully than most of those who stayed behind. Whether or not one wishes to call them radicals, the criticism by the volunteers of the society to which they have returned is of a radical nature; that is, it has to do with fundamental flaws within the entire American social structure and the present state of American democracy.

As they re-enter the system of education and the academic

culture, they and others like them find few persons there who match the degree of their interest in the world they have come to know; they find few who care to deal intellectually with the issues they wish to raise. Added to this, they find that the academic arrangements are so devoid of educational good sense that they must spend their time in a constant struggle with the inanities of the curricular requirements rather than engaging themselves in the kind of study and educational experience which would advance their intellectual growth.

They are joined by others whose political interests have been developed by service in VISTA, in volunteer tutoring, in the civil rights movement, in the anti-war organizations, in Head Start, in the volunteer social-action programs sponsored by the churches, and who come to the universities having been radicalized by their experience. They meet there an academic community which tells them that their insight and experience is irrelevant to the purposes for which the university curriculum has been established, and they look in vain for those who can match their interests and concerns with relevant educational programs.

These young people and others from the high schools are looking for ways of becoming educated which can continue a process of personal development which has already started. They are already fully motivated, and they wish to use their education as a means of becoming better equipped to act as agents of social change in whatever occupation or profession they may enter. To the half million of them in the colleges and universities, there will soon be added more, not to mention their allies among the non-students in the student communities, and the drop-outs from the colleges, many of whom will be back with stronger educational demands than they were able to make before dropping out.

The half million are the problem, along with the 6 million others who have very little concern for social or political issues, most of whom have not learned enough about their society to have a point of view about it. They all need a better education, as do the disruptives, who are expressing in overt action the feeling-tone of the others in the half million. If we do not wish to provide ourselves with the Latin American style of university that the university critics of the radical student movement keep warning us against, we must make the universities into communities where the young of all kinds, radicals included, can find the place they need in order to test their ideas in an intellectual environment which stimulates radical thought rather than blocking it.

A different kind of question would then be asked. What is the America the radical wants? How would it work? What are the merits of a system to replace the present one? What has to be done to install it? Is it worth installing? What is the place of the student in it? What kind of a university would best serve the new society?

Since they have not been able to find what they need in the present university, the student reformers are remaking it as best they can, often by ignoring the academic structure and organizing their own education by a combination of social action, self-education, research, and night-long discussions. But why should it be necessary for students to carry the main burden of an educational responsibility which rightfully belongs to those in the institutions of higher education who accept tuition money and public support for duties at variance with the true interests of students and the culture in which they live?

Michael Rossman of the 1964 Berkeley Free Speech Movement speaks for the main body of these American students when he says of the Berkeley affair, "We conducted a long struggle, assuming responsibilities we should not have been made to assume, heartbreakingly alone until the end, taking time out from our studies and our lives to do a job that should not have needed to be done. And we comported ourselves with dignity and grace, on the whole, unexpectedly so, and with good hearts, and trust and kindness for each other."

Since then, in the stress and conflict of the intransigence of so many students and university authorities in dealing with each other, some of the dignity and grace have been lost, the good hearts, trust, and kindness have many times been replaced by hard-boiled organizational tactics and ideological dispute. The genius of the earlier movements in civil rights and social action lay in the capacity of their student members to achieve an openness with each other, to become closer in personal terms because of their shared idealism, to develop the tactics and strategy of protest and reform through improvisation and spontaneous decisions reached in a spirit of mutual trust.

Theirs was an education in the emotions, a purification of motive down to the bone. The mystique of the anti-hero and the anti-leader had many levels, going from the refusal to consider oneself a hero by reason of risk of physical danger from the police and hostile citizens in the South, to an honest and unembarrassed acceptance of the idea of a community based on love between persons, and love as a political principle. White students working with black in the Mississippi summer of 1963 found themselves moving toward a philosophy which had no name and whose elements relied on no official spokesman in the history of philosophy but which grew from the experience of sharing a life of hardship and danger on behalf of an ideal.

There was no need in this formulation of belief for Marx or for Freud, Che or Marcuse. The contours of a new philosophy of nonviolence and social action formed themselves from the materials of experience, and the intellectual components merged with the emotional and social to form an aesthetic of pure action and pure feeling. This was not a split between intellect and emotion, but a fusion of the two. Personal values determined the content of a social philosophy which introduced deep psychic meaning into the idea of democracy. Without knowing it, or having decided it, the young had come to accept the classic definition of John Dewey, that "Any activity pursued on behalf of an ideal and against obstacles and in spite of threats to personal loss because of conviction of its general and enduring quality is religious in quality." [3]

Staughton Lynd has described the contrast between the formalities and futilities of theoretical discussions carried on by "full-time activists and full-time intellectuals" about the direction of political change, and the quality of intellectual experience available in practical situations like those of the Mississippi freedom schools of 1963 and 1964. Since then, activists and intellectuals have often been brought together "in the naive hope that the intellectuals could give [the activists] a magical something which they somehow lacked." Such meetings and conferences are very much like the daily situation of activist students in the classrooms of their universities.

In the freedom schools, says Lynd, "Northern white college stu-

dents and Southern black teen-agers had first to encounter one
another as whole human beings, to establish trust. This happened
in the process of finding a church basement together, deciding on
a curriculum together, improvising materials together, that is, in
a context of common work; and it matured in that context too, as
those who talked together in the morning registered voters together
in the afternoon. Please note that I am not advocating a narrow
pragmatism. What was read together in the mornings was often
James Joyce, what was talked about may have been French or al-
gebra as well as Negro history. But I must simply testify that the
context of shared experience (which meant, too, that teachers char-
acteristically boarded in their students' homes) made all the difference." [4]

Something of this feeling, in a variety of forms, came from the
shared experience of students in the Free Speech Movement in
Berkeley and elsewhere, and did not depend for its quality on the
necessity of having an enemy against whom to fight. It depended
on a need to join together with all others who held a view of what
life in a university could truly be if the teacher and the taught were
sympathetic allies in the cause of creating and sharing knowledge
which had meaning for both.

At that earlier stage in the psychological and aesthetic history of
the student movement, the tactics and strategy of opposition to
university policy emerged from situations which were constantly
creating their own successive stages. These then demanded immediate response through the extraordinarily complicated but simple
process of discussion and decision among student activists. The
spontaneity of response was the opposite of the studied tactics
developed within later modes of student action. These lack not
only the spontaneity but the gaiety and wit of the early Berkeley
style. To organize a march to the university administration at
Berkeley, with an American flag flying in the lead, of graduate
students who wanted their names put down by the dean for having
transgressed equally with undergraduates the rules against the dis-
semination of political pamphlets is not only a sound political tactic.
It is funny, an act of comic theater.

Michael Rossman, in a brilliant review of the events at Berkeley
from 1964 until now, which he describes as the "anatomy of a new
political style," has caught the flavor of the student movement in

the beginning and middle years.[5] Rossman contrasts the classic style of creating pseudo-events, as practised by the civil rights organizations (the 1964 civil rights march on Washington, for example, designed as rhetorical theater for the mass media), with the anti-rhetorical style of the Free Speech Movement.

> Though the movement paid some attention to its media image, almost all of its energy was turned into the audience of its actors rather than outward *from* them. It took shape in response to *their* needs, rather than to the supposed receptivity of others. The style might be called "therapeutic" rather than "anti-Rhetorical" theatre, for its success is measured by the changes wrought in the life of its actors. In the Spring of 1965, everyone I knew who had been deeply involved in the Free Speech Movement accomplished some major—and generally long-delayed—change in his life. Marriages were made or broken, school gladly attended to or finally discarded, academic disciplines switched, theses finished, paintings and novels begun.
>
> The Free Speech Movement was distinguished throughout by a fierce joy. When Mario Savio climbed onto the police car to begin the memorable dialogue, he first carefully removed his shoes, to a glad ovation. By the time the Victory Rally was held in the same plaza eleven weeks later, Savio was internationally famous and the community honored its "leader" by taking up a public collection to provide him with a suit of clothes and a haircut.[6]

[VII]

In a negative, carping time, it is easier to denounce white liberals than to develop workable programs, easier to condemn the middle class than to work out ways of making a classless society. It is easy to denounce the motives of reform-minded liberals as efforts to save the skin of the middle class and its leadership, and to say that the only course of action for the radical activist is to set out to destroy liberal democracy. The danger is that this means not merely the destruction of a system, but the destruction of the central impulse toward humanitarian action.

The question comes up in a special form among the students of the New Left when, in their meetings to plan tactics and organize programs, courses of action are argued on the grounds that the majority in the university community has no rights, that the civil rights of the opposition are mere bourgeois privileges to be swept away. If opposing political ideas must be prohibited from expression or advocacy, then at a given point the radical position loses its central moral point and becomes merely a rallying point for blind ideological action. The validity of a nonviolent revolution designed to make radical changes in the social order disappears, and what replaces it is a doctrine of violent revolution to impose one or another kind of political dogma by force.

If the system of liberal democracy in a post-industrial society is construed as a system of buying off the energies of its radical reformers, thus diverting them from their true business of pulling the system down, then what is left is not only the destruction of liberal democracy but the reassertion of the necessity of a class war with no clear vision of the kind of society which would emerge after the smoke cleared away.

It is possible to argue, in agreement with Herbert Marcuse, that the post-industrial society conditions its own members to accept what the middle-class majority have obtained in the present social system, and to consider that their own interests are best served by continuing the present economic and social system intact. But while agreeing that this is so, it is not necessary to fall into the Hegelian trap that waits for the individual in history and assume that individual action cannot change the system. Most of the students actively at work in American or European society to overthrow liberal democracy, whether capitalist or socialist, have managed to transcend the potential and actual rewards which, according to doctrine, should automatically have tamed their revolutionary spirit. If it is logically impossible for the radicals to work inside the system to change it rather than overthrowing it from outside, then *their* problem is to find ways of convincing others who are already outside the rewards of the system, and are excluded by it, *not* to want to get in.

The question then becomes one of whether it would be better to work toward the idea of including everyone in the benefits of the system of modified welfare capitalism, something which in theory, at least, is not hard to do, or to break up the whole enterprise. The grounds for doing so can only be that even if it were successful in giving everyone economic and social security the system would still be corrupt and would still be bad for those who received the benefits. I find myself fighting against Marcuse's abstractions, knowing that all abstract thought, once it leaves the particular human situation which gives body to its abstraction, dehumanizes the living person.

Marcuse's point about the way the system absorbs the revolutionary thrust of its opponents has been made in a different way by John Stuart Mill, whose formulation of the liberal position contains the seeds of radical thought and action, but without the determinism of Marcuse's philosophy of history. "A state," says Mill, "which dwarfs its men, in order that they may be more docile instruments in its hands even for beneficent purposes, will find that with small men no great thing can really be accomplished; and that the perfection of machinery to which it has sacrificed everything, will in the end avail it nothing, for want of the vital power which, in order that the machine may work more smoothly, it has preferred to banish."

It is the size of the men and the openness of the society which matter most of all, not the degree to which each adheres to social dogma. It has been the function of liberal social democracy, aside from producing its liberal heresy in Marx, to create a set of alternatives to coercion and violence, having rejected the absolutes of truth and the coercive acts which logically follow. At certain times these alternatives have led to armed revolution when other courses of action were blocked, but it cannot therefore be argued that the only way to achieve the goals of a humane society is by armed revolution and the destruction of democratic institutions, no matter on what economic base the institutions rest.

[VIII]

Another result of declaring war against the System is that it gives the warriors and activists an oversimplified view of what everyone is now calling the white middle class. The phrase now serves as an epithet rather than as a social or economic category and is applied to almost anyone who is eating regularly, has an income above the poverty level, is fond of his parents, and wears a collar and tie. We are told of the fact that the young student radicals have emerged from the white middle class whose values they reject, as if this were in the nature of a paradox.

Those who, like Kenneth Keniston and others, have looked at the matter more closely point out that the quality of relationship between the young and their parents in middle-class homes, where feelings of mutual trust and affection are more common than not, has given the intelligent young student a feeling for the kind of society which could exist if social authority were shifted from paternalism to participatory democracy. Or, on the other hand, in homes where the parents dominate as authoritarian figures, there is often a rebellion by the son or daughter against the domination, a rebellion inspired by what the young person finds in his relation with his friends in school or college, by having read about tolerant and affectionate families, or by having met the parents of other students. The commitment of middle-class youth to social change can be seen to have its origin mainly in middle-class values when these are analyzed more specifically than is common among the radicals.

I remember vividly a symposium at an Eastern college at which Robert Lifton, Paul Goodman, and I had been asked to speak in a panel discussion about the reform of education. As his part of the discussion, Goodman did a standard denunciation of white middle-class America, with special reference to the members of the audience. They, said Goodman, were middle-class students with middle-class parents in a middle-class college with middle-class teachers in a middle-class society, all of which, it followed, meant a certain kind of disaster for all those present and for their society. The audience was suitably cowed and made to feel the guilt of their transgression until one young man, bravely, I thought, stood to announce himself as a complete product of the entire system Goodman had just denounced—white, Scarsdale, WASP, Yale, everything—and that he agreed with everything Goodman had written about the System. "Should I lie to myself about what I am? Is my background a disgrace?" he asked.

In the panel discussion that followed, speaking as his friends, we asked about Goodman's own class, since by his credentials, appearance, and style of talking, we told him that he did not seem to be a member either of the upper class or the lower class. This left him publicly exposed as a middle-class anarchist keeping company with a liberal psychiatrist and a college president with radical views on education, neither of whose incomes was disclosed. The benefits in intellectual insight in the denunciation of white middle-class values have reached a point of very small return; the denunciation has for some time been redundant and intellectually counterproductive. Would it help to understand Theodore Roethke to call him a middle-class American poet? His father was a florist. Roethke lived in the suburbs and liked swimming, tennis, and lawns of grass. What would be accomplished by assigning him a social category so loaded with ambiguous negatives?

White, middle-class, racist America does exist. It *is* in control of American politics and American society. It does work its will through the full integration of its attitudes, values, and power within the economic system linked to government, the military, business, industry, technology, the mass media, and education. It is a System. It does try to cover over the real problems of America by rhetoric, entertainment, social rewards, patriotism, and appeals to self-interest. There are politicians who call for unity among the fifty states around the principle of What's in It for Us. Occasionally the System does allow us to see in full color its hideous grinning face with the open mouth speaking the hypocrisies and dangerous clichés of the preliminary stages of fascism among the papier-mâché buildings of Miami Beach and the barricades of Chicago. It does possess an ideological structure and an anti-human will which even the most violent of its denouncers—among the poets, the writers, the radicals, the social critics, the revolutionaries—can barely overstate.

[IX]

But that is the beginning of it, not the end or the whole of it. These are the data which have to be taken into account; this is the situation which sets the stage for social action. The American middle-class values include some observable and verifiable characteristics, including friendliness, inquisitiveness about other people's affairs, social and sexual propriety, kindness to children and animals, cleanliness, orderliness, a sense of responsibility, appreciation of official and popular art, appreciation of education, sincerity, love of family, of country, wanting to be liked, to be comfortable, to get ahead, to own property. Out of the curious mixture of these and other qualities have come, among other things, the main body of American radicals, dissidents, scientists, avant-garde artists, the New Left, the electric circus, the rock musical, the underground newspapers, the little magazines, the underground film, off-Broadway theater, draft-card burners, Peace Corps volunteers, VISTA workers, poets, new styles of communal living, and the major critics, writers, and film-makers whose ideas and opinions set the standards of taste in the arts and letters for anyone who is serious about art. The possession of an automobile, a television set, a radio, furniture, a washing machine, or a refrigerator creates no necessary handicap to the intellectual and moral powers of its possessor, and does free him from quite a few other handicaps to convenience without automatically damaging his humanity or political good sense.

The teachers, the workers, the managers, the clergy, the lawyers, the professors, the students, and all the rest of them are in the middle class together, everyone except the poor and the rich, most of whom usually hold fast to what are so constantly called middle-class values. As Stephen Spender has pointed out, the Czech revolt of 1968 against the authoritarianism of the Czech government was a protest against the lack of consumer goods as well as against cultural and political oppression. In this case, the political system had choked the economic system, and it would do no good to argue with the Czech reformers that for the sake of the socialist ideal the economy should be allowed to work badly enough not to produce and distribute the consumer goods needed by the citizens.

To be precise about it, in 1936 the middle class in the United States, defined as the class of people whose incomes are above the poverty line, were 13 per cent of the population. In 1967 they were 60 per cent, with a national family median income of $8,000. That still leaves us with the desperate problem of 30 million people, a third of whom are Negro, two-fifths of whom are children, who are living in rural or urban poverty. But the values of the poor or the middle-income groups cannot be lumped into a single category as if the members of the income group had all assembled themselves there like lemmings going to the sea.

The injection of new values into the middle-class section of the society can be accomplished by education, if education is designed for the development of social values going beyond raw economic utility. In contemporary society, some of this is already accomplished among the 6½ million families attached to sons and daughters who attend colleges and universities from which, the record shows, a fair proportion bring back new views and deviant opinions about how to live. The middle-class student in the middle-class college can and does turn out to be the radicalizer of his parents as well as the teacher of the educators.

In view of the ambiguities involved, we would be better off not using "middle-class" as an adjective defining a category of aesthetic, political, or social dogmas, and to speak in more precise terms about what the values actually are in human terms. You can be rich and radical, poor and conservative, middle class and progressive. In any case, for the foreseeable future on the college campuses, the radicals will be coming from middle-income families with enough money to make possible the freedom of youthful political action which goes with not having to work while in college and not having to withhold opinion or action in order to hold a job. Their ranks will be increased by the radicals from poor families, black and white.

Because of the very nature of their student bodies, the universities and colleges have a magnificent chance for educational leadership in bringing about changes necessary not merely to improve the quality of life in the university community, but for the enrichment of liberal and radical thought in social and educational change. The greatest of all humane learning is the kind which comes about when the tension between minds is heightened, not by the hostility of opposite purposes, but by a mutual concern for finding answers to urgent and honest questions. The radical student movement needs confrontation at that level if it is to contribute what it has to offer to the improvement of the society it is now attacking. Students of all kinds, particularly if they are radicals by self-definition, need a chance to be forced to look at the full range of implication in the ideas with which they have become engaged. They need to learn how to keep the passion of their commitment without having constantly to revive their passion through the method of antagonism.

5: The Radical Element
in American Thought

I come now to the special meaning of the word "radical" which has been built into the consciousness of the new student movement. To be radical in this sense is to judge the quality of life and society by its reality as perceived in experience, not to accept anything that is said about reality by accredited authorities, inside or outside the universities. It means to judge the quality of an act or an idea by its consequences in the lives of persons, not by its relation to the ideology of liberal democracy, democratic socialism, or the varieties of contemporary communism. It is to judge one's own life by the same radical criteria, and to ask whether the ideas and acts which make up one's own self and psychic continuity have the purity of motive and consistency of belief which is demanded of others as the measure of their quality.

In all this I see a return of the young to the deepest traditions of the American experience and to the poetry, philosophy, and central perceptions which go to make up what has been new and original in the American approach to the world. In talking, thinking, acting, and perceiving themselves as they do, the young radicals are inventing their own forms of a radical empiricism and rediscovering an American tradition which has been in danger of being lost. In their case, the young have not gone back to the texts for the discovery or confirmation of their ideas; they have created the ideas out of their own experience with their own culture. The result can be seen in a new and intense statement of attitudes and perceptions also to be found in Emerson, Mark Twain, Whitman,

72

William James, and John Dewey. The young radicals have found their way back to American ideas which can be called American because they had something fresh and original to say about human experience in a new environment, not because they are expressions of an agreed-upon American national character.

They have also found their way back to the arts and purity of expression among the Negro and white folk musicians and folk singers, and have developed their own poets and singers in a tradition they recognize as theirs. It is a tradition which refuses to identify art with the conventional models and classical standards of organized American culture, and, as in the case of avant-garde dance, jazz, the rock musical, mixed-media happenings, American painting, and post-modern theater, presses toward an intensity of personal expression within the context of American experience.

In this sense, the writers and thinkers who have had most to say in the past about the American experience have all been radicals. The base line for conventional Western thinking has been in European thought, and the deviations in the direction of American originality have come from rejecting the European base line as the measuring point for intellectual norms. The major American heresy is to think of practical thought and pure thought within the same concept, against the European tradition of a separate class for ideas as well as for intellectuals. What is radical in American thought turns on the American habit of judging ideas and acts by their consequences.

The pragmatism of James and Dewey is not, as so many Europeans and Americans have led themselves to believe, a rationalization of the native American temperament for getting ahead, beating down the environment, practising the doctrine of materialism, being "pragmatic." Pragmatism as James stated it and Dewey constructed it was a radical way of talking about and judging ideas, judging them by their ability to hold up in experience, to work their own way toward affirmation in human minds, by their adequacy in meeting a variety of tests beyond the standard test of rational consistency and logical coherence. James was investigating the nature of rationality itself; Dewey's investigations of logic were in many ways an anticipation of the movement toward linguistic analysis—the testing of ideas and their expression in verbal symbols against proper tests for their validity.

When the big public questions of educational reform were being debated in the nineteenth century, and the university presidents and faculty members were defining the role of the university in society, the major conflict of philosophy came not as a result of the application of philosophical systems to the solution of educational problems, but from arguments based on actual functions the university had been performing all along and on practical questions about what it should or should not do in the future. In many ways, the questions and answers had to be practical ones. In a system of higher education with such variety in it, to argue impractically about the future of one's own university might mean that you argued your university out of a place in the national society.

At the same time, the question of how the universities, the colleges, and the schools should serve their society is a philosophical question, and the experience of dealing with the problems of education is a special kind of practical training in answering philosophical questions. Merely to ask the extent of the obligation of colleges to control the personal and social life of its students and faculty members is to ask: How should man live? Is the style of life advocated and imposed by the colleges a better one than that possible in the communities outside the colleges? To decide to add a business school to an existing university rather than an education school for the disadvantaged is a practical answer to a philosophical question; to decide to install a research institute in space technology rather than a center for the performing arts answers another question.

This is what John Dewey and the progressives in the tradition of American philosophy were saying about the nature of philosophical questions—that they were questions which had their roots in the reality of social institutions and human experience. Institutions, said Dewey, were built around the answers to philosophical questions. But instead of asking the questions in the terms of the nineteenth-century utilitarian concept—what pleasures and pains, rewards and punishment, goods or evils are the result of this or that institution—Dewey wanted to know what sort of individuals are created by the institutions.

> Just what response does *this* social arrangement, political or economic, evoke, and what effect does it have upon the disposition of those who engage in it? Does it release capacity? If so,

how widely? Among a few, with a corresponding depression in others, or in an extensive or equitable way? Is the capacity which is set free also directed in some coherent way, so that it becomes a power, or are its manifestations spasmodic and capricious? Since responses are of an indefinite diversity of kind, these inquiries have to be detailed and specific. Are men's senses rendered more delicately sensitive and appreciative, or are they blunted and dulled by this and that form of social organization? Are their minds trained so that their hands are more deft and cunning? Is curiosity awakened or blunted? What is its quality: is it merely esthetic, dwelling on the forms and surfaces of things or is it also an intellectual searching into their meaning? Such questions as these (as well as the more obvious ones about the qualities conventionally labelled moral), become the starting-points of inquiries about every institution of the community when it is recognized that individuality is not originally given but is created under the influences of associated life.[1]

[II]

The radicalism in Dewey had its roots in the radicalism inherent in all appeals to direct experience and the contradiction between what is generally known and believed and what is found to be true in the experience of the informed and sensitive observer. Dewey's views about the responsibility of education to society were the result of the same kind of thinking the nineteenth-century educators were doing as they made their decisions about what to do next, what to teach, how to teach it. Dewey's theories of education were radical because they extended into theory the results of practice, and persistently asked the question, How do these institutions respond to the needs of the individuals for whom they were designed? What sort of individuals are created? That is the radical break with a European educational tradition which persistently asked its own question: How can these individuals be made part of the tradition?

But the break with European education had been made long before Dewey developed the philosophy which gave expression to new American thought. While the European style of university was being introduced at Johns Hopkins in 1876, with its own college to feed students into its graduate schools, and the stage was being set for John D. Rockefeller to back William Rainey Harper's conception of the University of Chicago in 1892, and the concept of the Ph.D. as the king of the academy had been launched at Yale in 1861, the people were organizing their own people's university without benefit of philosophical theory. What they had was a Jacksonian sentiment linked to the straightforward Jeffersonian proposition that "the state is bound to furnish the citizen the means of discharging the duties it imposes on him; if the state imposes duties that require intelligence, it is the office of the state to furnish the means of intelligence." [2]

The break with European thinking about the university was made by applying the unashamed arguments of practical men working their way through the experience of nineteenth-century American life, and applying to education the radical concept of the land-grant university. That concept had emerged almost inadvertently in a contract made in 1787 between the government and the Ohio Company, a group of New England speculators and settlers. To tempt settlers and new enterprise into the Midwest, the government included grants of land in the contract, and Ohio University in Athens, Ohio (1807), and Miami University in Oxford, Ohio (1809), were the first results and the first prototypes of the idea of the citizens' university. [3]

The land-grant idea is a radical philosophical principle. But it is so much a product of American experience, of the American temperament, and of the local American conditions at the time of its origin that any attempt to cite a philosophy which could be said to have directed its educational wisdom would be intellectually impossible. It did of course rely on populist sentiment, and it did express a bold educational theory. But the philosophy and the arguments to support it as congressional legislation in 1863 emerged from the American situation of the nineteenth century. The land-grant proposal did not furnish a coherent set of arguments which could be expressed in a philosophy until later on, after it had formulated its own meaning through experience in educational and social action. It found out what it was through discovering what it was doing.

Consider, for example, the use of land as a basis for the national support of universities to be administered by the states. Although the idea turned out very well, it was not produced as an educational or social concept, but by the fact that the political situation in the 1860s was one in which (a) it could be argued that what was being done for the children of the businessmen and the well-to-do should be done for the children of workers, farmers, and the common man; and (b) that it could be done without increasing taxes or taking revenue away from business and industry, simply by giving away land, of which there was a great deal around, and letting the states make what use of it they could, for revenue and economic investment. Had the Morrill Act proposed a national tax to make its educational program possible, it would have died early.

Or consider the philosophy of service to all citizens which flowed from the land-grant conception and grew into the strongest social and economic instrument the universities of any country have ever had. The philosophy did not spring from the minds of intellectuals for use as an American doctrine. It grew from the particular nature of American social and economic expansion, which, given the elements of a capitalist liberal democracy, had to create its own kind of educational instruments if it were to be successful in its expansion.

If I had a choice as to how I would like to see an educational system developed—by educational plans linked to a clear social philosophy and made by intellectuals, or by starting with the needs of an expanding democratic society and making institutions to meet those needs as the society went along—I would unhesitatingly, gladly, enthusiastically, and irrevocably choose the latter.

Having made that choice retroactively, I would unhesitatingly defend it and the educational consequences in America which have flowed from it, as a philosophy of education we were fortunate enough to have invented from the materials of the American experience. The nineteenth-century debate was between the utilitarians in support of the practical functions of the university in serving its society, and those on the other side who supported the conception of the university as the sanctuary of scholars and the home of the disembodied intellect. The debate helped to resolve the question into its practical answers, and it made clear that the distinction itself was false. Unless the university could extend the range of its service to society by moving into the broader areas of scientific and scholarly research, and at the same time could reach out to the communities and their members to minister to the intellectual, cultural, and educational needs which existed there, it could do neither one with any great success.

One reason was that the citizens, if they were to support the

public universities, had to be able to see what they were getting
for their money. They had to believe in what *their* universities were
doing, and it would be very hard indeed to convince the uneducated American citizen that he should pay for the education and
research training of an élite of Americans who would use their
education and intellectual privilege either for purposes exclusively
their own or for running the country in ways which they, as an
élite, thought advisable. This is not anti-intellectualism on the part
of the citizen. It is the natural response of the citizen in a democratic society whose institutions are conceived as servants to the
people and not as agencies for expressing the will of an intelligentsia. The form of the polity produced the form of its education.

What seems to me to have now happened is that the primary
insight of the American conception has slipped out of the minds
of those who now conduct the contemporary debate. In any number of ways, it is of the highest degree of importance for America
that controversies such as those developed in the state of California over the present and future of higher education should have
reached the stage they have in public visibility and public importance. It is a controversy about how American life should be lived
and what shape the American future should take. The presence of
Governor Reagan as the political symbol of American materialism
and authoritarianism is as important as the presence of the student
protest movement against it, since it makes clear the fundamental
issue around which the most serious educational and political questions must be raised.

A controversy of this magnitude in one state is an educational
factor in the politics of all states. Having worked its way from the
Berkeley of 1964 toward some kind of resolution about the nature
of the public obligation of the public university toward its students
and its citizens, there is a kind of historical inevitability in the fact
that the same kind of test has been put so clearly and forcefully
in the public obligation of the private university in the case of
Columbia University in 1968.

[III]

I return to the role of the younger generation in raising these issues
in the terms they have chosen. It is clear from the history of the

contentious four years of the immediate past that those who should have been conducting the public enquiry into the national purpose and the relation of the national purpose to its institutions of higher learning—the university presidents and their colleagues among the scholars—have failed to come to grips with the real issues. These are not simply the issues revolving around student rights and student involvement in educational policy-making, or even about the relation of the university to the national government. They are the issues which have gone by default into the hands of students because the students are closer to the working areas of the society where education deeply matters, and where the presence or absence of opportunities for getting an education exerts a control over the future lives of the coming generations and the place of America in world society.

Once more, it is not a struggle between the utilitarianism inherent in the land-grant conception of education, as against the ideal of the higher learning as an expression of the disinterested intellect. That struggle has been won. The American institutions of higher education, all 2,300 of them, with more coming every week, have accepted the sensible proposition that in one way or another the needs of citizens of all kinds must be met, and that meeting these needs calls for a quality of intellectual and social effort of the highest possible kind. That these intellectual resources are not yet available in profusion, and at the height of quality necessary to meet the needs, is a fact of history; but it is a fact which recommends certain kinds of action, not a mood of social despair or apocalyptic prophecy. The struggle now is a struggle over who shall have the use and benefit of knowledge, not over whether certain kinds of knowledge are useful or beneficial.

That is why it is so important that the students have joined the struggle and that they have become part of it while they are still undergraduates. They accept the philosophy of land-grant education instinctively, and are adding their own ideas to those of the educators about what kind of knowledge is most useful to the variety of people who need it, themselves included. Rather than waiting for someone in the university to make a new curriculum more in keeping with their ideas of what is needed, they are making curricula of their own, conducting their own courses, and making their own decisions about what is relevant and what is most useful.

Without having turned to the texts of educational philosophers for guidance, they have simply begun to make their own plans, and in the process have produced philosophies which when analyzed show a direct and deep affinity with the concepts of James and Dewey. "The aim of education," says a statement from one student group, "is to foster experiences, both in activity and thought, [which will] enable men to become rulers of their own lives, genuinely creative in their world, being totally responsible for themselves and their fellow men. . . . Therefore the course of study must be decided upon by the group together rather than forced upon it by one member of the group or by an outside force. When people are free to choose what activities they will pursue, they will then be in a position to take real responsibility for what they do. . . ." [4] Following this preamble, a set of practical proposals is developed for starting projects inside the university which could lead to its reform.

Although not all student activists and radicals agree on a philosophy as close to Dewey as this one, their ideas for reform move in the progressive direction, and are usually accompanied either by practical proposals for reform in the universities where the students are enrolled or by actual research, course outlines, reading lists, study guides, and suggestions for educational projects. In nearly all of them, the central theme is that education must move from a consideration of what the student already knows toward what it is he needs to find out. There is constant assertion of the idea that direct experience with society and with other persons, direct experience in the arts and in life, is the beginning of education, and the basis on which the student can learn to choose an intellectual course of action and to work as an independent intellectual.

There have already been some important effects of the involvement of students in their own educational planning, and the effects will grow in influence very quickly now that some of their experimental projects have already proved successful. One of the effects already apparent in the radical student movement is to break down the distinction between undergraduate and graduate education within the formal university system on the campuses where projects have been in effect. Sophomores and juniors who are activists work just as freely with seniors and graduate students as they do with freshmen. Academic status has little to do with their talents and their capability in organizing or teaching.

The student movement has made no hierarchies except in terms of talent and willingness to work, and even here, the student attitude to leadership within the movement is to accept as a leader anyone whose talents at a given point fit him to do whatever task is necessary and which he can persuade others to join him in carrying out.

It has also meant that field work in the social sciences, usually formalized even when allowed in the university curriculum, has already been made part of the education of students in the movement. It is as natural for undergraduates to spend a summer in the ghetto, tutoring, teaching, organizing, or working in the arts as it used to be to take a job in a construction company or to work in a summer camp. The difference is that the experience off the campus and out of the classroom is a part of the student's conscious development of his own education, and that what he learns makes him better able to understand the nature of his society and the place of his own education in it.

The result of this is to be seen in the high degree of pressure the student exerts on the university he attends to bring its work to a level to which he has already brought his own, with the help of his fellow workers in the field and sources of direct information among his friends in the community. The student ideas, radical or not, grow from his own experience. It is his experience, not his academic status, which determines his readiness to test his own ideas against those of formal studies in the curriculum. At present he is unlikely to find very many of those who teach him in courses in the social sciences and the humanities who can match the activist's experience with their own.

The same is true of graduate students who are activists and who also teach. Many of them have had months of experience with social and educational reform in poor communities, working with other students, both older and younger than themselves.

In another dimension of initiative, many undergraduates have worked out research projects of their own in the social and natural sciences, one of the most interesting of which is an example drawn from student work at the California Institute of Technology. There a twenty-year-old president of the student body, with financial support from the Department of Health, Education and Welfare, has organized a research project on air pollution, with seventy students involved in a series of investigations which use each student's talents and background, whether in the social or natural sciences, to develop lines of independent research on the main issues.

When they teach undergraduates in the freshman and sophomore sections of departmental courses, the students of this degree of talent bring with them a new and progressive attitude to teaching which creates a new spirit among those in their classes. They have transferred the spirit of cooperative social action into the academic curriculum.

[IV]

The psychic distance between the undergraduates and the academic faculty is thereby shortened. The student who has been taught by a talented graduate student, whose mind is active and whose teaching has benefited from direct experience with the problems he is talking about, need no longer think of all professors in conventional terms. He has something to compare them with. The graduate student who teaches a freshman and sophomore seminar serves as a different kind of model for the university intellectual. The professor, who by his role in the university and in the classroom is put in the position of an authority, to judge, to convey the knowledge of scholars, to supervise the work of the graduate students, then receives a different kind of test from graduate and undergraduate students alike.

The mind and intellectual interests of the professor must be at least as active as those of his junior partner in the graduate school. His judgments must be as informed, his concern for what his students are learning as great, at the risk of being found wanting in the necessary qualities of a teacher and a scholar in his field. As the number of graduate students with practical experience in social and educational reform increases, as more of them are taking to writing poetry, novels, plays, underground newspapers, television scripts, research reports, and making films—all as undergraduates—the quality of graduate education and university teaching must change, from the sheer intellectual force of the new graduate students and their pupils.

The radical question which students are now asking themselves about their professors is, What does he know that we do not, or that we could not quickly learn for ourselves? What can he do intellectually that we can not do, and what can he show us to do that we do not already know? If the professor does not have a fairly good margin in both of these matters, he can not be expected to exert much influence on his students; it is the residue of knowledge and ability remaining in the hands of the professor, over and beyond what the students already possess, which decides his size in the eyes of the student. It is a fair criterion. Ortega has put it beautifully. "Scarcity of the capacity to learn," he says, "is the cardinal principle of education. It is necessary to provide for teaching precisely in proportion as the learner is unable to learn." [5]

An accomplished student, undergraduate or graduate, can do most of the things he is asked to do, and anything the student can do for himself he should be asked to do in the regular course of instruction. The quality of the asking also becomes a criterion by which the student measures the quality of his instruction. Trivial or banal assignments which require only conventional responses, or assignments which tell the student what he already knows or could quickly find out, are factors which now go into the judgments students are making about their teachers.

It is in this sense that the informed students are asking for a radically new kind of relation with their instructors, one in which each man recognizes the other for what he truly is and takes his measure without the interference of categories of status, age, reputation, or position. The youth want to show who they are, what they know, and what they can do; they want to be judged by their performance in intellectual action. They want to be taught in such a way that the reality of their talent is taken into account. They know what they can do. They know, better than ever before, what others are doing and are capable of doing. They are expert in assessing experts, and they give their respect to those who demonstrate who they are and what they can do without the need for the support of status. They are sensitive, to a degree unknown in previous generations of students, to the attitudes of those who instruct them.

This is the real nature of the generation gap. It is a gap which exists when a member of either generation gives to himself certain attributes and prerogatives by reason of his youth or his age, and assigns himself to a privileged category. It is not the fact of youth or the fact of age which is at stake. Each generation has its own truth, created out of the events, occasions, and experience of its own time, and its version becomes part of the whole process of truth-making as the generation enters its own place in history. The gap opens when an older generation fails to recognize the reality of the truth perceived by the young, by not taking that truth seriously, by putting it over against an older and better truth in the possession of older persons of more experience. The young assert an equality for their own ideas with those of anyone else; the testimony they bring from the life of the child growing up in the 1950s and 1960s is unavailable except from them. The relation between the older and the younger becomes false when either asserts the authority to speak for all truth.

The present system of the colleges and universities is an organized way of keeping the generations apart by consolidating all the truth-saying in the hands of the academic faculty. Most of the faculty accept the role the system gives them. So do most of the students. It is the new radical group which does not. The academic professional makes a distinction between the professional and the amateur in scholarship and learning, and few of the professionals are willing to accept the fact that many of the new amateurs play the game at a level comparable to the professionals, and in some cases and in some ways go beyond them. When the question of students' sharing the educational policy- and curriculum-making come up, most professionals argue that students do not know enough to make decisions. They are students, not educators; they are raw amateurs.

Professionals in the arts, in sports, or in politics are less likely to take a negative point of view toward the young. When faced with the observable talent of a young musician, an actor, a tennis player, or an organizer, they accept it as a fact and accept the young as colleagues. The young artists and athletes make their judgment about the qualities of other artists and athletes by a direct awareness of how good they are in action. They too have a sense of colleagueship among old and young. That is the way the informed student takes the measure of his elders, inside and outside the university, in the same way that he measures himself and his friends. He judges a man by what he does with his life, and he finds few among his professors whose lives reflect the values implicit in the ideal of humanist scholarship.

For the young, the older generation inside the universities exercises the authority of the institution, not the authority of a life. The intellectual authority of a teacher's mind exerts its force by coming to terms with the lives and needs of students who share with the teacher in the culture of their time. This is the only kind of authority which counts, one which is not imposed but which draws acceptance toward itself by the authenticity of its actions and the persuasiveness of its example. "What the elders have that they can offer the young," says James Baldwin, "is the evidence, in their own flesh, of defeats endured, disasters passed, and triumphs won. This is their moral authority, which, however mystical it may sound, is the only authority that endures; and it is through dealing with this authority that the young catch their first glimpse of what has been called the historical perspective." [6]

The true teacher is one who can stand before his students and before the world in the full reality of his own intellectual character, affirming his authenticity by taking the radical risk that the disclosure of himself in the fullness of his certainties and ambiguities will show that he means to be what he is. When he stands that way, he stands with the students, and they with him.

PART TWO

Mass Culture and
the Academic Mind

6: The Culture and
the Professionals

One of the reasons for the growing strength of the student movement is that it has its base in the mass culture as well as a special base inside the educational system. When students raise issues about war or about racial and educational injustice, they speak not only for themselves but for a large section of the society which does not have as direct an access to the mass media. In former years, the universities and colleges dealt with students as students. Now they must deal with them as a new constituency with a political and social base in the society at large. One result is that the students cannot be controlled by unilateral administrative directives or threats of discipline. What was formerly a private matter between students and the college authorities has developed into a series of issues of public policy discussed by everyone from Congressmen who want to cut off scholarships to activists, to parents who want the deans and presidents, not their sons and daughters, dismissed from the university.

As the French and Soviet authorities have discovered, in company with their American counterparts, you cannot raise the level of human capacity on a broad scale in any dimension—you cannot give a large proportion of the younger generation the instruments of conceptual thinking and a set of practical social skills—and then keep their minds from turning to critical questions about the environment in which they exist. The vital force in the revolutionary movements now growing in post-industrial and industrial societies lies in that sector of the educated manpower which combines trained intelligence with social passion. Ideas in that sector are now being affected in the United States by the passionate spokesmen of the intelligent but untrained. The students have become their intermediaries, not merely spokesmen for student rights and educational reform, but spokesmen for others in the society to whom the public is less likely to listen.

In this situation, the clue to the reform of the universities is to seize upon these facts and accept, with the students, the legitimacy of the social revolution. By this I do not mean giving up the objectivity of the scholar or turning the university into a revolutionary center. I mean what Herbert Block meant when he spoke of the spurious objectivity of those who don't want to become involved with the race question, and said that it is like watching people kick babies and saying that half the time the kickers are right, the other half the babies. Nor do I mean a grudging acceptance by the universities of the fact that students already have power of their own in determining their own goals and values, both inside and outside the universities. I mean a radical alteration of the entire philosophy according to which the colleges and universities have been operating in the past.

What is at stake is not a slight modification in the governing structure, with students added to faculty and administrative committees to appease the student protestants. It is a reformation in the idea of what a university is for, one which takes account of the place the university occupies in the altered circumstances of a mass technological society. The new generation is used to technology; it has known little else and is happy to use it for social ends. The large sector the new generation occupies in the national society, soon to be larger when the next children grow up, includes very few who follow the doom-ridden statements of those who see technology destroying individual lives. The student activists have found their own ways of breaking down the impersonality of the collective society. They take as their assumption that bureaucracies of any kind are objects of suspicion and the enemy of life.

They make another set of assumptions about authority and leadership. They have discovered that one way of dealing with authority, aside from ignoring it, is to withhold support, since the power of a leader or an authority is only as great as his capacity to persuade others to do what he asks or what he directs. These are the grounds on which the students choose the leadership of their own groups, and they have begun to look at all other organized groups, especially in the university administration and faculty, in the same way. In the lesson book of activists, noncooperation can be as effective an instrument of change as other forms of nonviolence. It is the active side of apathy, which is itself a powerful weapon against any kind of educational system.

When student activists consider their place within the university and speak of taking a role in the decision-making that goes on there, they, like their counterparts in the black-power movement in relation to the whites, are thinking of a situation of equality in which their views are not merely to be listened to, but are to be confronted. If certain ideas and proposals are not possible to accept, then why not? They do not wish to be advisers to deans, witnesses at faculty committees, suppliants to presidents, junior members of a boys' town, but to be taken seriously as informed educators with serious commitments to certain kinds of educational reform which they believe would make the university and society a better place. They are tired of not being taken seriously when they are genuinely serious.

[II]

Christopher Jencks and David Riesman, in their book on the Academic Revolution,[1] have described the rise to social and cultural power of the academic profession in the United States and the place of the university in the American power structure. In doing so, they have presented the case for the continuance of that control, for not taking students seriously, and have provided some of the reasons why the student movement has met so high a degree of resistance to the reforms it now advocates. The revolution to which Jencks and Riesman refer is not a social or intellectual revolution led by academic professionals, but a revolution in the sources of power through which the society is now run. As a result of it, the academic profession has established itself in a controlling position from its base in the graduate schools over the development of the entire educational system and, to this extent, over the development of the society as a whole.

Having established the facts of that control, Jencks and Riesman leave them before us as if they were idle sentences from a discarded faculty report. They note that there is some scattered resistance to the use the academics make of their privileged position—by "young people who resent adults, by provincials who resent cosmopolitans, by the devout who resent heretics, by the upwardly mobile who resent the arrived, and by the wealthy who resent the application of meritocratic standards to their children. But this resistance is for the most part poorly organized, poorly financed, and poorly thought out." [2]

A more inaccurate and misleading set of casual observations presented as sociology could hardly be put together in two sentences. Even a survey of responsible newspaper and magazine writing would produce the evidence, from sheer volume of reporting, that the resistance on the part of students to academic control is deep-rooted, growing in intensity, and valid in its aims for exactly the reasons the authors point out elsewhere in their study. Must everything be well organized, well financed, and well thought out in order to qualify as a valid revolution? Is the Berkeley revolt less significant because it began without prior organization or finance, by the spontaneous combustion of all the elements so fully described by Clark Kerr in his clinical description of the modern university as the center of the knowledge industry?

It would also be useful to have in so crucial a matter some old-fashioned, head-counting sociology to distinguish first of all what an adult is, and then to determine the approximate number of young people who object to the sterility of the academic curriculum because they resent adults, as against those who object because in their association with fellow adults (those over twenty-one, for example) they have learned that you don't have to accept boredom and banality simply because it has been sanctified by the academic profession.

It is true, as Jencks and Riesman have pointed out, that whatever the virtues or defects of the academic system, it has produced a generation of educated young people which is the best we have ever had, and perhaps the best that any country has ever had. The members of the present generation know more than their predecessors, they have more talent in every dimension, from the creative arts to the sciences and social technologies, they care more, and they express themselves with force, in language, art, and social action.

But this is not due entirely to the efforts of the academic profession to educate them, but is in many ways in spite of it. By reason of their experience within the total culture, of which the academic is merely one unavoidable part, the youth have gained fresh insights and the capacity to make intellectual and social judgments by which to test the validity of what the academic system has imposed on them. In a real sense, they have left their academic mentors behind. Yet all we are given by these authors, who represent the general point of view of the academic profession, is a vote of approval for those left behind, along with a statement of despair about the ingrown attitudes of the academic community and "the inadequacy of the faith most academicians adhere to."

I would prefer to call this not an inadequacy but a bankruptcy. "The two great challenges," say the authors, "are therefore to devise colleges that can touch the lives of those who are now merely going through the motions, and to devise graduate programs —and indeed a style of faculty life—that better develop and exemplify the possibilities of the life of the mind. At the moment very little effort is being made on either front." [3]

This is, of course, observably untrue. A great deal of effort is being made on both fronts, although not much by the academicians. According to Jencks and Riesman, the academicians have such a tight control over "the natives in the undergraduate colleges" that opposition efforts could succeed "only if they had the support of outsiders." The basic responsibility for change rests on established members of the academic profession. Having found ways of deprecating some of the liveliest and most important movements of reform now in progress, developed by students, in counter-curricula, educational research, experimental student courses, free universities, social-action projects across the country, and having dismissed with the epithet "off-beat" a serious and sustained effort by experimental and progressive colleges of all kinds to invent new educational forms, Jencks and Riesman express the general attitude of American contemporary educators that nothing much can be done. They have missed the meaning of the revolution that is not academic.

It is precisely because the reform of the universities *has* the support of outsiders that the movement toward reform has gathered strength and is now challenging the academicians in the heart of their citadel. The students are the outsiders, representatives of a mass culture which has provided them with new weapons and strategy, and has dropped them behind the enemy lines. Jencks and Riesman have provided a map of the battlefield and a position of the defenders, but have mistaken the location and quality of the adversary and the nature of the battle. In doing so, they have illustrated by a variety of examples a fundamental failure of the academic profession and its administrative officers. It is abuse of academic power and its use on behalf of the interests of the academic profession that marks the present failure of the university as an educational institution. The university has lost its ability to educate by turning its resources to other uses, at exactly the time an educated generation it has helped to create has risen to a level of cultural and social achievement which, if aided by the universities, could build a different world and a better one. In retaining an inverted conception of its duties to itself, the university has lost touch with the mass society to which it is ultimately responsible.

[III]

If the problems of this society were the same as those of the nineteenth century, the situation would not be as alarming. There were a sufficient number of institutional ways—through the church, the political system, the colleges, the schools, the smaller units of local government—to ensure some kind of unity of purpose in the national life, even if that unity were achieved by the exclusion of the potentially disruptive poor and ignorant from a place in the decision-making. Now we have both the advantages and the difficulties of a mass society without the benefit of social leadership from the existing institutions.

Instead we have a mass culture surrounding the universities and an academic culture inside them. We have outsiders and insiders. If you want to join the insiders, you must give yourself up to their regime, you must prepare yourself, preferably from birth, to develop those professional skills and vocational aptitudes which make for success in the academy. Although much of the preparation, especially in the undergraduate years, is said to be education in the liberal arts, it is not liberal and has little to do with the arts. It is vocational, a training in a skill. Once one becomes a professional member of the academy, it is almost impossible not to be caught up in the modes of intellectual behavior, concerns, and issues which the academic culture generates within its own organization, and not to be caught up in the allegiance the organization gives to the existing social order. If not, among other things, the rewards of the system are not yours, and you move from one year to the next as a perpetual outsider whose satisfactions, including that of being an outsider, gradually diminish in quality.

The outsiders in the mass culture are a different breed. They are the poor, the artists, the blacks, the novelists, the actors, the radicals, the hippies, the workers, the businessmen, the sailors, the students (who are both outside and inside), and anyone else who either wants to stay outside or is forced to stay out by lack of qualifications. Among the outsiders are the non-students and young intellectuals without credentials who have a vocation for ideas but cannot stand the academy.

As George Steiner has said about Herzog in Saul Bellow's novel of that name, Herzog "lives the life of literary and philosophical ideas in a civilization where such life has no anchored place, where it has to be continually justified and reasserted by force of irony and passion. He seeks to uncover the laws underlying his own unquiet being." [4] There are few places within the academic culture where this kind of seeking is possible, or where the attitudes which go with it can find their authentic means of expression.

Membership inside the academic culture confers its benefits and extracts its tolls. Membership in the outside culture does the same thing in a different way, with more room to move. But what is seldom noticed by the educators is that the students are the connecting link between the outside society and the academic culture. The students bring directly into the academic culture the reality of the society itself, with all its richness, its vulgarity, its contention, its blandness, and its presuppositions, since the students are perfectly formed representatives of a large and dominant sector of the society at large. They represent the bright, the dull, the average, the above-average, the conservative, the liberal, the radical, the know-nothing, the motivated, the unmotivated, the disruptive, the cooperative.

They bring with them into the universities whatever they have learned on the outside, and if they have learned to be critical of the society and its educational system, they bring that too. On the other hand, they take from the academic culture whatever is good, useful, enlightening, trivial, false, true, conventional, banal, beautiful, or invigorating to be found there. They take whatever they have been able to create for themselves out of the academic culture and put it to some kind of use on the outside.

They are therefore the transforming agents of the mass culture, as far as it can be transformed by anything the universities do, since they carry into their lives what they have learned. If they have been poorly taught, if they have learned very little, they still act, in this case as neutered examples of what education does, or perhaps as irrational, stubborn representatives of the common culture. They are, all of them, potentially able to change the society and the content of its culture, and whether or not they make the effort is a matter of how they live their lives. Societies are changed when a given number of its members begin living in a different way. If the colleges and universities have no effect on the attitudes and values of their students, or if they have a neutralizing effect, the place to look for the reason is not in the students or in their society, but in the educational arrangements of the colleges and universities.

The crux of the matter lies in the absence of a philosophy which links the purposes of the university and its fragmented units of bureaucracy to the larger aims of civilization. One of the frustrating things about the Jencks-Riesman analysis of the universities is that so much of what they say is true and has been generally known for some time, yet neither they nor their colleagues among university administrators and faculty members have moved to the deeper levels of discourse where the bigger questions lie.

Is it true that all we can do is to describe the power structure of the university and the nature of the society it serves, and then go on simply to describe the pluralism of purposes that such service entails? Must all that massed brain power be put at the service of whatever ends society seeks? Are there not some ends which command a higher value than other ends? Is not the major end of all learning to enrich the life of persons and to create a world in which such enrichment is possible? Is the greatness of a university to be measured entirely by its competitive success in hiring the largest number of scientists and scholars with the highest degree of academic prestige and productivity in research? If a technological society is dehumanizing the lives of those who inhabit it, do we have to feed the monster simply because the enterprise is profitable?

[IV]

To review the literature of university education is to find not only that the deeper questions are seldom asked but that the answers already given deny the significance of the questions. Even the question of greatness is begged at the start by the fact that it is answered sociologically. Which are the great institutions? Those which are identified, in a high form of self-congratulation by the academic profession itself, as the ones which have the "strongest" departments, that is, the greatest number of research scholars and scientists whose work is recognized by academics. Columbia University and the University of California at Berkeley are great institutions as certified by the opinions of the academicians and the statements of their presidents. But greatness in what? And for whom?

Clark Kerr has given the general American answer, and one which has yet to find its refutation or even its serious challengers among those who dominate the discussion of major educational issues. Greatness lies in adaptation, he has told us in *The Uses of the University*,[5] the basic document stating the case for the university as a "mechanism held together by administrative rules and powered by money." The university exists to meet the demands of the society for certain kinds of knowledge and knowledgeable people to move the society toward the goals it has set for itself. "The process cannot be stopped. The results cannot be foreseen. It remains to adapt." The universities able to adapt quickly and effectively will be the great universities of the future.

A comparable sociological fatalism lies in Mr. Kerr's analysis of the university structure. The president, he says, presides over a loosely held set of bureaucracies. His duty is to mediate the forces at work among them, feeling their strength, deciding which ones are to be encouraged, which ones blocked, which ones are so powerful that they would, if opposed, sweep the president away with them. There are varieties of interest groups, all of them legitimate—the faculty, the alumni, the voters, the community, industry, agriculture, the government, the state legislature, "society," the students, among whom "the walking wounded are many." The president must see that each of the interest groups has its fair hearing, its fair share of attention, and that it remains in balance with the others.

The president is therefore not an intellectual or educational leader, seeking new forms of social thought and educational action. Nor should he try to be. The faculty would not allow it, and his duties in real estate, business management, public relations, and politics prevent it. Mr. Kerr is suspicious of "vision," as he puts it. That day is over. The president is now a "mediator-initiator," and although he has the *opportunity to persuade* (original italics), he must remember that the mediator-initiator "wins few clear-cut victories; he must aim more at avoiding the worst than seizing the best. He must find satisfaction in being *equally* distasteful to each of his constituencies; he must reconcile himself to the harsh reality that successes are shrouded in silence while failures are spotlighted in notoriety." [6]

But why not seize the best? Why be equally distasteful to all constituencies? Is not the ultimate constituency the human race? Is the educator condemned by his position of leadership never to utter those clear, passionate words of men who believe in man, who believe in the power of the intellect and the imagination to push back the forces which clearly threaten to engulf us? Must he always assert propositions cleared in advance by everybody?

"What is desperately needed," said Tom Hayden, in his early days in the student movement, "is the person of vision and clarity, who sees the model society and the pitfalls that precede its attainment, and who will not destroy his vision for short-run gains, but instead, will hold it out for all to see, as the farthest dream and perimeter of human possibility."

If students proclaim that desperate need and, failing to find it fulfilled within the university community, turn to others, among themselves and elsewhere, to devise the elements of a model society, are they not justified in allying themselves against a system whose spokesmen proclaim such little faith and set so narrowly the limits of human possibility?

We owe to Mr. Kerr and his book one of the best, most succinct, and most influential statements in recent years of the character and power of the organized intellect to determine the future of society. We are in his debt for making available so accurate an account of the disintegration of central purpose in the work of the modern university. He has provided the rationale for the multiplicity of purposes which already exist and has opened the way for more to come. What he has not done is to describe the way in which the power of the organized intellect can be directed toward ideal ends. That is the heart of the matter, and the place where the heart should be is empty.

"The ends are already given," says Kerr, "—the preservation of the eternal truths, the creation of new knowledge, the improvement of service wherever truth and knowledge of high order may serve the needs of man. The ends are there; the means must be ever improved in a competitive dynamic environment. There is no single 'end' to be discovered; there are several ends and many groups to be served." [7]

But the ends are not already given; they are not "there." The eternal truths alter as we look at them or even as we state them— the nature of man, the nature of the universe, the nature of truth itself. If they are to be preserved at all, they will only be preserved by their reinterpretation in the light of new knowledge and in the beliefs and actions of the new generation. The means determine the ends; the two are indissolubly joined.

If a university president buys scholars, his coaches buy football players, and his scholarship officer buys students, all according to the conventional rules of the competitive university game, this defines the ends his institution is seeking—prestige, power, and money. If the president is simply an executive with the acquired skills of a mediator-initiator, and his twin purpose, as Kerr says, is "the keeping of the peace and the furthering of progress," how does he choose particular means for these particular ends? How does he decide what kind of peace is to be kept, at what price, and what kind of progress is to be made, at what price and in what direction?

Or, for that matter, who decides, among all those powerful ones administering half-billion-dollar budgets and tens of thousands of students, what education is, what direction it should take, and what are the means to its improvement? Not the faculty, who have already decided that education is a matter of giving courses. Not the students, who are the ones to be educated. Not the vice-presidents and deans, who, under the present system, are middle-management mediators in their own right, administering their subsections of the knowledge industry.

Then who? The board of regents? The state legislature? The governor? The alumni? The public? A national committee of experts? Or a consensus achieved among all the elements, fragments of ideas and opinions congealed into policy by the machinery of university politics?

A university, no matter how big, must be a university, not a multiversity; and if it exists as a collection of activities held together only by a common name, if, as Mr. Kerr says, "it has been embraced and led down the garden path by its environmental suitors," is it not time that it shocked itself into self-understanding by the facts of its own situation and discovered at last "whether it has a brain as well as a body?" The pluralism of American society and the pluralism of the big university match each other in the opportunities they give individuals for alternative courses of action, preferences, institutional arrangements, failures and successes. Mr. Kerr and those who assent to his views are right in stressing the significance of pluralism and its advantages to democracy.

But what is taken for granted about the pluralism is just what should be examined—the economic and social structure in which it exists and the cultural habits it has produced. Taken all together, both the structure and the habits have combined to create an implicit ideology of competition, and the economic model of corporate capitalism with its links to government funds on the one hand and to a consumer market on the other has its counterpart in the agreed-upon conception of the university in society. The universities compete with each other in ways which parallel the competition of the corporations. So do the members of the academic profession, as Mr. Kerr points out, in ways leading to manipulations and stratagems among professors, departments, and institutions. So do the students, who are caught in a competitive system in which academic credits are the exact equivalent of dollars—they are paid for at so much a point and the man who gets the most soonest, from elementary school to the end of the doctorate, is the man who wins.

If the universities are organized so that success is measured in the same terms as is competitive success within the economic and social structure—that is to say, high grades and academic prestige for students; high rank, salary, and prestige for the faculty members; money and prestige for the institution—then the entire value structure and ideology of corporate capitalism, complete with its metaphors, has been taken over by the intellectual community. The university becomes an indistinguishable part of a homogeneous culture. Then from what corner of the entire culture, if not from the universities, will come those ideas and forms of higher criticism about how life can be lived which can take society out of its narrow orbit of self-acceptance?

[v]

The big universities have changed in precisely the ways Mr. Kerr has described, without, as far as the historians of education can tell us, having decided to become what they are. They have been organized for efficiency, not for true public service. At the time they should have been creative centers for the development of strategies for peace, disarmament, and world unity, they were expanding their work with Defense Department contracts. When the educational problems of the black community were getting worse by the day, they were busy making admission requirements more and more favorable to white students with high scholastic aptitudes.

While the problems of the cities were multiplying and their situation was mounting to the level of catastrophe, the universities were busy with the construction of buildings which disrupted the lives of citizens and whole communities. While scholars could have been at work on the social technologies and social science of the city, they were working on problems dictated by fashions in the profession. When the public schools were groping for ways of improving the intellectual content of their curriculum and bringing a fair distribution of education to the whole population, the universities contented themselves with sneering at the teachers colleges and schools of education as the province of the intellectually unfit and the spiritually slothful. At a time when right-wing ideologues and agitators were promoting dangerous attacks on democratic values and intellectual freedom, the universities did their best to inhibit political action and expression on the part of their students.

I do not see how the university president and the university faculty body can run away from all this and absolve themselves from responsibility for defining clearly the aims of a democratic society and the choices they are prepared to make in using their intellectual and institutional resources in achieving those aims. In the nineteenth-century university, the issues were publicly argued by university presidents who took sides and whose social philosophy expressed itself in the administrative and educational policies they adopted. What they decided then has had a great deal to do with what we have now. They could hardly be expected to have done our present thinking for us.

In the absence of public expression of serious conviction by educational leaders, and in the absence of initiative toward action on the most serious questions of public policy and social change, the students have formed their own enclaves and movements, have found their own way to their own kind of truth and life-style. They have also found, in the resistance of the universities to the possibility of reforms which would take account of their criticisms, exactly the situation suited to their own emotional and political state. The resistance to student action rests not only on the inherent conservatism of the university structure and ideology, but on a lack of understanding of the political and social grounds on which the students rest their case. The students are therefore presented with authority figures who offer themselves as targets for student opposition. The authorities make possible the dialectic of political controversy by automatically taking the other side, and act out the roles in which the students wish to place them.

"Our young people in disturbing numbers," said President Kirk of Columbia University two weeks before the student revolt at his institution, "appear to reject all forms of authority from whatever source derived, and they have taken refuge in a turbulent and inchoate nihilism whose sole objectives are disruptive. I know of no time in our history when the gap between the generations has been wider or more potentially dangerous."

Of course the gap is wide, and no wonder it exists when the members of the older generation talk and think this way, and are so little in touch with the issues around which the student protests move. If the university and its leadership fail to act, either on behalf of world peace, racial justice, the reform of an archaic curriculum, the grant of legitimate student rights, or refuse to take their students seriously as educational reformers, and if the leadership communicates its point of view to students and everyone else through the public relations office and the press and television, what else can serious young people do other than move beyond acquiescence into protest and resistance?

Since the university *is* linked to the established economic and social order and *is* carrying out its purposes, thoughtlessly more often than not, in ways Mr. Kerr and others have described, that is what the students are objecting to. The student protest and militancy has a basis in a serious intellectual position which should be no secret to scholars and educators whose own work should bring them in touch with such phenomena.

If among the student radicals there are those who have prepared organized plans to deal frontally with the achievement of their goals, by sit-ins, demonstrations, strikes, take-over of buildings, and other tactics practised in the 1930s by union organizers, this is a situation which, again, in the absence of an educational or social philosophy, it is almost impossible for the university to deal with at the very moment of confrontation. The resistance of the American corporation to the organization of the workers in the 1930s marked a period in American social history in which the ideology of the capitalist system had not yet defined itself in relation to the validity of the rights of labor. As the resistance to reform in the ideology increased, so did the militancy of the workers, until new institutional forms were developed to give to the unions the power and rights they claimed as their own.

[VI]

In the case of the universities at this period in American history, the problem comes when, having neglected to take account of major intellectual and political forces at work within the American student body, the university is suddenly confronted by students who make demands and back them up with direct action. If at that point there has been no serious effort to come to grips with the issues raised by the protest and no direct access by the students to those who make the basic policy decisions about those issues, the student action gathers strength by the support it receives from other quarters in the student body, faculty, and public.

The dilemma of the university then is that everything it does is too late. An additional dilemma arises when it becomes obvious, after the struggle is over, that the issues raised by the students were real and that the tactics of civil disobedience have actually produced serious attention by the university to matters previously neglected. The attention would not have been produced without the extreme measures to which the students resorted. On the one hand, this encourages an escalation of student militancy on any matter at all, from dormitory rules to the grading system, and the introduction of a kind of blackmail to replace rational discourse. On the other, in most cases it results in faculty and student involvement in serious educational issues which are seldom discussed seriously until a crisis is caused by student action.

It is here that a deeper analysis of motivation and aim within the culture of contemporary youth is crucial if the universities are to fulfill to any degree their responsibility for education, and if they are to find the ways in which the extraordinary strength and idealism of the present student generation can be put to the use for which the students intend it. Without that analysis from which a philosophy of education can emerge, all policies become transitory, all reforms are simple reactions to present threats and pressures, serving both universities and students badly.

In the following passage, Erik Erikson sets the terms of a wider perspective. He is writing on the theme of fidelity in the lives of the young, "the strength of disciplined devotion" and how it is achieved.

> The evidence in young lives of the search for something and somebody to be true to is seen in a variety of pursuits more or less sanctioned by society. It is often hidden in a bewildering combination of shifting devotion and sudden perversity, sometimes more devotedly perverse, sometimes more perversely devoted. Yet, in all youth's seeming shiftiness, a seeking after some durability in change can be detected, whether in the accuracy of scientific and technical method or in the sincerity of conviction; in the veracity of historical and fictional accounts or the fairness of the rules of the game; in the authenticity of artistic production (and the high fidelity of reproduction) or in the genuineness of personalities and the reliability of commitments. This search is easily misunderstood, and often it is only dimly perceived by the individual himself, because youth, always set to grasp both diversity in principle and principle in diversity, must often test extremes before settling on a consid-

ered course. These extremes, particularly in times of ideological confusion and widespread marginality of identity, may include not only rebellious but also deviant, delinquent, and self-destructive tendencies. However, all this can be in the nature of a moratorium, a period of delay, in which to test the rock-bottom of some truth before committing the powers of body and mind to a segment of the existing (or coming) order.[8]

It seems to me that Erikson here, and elsewhere in his work, gives a basis both for understanding and for dealing with the educational questions now being raised by the student generation. These questions provide the place for the beginning of an educational philosophy. If student action is a way of seeking out and testing the authenticity of belief and honesty of motive in the response of educators, the educators who proclaim no principles other than those of law and order become vulnerable to continuing attack, since they do not understand the nature of their test. Conciliation on their part is seen by the tactical militants as a sign of weakness. So is the use of police power. The rest of the students and the faculty, whose decent opinion the militants must have if their actions are to be successful, then become the judges and final arbiters of the conduct of the educators. If, in sufficient numbers, they follow the lead of the militants, they can impose their collective will on the policy-makers of the university. It is a play in which the audience decides how the plot will unfold. In the case of the educators, what is required is an act of faith that once the issues are out in the open, the students and faculty will find authentic solutions to the problems raised, no matter what the circumstances may have been in the original controversy.

To continue the Erikson theme, it is characteristic of those who are beginning to define a role for themselves, in this case a role as radicals and revolutionaries, to act in such a way that their actions appear, at least to themselves and to those of their own group, to have a universal quality. They are intentionally and consciously joining history and making it. They call up the spirits of the radicals of the past who were scorned, put down, jailed, and denied. They have something else which their spiritual antecedents did not have—access to the mass media, and a fair degree of sophistication about how to create situations in which their actions will be widely reported to the public. Their tactics have been based on developing confrontations on issues which can attract sizable numbers of demonstrators, since the size of the demonstration, its indication of the extent of student feeling and support and the evidence of a will to prevail, determines how much attention the mass media will give to the action.

If, as has been the case in the plans and tactics of the militants in SDS and the Progressive Labor Youth, the approach of the militants has been technical, consciously based on a metaphor of guerrilla warfare, comradeship within a small group of determined men who form their cadres outside the society and make raids on it, this should not surprise the educators. Nor should it dictate the kind of response the educators make to those who are attacking them. If the educators adopt the conventional posture of counter-insurgency, they then play the role which the insurgents have assigned them, and if the educators can be persuaded into police action against the students, they have played into the hands of their adversaries.

In other words, if youth demands to know what its elders stand for, and find that in the absence of social and political principle, to say nothing of educational philosophy, what their elders stand for is counterinsurgency rather than confrontation with the real issues, then the insurgency spreads to include moderates of all kinds, who, simply because they are not radicals, are not excluded from the category of those who want to know what their elders stand for. The moderates become radicalized according to the intention of the insurgents. The question of whether the insurgents are idealists or political manipulators then becomes irrelevant, since the educators are by that time put in the public position of demonstrating the inadequacy of their own philosophy.

[VII]

In another sense, the insurgency is an educational experience for all concerned and should be looked at that way by the educators involved in it. The testimony of hundreds of students who eventually became involved in the Columbia and Berkeley actions after classes were shut down was that for the first time they felt themselves to be part of a genuine university community, where major issues affecting their lives were discussed and freely debated among intelligent and concerned persons both from the faculty and the student body.

Just as the teach-ins on Vietnam developed a new educational form for raising serious questions about the nature of contemporary world politics, the student protest movement has created new kinds of student groups whose influence has been in the direction of stimulating student research, thought, and education on the very questions with which it is the business of the university to deal. Never in the history of French education has there been as vigorous, free, and open debate among students on philosophical, political, and cultural questions as those held in the twenty-four-hour free-for-alls at the Théâtre Odéon in the spring of 1968. Is there not some way, short of student take-over of buildings and disruption of law and order, to inject the reality of contemporary intellectual issues into the life of the university? Can the university not build a social structure which, as Erikson says, "grants a given age group the place it needs—and in which it is needed"?

It has been my experience in working with students that when there are educational policies governing the behavior of the university community which have grown from the mutual involvement of students, faculty members, and administrators in creating them, there is little possibility that insurgency either of a political or a physical kind can mount a successful program of disruption. In this case the student body has already established its own kind of authority and responsibility; student loyalties cannot be won to a cause which is not theirs. Prior commitments have already been established.

The mistake is to deal with insurgency when it arises by tactics and counter-strategies rather than by educational principles. When President Kirk was asked during a television broadcast what he might have done differently in meeting the student demonstrations at Columbia, he replied, "Perhaps we ought to have been able to foresee a little more clearly the possibility that we might have been involved this way. We were all conscious of what had happened at Berkeley. We felt that our differences were such that, with a small undergraduate college, sixteen faculties with varied, diverse interests, an overwhelmingly graduate-student population, we thought that this situation would not be one that would be as

fertile for trouble as the Berkeley situation had been, and in this, of
course, by hindsight, we were wrong. [We had] a fairly small number of people in non-tenure staff positions by comparison with the
teaching assistants at Berkeley, and so on." [9]

In other words, the question for Columbia University was not
whether there was substance in the student criticisms, but whether
the student critics had a power basis in the fertile minds of a
sufficient number of underpaid graduate assistants, transient and
therefore younger and possibly bolder faculty members, and undergraduates. Once a university begins to plan its educational policies
by reference to power politics, not only are its policies bound to
suffer, but its moral leadership has been lost.

Nor is it sufficient, as so many have done, to refer to the spiritual
ancestry of the student revolutionaries in the roster of Mao, Che,
Castro, Fanon, Ho Chi Minh, Marcuse, and others as a way of
proving the dangerous and nihilistic character of the insurgents.
It is perfectly natural for young Americans to identify with revolutionary heroes if they are convinced that the policies of the
present government of the United States are reactionary and
counterrevolutionary in the support they have given to the non-
heroes Batista, Chiang, Diem, Ky, Thieu, Perón, and Franco, for
example.

If the surge of militant rhetoric then identified President Johnson, Mr. Rusk, Mr. Rostow, and General Westmoreland as fascists,
imperialists, and bloodthirsty criminals, the reply need not be
given in terms of a psychological or intellectual equivalent. Rhetoric in that style convinces few, and informed students know fairly
well that we are in a situation in which there *are* George Wallaces
and Senator Eastlands; we *are* fighting an immoral counterrevolutionary war; Che Guevara and Ho Chi Minh *are* men of higher
principle than Diem, Ky, or Franco; this *is* a white racist society,
and that is where the problems are.

The difference in the case of American radicals is, of course,
that those who choose to use the clichés of extremist rhetoric are
not likely to be jailed and shot as traitors in the manner of Mao's
cultural revolution; and the comparison of the United States as an
imperialist reactionary power of the same character as Spain, Portu-
gal, Hitler Germany, and fascist Italy, while a source of exhilaration
to those who assert it, is unconvincing as revolutionary doctrine
even among the student revolutionaries who use it.

Consider, for example, the message from Michael Klonsky, national secretary of Students for a Democratic Society to the Cuban people as a 1968 Fourth of July message from his organization:

> Hundreds have been killed in the streets of Harlem, Watts, Detroit, and Cleveland and on the campuses of many black universities [fighting for the ideals of 1776]. The student movement now faces the same type of repression. Hundreds of Columbia University students are facing long prison terms because they dared to struggle for an end to university complicity with the racist and destructive system of world imperialism. At this very moment, students at Berkeley are being attacked by police because they wish to demonstrate their support for their brothers in France, fighting against French fascism.

The general effect on the American student movement of rhetoric in this style is to lose for the militants the support of the activist students who have retained the capacity to make distinctions between the response of American officials to the law-breakers in the Columbia University insurgency, for example, and the response of the Cuban, Chinese, Polish, and other Communist governments to students who demonstrate against them. The radical student movement must have for its effectiveness the support of those able to make such distinctions, the support of students who are no less radical in their thinking while retaining their ability to nail down the facts and issues in accurate terms.

These students are a much more powerful sector of the movement in their political and social influence on the campuses than those who overload the facts with a burden of ideological rhetoric. It is therefore important for educators in looking at the actions of student radicals to be able to distinguish, in the midst of the general confusion, between what is said in the clichés of revolutionary diatribe and what is real in the situation to which it refers. The answer to student "nihilists" is not simply to assert that the analysis they make of the historical and political realities is false, but to provide opinions, judgments, and analyses which bear the mark of serious and sophisticated thinking about the problems which agitate the radicals.

This has become a different kind of issue in the case of the tactics of Black Student Unions and other organized student groups who started out with the assumption that the way to achieve immediate change in university policy and student control of program of black studies, control of faculty appointments, the immediate inclusion of large numbers of non-white or Third World students in the student body, is to present a list of non-negotiable demands, backed by threats and acts of violence. If the university were to accept these tactics as a permissible way of making educational policy, it would very soon destroy itself, since it would not only open the way to the solution of all policy questions by the use of violence and intimidation, but would be declaring again, this time in despair, the bankruptcy of its educational philosophy.

Mr. Jerry Varnado, coordinator of the Black Student Union at San Francisco State College and a graduate student who lectures in black studies there, has put the position of his Union bluntly: "We will use any means necessary to uphold the principle that people of the third world have a right to determine what kind of human beings they want to be. Violence is the best means. It disrupts and terrorizes, so that if people of the third world are not allowed to determine their own kind of education, then nobody else on that campus can get any kind of education."

The issue as Mr. Varnado states it then becomes much simpler, and should be distinguished from the other issues. On its part, the university has the obligation to make certain that the interests and insight of the non-white students, along with the white students, militants and moderates alike, are given full and equal representation in the process by which decisions are made about appointments to the faculty, changes in the curriculum, methods of admission, and university policy in general. If, as has been the case at Wayne State University, the black students, with the appropriate faculty, student, and administrative bodies, conclude that the establishment of a separate black studies institute is in the best interests of the university and its students, the issue has been resolved according to certain principles of educational philosophy. On the other hand, if organizations of black or white students refuse to accept responsibility for collaborating in a fair and equitable way with others in an agreed-upon system of decision-making, and if they assert that violence is the best and only way of achieving what they want, then the university is forced to consider violence in its own terms— as the destruction of rational means of reaching agreement in educational policy.

It then becomes a question of organizing the university in such a way that those who work as activists in trying to run the university by violence are barred from membership in the university community. But their educational views, as stated in non-negotiable demands, must be taken seriously, not because they are backed by threats and violent actions, but because they are representative of the views of one sector of the American community whose educational needs, opinions, and demands have until now been almost completely ignored. They are providing, rightly or wrongly, a new set of dimensions for educational and cultural thought by asserting the validity of the claim that a black culture and a black mind exist and must be taken into account.

What is needed is a clear policy which holds students accountable for their actions while giving them equality of power in making the policies which affect them. Coupled with this must be the machinery for settling questions of accountability and behavior in the university community. Once the policy is set, whether it be one of encouraging black separatism within the student body and curriculum, granting to students the power of faculty appointment, deciding that all black studies should be conducted by black faculty members, or the opposite, or variations of all these, the policy must be applied in such a way that when it becomes necessary to protect the rights of the community against violence by calling for police action, it is a matter of agreed-upon principle and policy, not of *ad hoc* administrative action. Unless the faculty and students are made responsible for deciding on the rules according to which they guarantee to govern themselves, they cannot be asked to have anything to do with the governing.

[VIII]

To sum it up, the flaw in the response of the educators to student disorders has been that the response has been based not on educational principle but on legal attitudes and administrative codes. Instead of looking at the circumstances of the disorder to decide what in fact is being said by the overt behavior and asking the question, Is the action based on a commitment to something serious, fed by grievances which are genuine?, the universities have looked to the rules. Is the insurgency the joint action of persons who need some kind of aggression to test themselves out as members of a generation they have read about in the magazines? What part of the situation of disorder is creative; what part of its internal energies are useful for change; what is there in it which can be used to teach everyone concerned—the administrators, the faculty, the students, the public—about the nature of genuine educational reform?

To take the other path toward the strategy of imposing law and order means that every time a rule is made, the rule gives the students another chance to test its validity and its enforcement possibilities, new opportunities for challenging authority, new means for devising tactics to overcome the new rule. When the principles of an educational and social philosophy are applied in a situation where surely one would assume them to be relevant, at an educational institution, what may seem to be a retreat before threats is transformed into an educational policy whose purposes can be reasonably explained and fairly acted upon.

In the absence of profundity of philosophy and clarity of principle, the administrator is reduced to the application of administrative and legal codes to which he is asking the students to be loyal in a situation in which loyalty can not be given. The codes are artifacts of administrative policy rather than the outcome of mutual agreement. The demand by the university that *de facto* codes be accepted is of the same order of arbitrariness in the eyes of the student as the endless requirement of subject-matter courses and the punitive system of tests and grades, which are also administrative codes rather than products of a sophisticated and imaginative approach to education itself.

When, in addition, the university president remains, either by inclination or press of duty, remote from the concerns of the students and the internal life of the campus, the way is then open for the students to confer upon him whatever image their inclinations and interests may dictate. If the university president, again by inclination or press of duty and the need for business and financial connections of use to his university, serves on the boards of directors of business corporations, government advisory bodies, and quasi-military research institutes, the students, having no other clues, even if they wished to use them, can construct a verifiable image of the president as a capitalist-apologist for the American business society.

If, at the same time, the president in his public statements never addresses the student body directly on matters of educational or social substance, and acts out exactly the role of the defender of the American establishment, the students are then given exactly the role they are expected to play, with the script marked for their exits and entrances. They are explicitly placed in the role of young radicals who are fighting against the power of the organized business community and against the control of the universities by its representatives. The concerned students are ready for something to be true to, and when they do not find it in their university they search for it elsewhere or create their own imagined version of a university they could be true to.

This was very clear in the behavior of those students at Columbia University who, after the first outbreaks, formed their own organization independent of the black militants and the white SDS activists, entitled Students for a Reconstructed University. In the counter-Commencement which they organized as an alternative to the regular 1968 Columbia University Commencement, the most striking fact about their ceremonies was the degree of genuine happiness, gaiety, and commitment which the participating students showed toward their university and toward themselves as students. After leaving in the middle of the regular Commencement to attend an outdoor celebration of their own, to hear speakers whom they had selected and invited, they marched, still dressed in their caps and gowns, sat in the heat of the New York afternoon sunshine on the steps of their university library, and paid tribute, by a ceremony of their own devising, to their sense of loyalty to the community of scholars and to Columbia University, the institution which had somehow taught them to want to reconstruct it.

7: The Moral Energies
of the Academy

What is encouraging in the history of university conflict over these past five years, once one goes beneath the surface to see where the eruptions are coming from, is that the conflict is forcing a redefinition by the academic profession of the nature of its own commitments. No matter what else is said about the size and immobility of the faculty bureaucracy, it provides a location for the development of humanist sentiment. If that sentiment is to express itself in social change, both inside and outside the university, it will be because of an increased sense of responsibility on the part of the faculty members toward their students and toward the issues to which the students have drawn attention.

In most cases, failure to act in these matters has not been due to a decision by scholars and scientists not to act, but to a community structure which shields the faculty from a direct awareness of the reality of student life and student commitments. As Albert Goldman of the Columbia University faculty has pointed out, even the engaged faculty who became involved in efforts to deal with the substance of the student protest at Columbia eventually withdrew and left the issues in the hands of the administrators. "Their motives were not selfish," said Professor Goldman, ". . . their problem was, as it had always been, that they had no concerted will and no organs for the expression of their tentative and divided consciousness." [1]

On the other hand, it is a matter of crucial importance that the colleges and universities have acted as the center of the resistance movement to the war in Vietnam, and that around the issues of the war has grown a new national community of university intellectuals who have taken the initiative in public and community action to alter American foreign policy. This kind of initiative showed itself among the natural scientists following World War II, in actions having to do with controlling the use of nuclear weapons. Later, the scientists combined forces with others in the universities to explode the mythology of the fallout-shelter movement and to explain to the public the necessity of a nuclear test-ban treaty. In doing so, they contributed a style of political action which was true to the tradition of humanist scholarship.

It was action which invoked the authority of the rational mind on behalf of the aims of peace and world unity, and its efforts in political persuasion were based on informed arguments developed by serious thinkers addressed to the public and to the government. A new style has developed in the academic profession since then which ranges from writing speeches for political candidates to providing position papers on public issues and becoming actively engaged in election campaigns.

John Kenneth Galbraith in his analysis of the new industrial state [2] has described this constituency and has restated the facts about the link between the intellectual community (in his words, the educational and scientific estate) and the power centers of the post-industrial society. He argues that this estate is the center of what hope we can have for the humane use of the instruments and controls of the national society.

What is missing from Galbraith's analysis is a specific plan for generating a concern for social responsibility within the academic profession. The academic profession in its image of itself already shares Galbraith's élitist view that the academic classes have not only the power but the wisdom to arrange the society according to a higher set of conceptions than those of politicians and industrialists. But at the moment, most of those conceptions fit squarely into the dominant patterns of established social policy and, as far as social vision is concerned, are doggedly and essentially conservative.

The academic profession shares in some degree Galbraith's concern for the use of American material resources for improving the quality of American life in its aesthetic and social aspects. But among the academics, these are the values of art as product in an expanding cultural market, not art as experience, insight, subversion, insolence, negation, mystery—the art of the artist. Galbraith's is a philosophy of Kennedyism, which relies for its short-run effectiveness on recruiting distinguished academics to serve in the decisions and planning of the government and in running election campaigns. It has only an indirect relation to the total process of building a new mass democracy with the participation of all its citizens.

It leaves education in the hands of the academic profession, ignores the students, and consults the citizens only when it seeks their votes. In the limited form in which the philosophy was applied in the Kennedy and Johnson administrations, it recruited academics whose thinking and planning involved us among other things in the most disastrous war in the country's history, and then sought the means, with the help of other academics, to persuade itself, the country, and the world that this was a necessary and desirable step to take on behalf of world peace and the self-determination of nation states. In a straight choice, I would prefer to take my chances with the politicians.

The trouble with the Galbraith proposal is that it does not go far enough. It makes no provision for energizing the social conscience, either by building into the present academic structure a new set of aesthetic, moral, or social incentives or by providing a means for shifting the philosophy of education in the direction of social imagination. What is most promising in the proposal is that it considers the mass of organized brain-power in its present state of employment as the potential servant of humanist goals. It remains only to consider how the academic profession can be blown out of its curious mixture of intellectual arrogance and moral complacency by a combination of students who are attacking the basic structure of the academic estate and that small minority in the academic faculty who are busy with the same enterprise—in other words, the radicals.

After the attack, after the injection of spirit into this dead body, then the educational and scientific estate may very well shift its attention to the issues which matter desperately. This could increase the number of those in the university who do *not* want to establish links with the center of power in the government and in the industrial state, either as advisers, policy-makers, or research scholars. Work at the center of government power has the effect of neutralizing the effort of the critical mind by smothering it with government policy.

Those of us who have had the experience of trying to persuade members of the academic profession to turn away from their regular pursuits and devote at least part of their research and teaching to the issues of war and peace have found that unless some way can be found to make this a part of the regular academic reward system, few volunteers are forthcoming. From the point of view of the academic profession, there is no future in peace, no money in it, no reward in it. This is not to deny the fact, restated by Galbraith, that the center of opposition to the present war is to be found on the campuses. It is to correct the thesis that the initiatives came from the academic profession itself or that they are likely to come from that source in the future. The initiatives came from large groups of student activists working with a limited number of academics. It is the combination of that internal community, linked in every way possible to the activists in the communities of the blacks and the poor, that shows what promise there is of a use of the academic profession to keep the technological society honest and humane.

[II]

There is a line of development within the academic profession which parallels that in the student movement. It goes back to those years from 1960 to 1964 when faculty members across the country began to take a serious interest in the issues of peace and disarmament as they were presented so vividly to the communities in the form of civil defense programs. So absurd were its presuppositions, and so sinister its implications, that the civil defense program roused both the moral antagonism of liberals and the intellectual antagonism of scholars and scientists not normally drawn into political issues.

The bland assumption of the American military that they could go on testing any number of nuclear devices and releasing strontium-90 into the atmosphere, there to be blown around and eventually settle on the land and in the living organisms of this and other continents, was for many faculty members the first confrontation they had had with the military mind at work. When this assumption was followed by the next assumption, that all the data as to the dangers from nuclear fallout should be distributed by the military and their colleagues of the government research establishment, and that contrary opinions as to potential danger to all living things from fallout were of no importance, further affront was given to the organized intelligence of the university community.

The government policy at that time was to try to convince the American people that they should learn to live with the bomb and all its dangers, not worry about the fallout until the level of strontium in the atmosphere became clearly lethal, and prepare to move underground. It was not until the scientists, scholars, and critics outside the government began to examine the implications of government policy and to work out in detail such neglected questions as the actual effects on the lives of millions of one or two hydrogen bombs dropped on centers of population, that a national citizens' movement was mobilized against the whole nuclear war policy of the government.

For mothers and fathers of children, for college students, and for faculty members, the civil defense issue was an organizational point for citizens' action which had its center of origin on the campuses. An entire cluster of issues was uncovered once the civil defense policy was exposed. Even those without a week of scholarly training in political science or nuclear physics could see that if American foreign policy were based on anticommunism and a Cold War posture, the logical outcome of continuing it was to make America into a garrison state in which the citizens took up permanent residence one-half mile underground. If that was to be the consequence, then it was clear that there was something wrong with the policy.

It was also clear that there was something wrong with the attitude of the American government to its citizens, when millions and millions could be spent on propaganda and organization for a massive civil defense program which had not even examined its own assumptions. For the first time the outline of a new pattern of university service to the community emerged. The scientists and scholars, working at their proper tasks of research, analysis, and study of political and scientific issues, were reporting their findings directly to the people, not merely to their own internal community or to government contractors. They were also taking responsibility for their findings by organizing themselves and the communities to make the results of their research known on a broad scale so that action might be taken for the redress of citizens' grievances.

From this beginning, a community of concerned persons among the members of the academic profession began to emerge as a national phenomenon, and those who had originally joined together in a national information network in exchanging reports, pamphlets, and descriptions of action programs continued to deal in cooperative research and action projects with problems of disarmament, war, peace, and American foreign policy. Graduate students also became involved. They turned in many cases to thesis topics and student–faculty-initiated seminars within the regular graduate program in which the issues of war, peace, race, American foreign policy, and American education were the subject of student-faculty research related to the interests of student activists.

One of the centers of intellectual energy for the movement was in the University of Michigan, where, for example, the Center for Conflict Resolution had given undergraduate and graduate students a chance to work inside the university curriculum on issues of broad-ranging significance in social, psychological, economic, and political conflict. Later, the Radical Education Project, formed by a group of graduate students related to the tradition of SDS at the University of Michigan, developed student position papers, research and study guides, in what they referred to as a counter-curriculum, and circulated them to other campuses after using them in their own university.[3] Another source of intellectual nourishment for this and other movements has been in the Mental Health Research Institute at the University of Michigan, several members of whose staff share the view stated by Kenneth Boulding that war is a public health problem.

As the attention of the country became concentrated more and more on the Vietnam war and its effects on the fabric of American and world society, the same pattern of intellectual organization was applied to issues which went far beyond the nuclear-war issue into every aspect of American life. Out of this pattern emerged the close collaboration between university students and faculty members in organizing another form of public education and action—the teach-in movement which began on the campus of the University of Michigan in March of 1965. This too involved a network of communication for the country's campuses. Documents, reports, and position papers were circulated, and scholar-activists appeared in the press and on television, most dramatically in the major confrontation with government policy of the Washington Teach-In of 1965.

[III]

The history of the organization of an internal community of this kind working within the framework of the national system of higher education suggests one kind of extension and alteration in Galbraith's approach. The line of connection between the academic profession and the System, which now goes through the controllers of the technological society in the economic and social power centers, should in fact be going through the students and from there to the community. It should make its own links with the wider community rather than with the managers. In the case of the civil defense issue, the line was clear, the issue was understandable, the moral obligation fully visible. In the case of the Vietnam war, although the issues have now become cruelly clear, the lines of connection to the instruments of change are less clear, since they apparently cannot go through the organized political parties or the economic and social establishment, and the political strength of the dissenters has no large-scale organization to press its views.

There is accordingly a long-run problem of defining the university and the academic profession. The problem will certainly not be solved by giving up the role of the university as the center of dispassionate enquiry in every aspect of human concern. Without that, we have lost the basis for everything else. What the society needs is a university which acts as a central community for sensitizing its students and scholars and the community at large to the moral and social issues on which responsible citizens everywhere in the world should be taking humane action.

No matter where we look in the documents and reality of the contemporary world we find that we have all the direct information we need in order to understand the conditions in which the world lives. From the United Nations alone comes a stream of documents, reports, and analyses of what exists, what is wrong with it, what causes the difficulties, and how they might be eliminated. From the universities and research centers of the world the flow is impossible to stop, impossible even to absorb.

What is lacking is also known. We say it to ourselves in a hundred ways every day. It is the lack of a collective will in the world to act humanely on the knowledge we already have. Where will we get the energy to act? From what source will come the impulse toward moral imagination, sensitivity to the needs of others, and toward specific and magnanimous action? If not from the centers of education, the colleges and universities, then where? If not from *American* colleges and universities then from whose?

As in the case of the social responsibility accepted by a minority of the natural scientists for affecting public policy, the professional associations in the social sciences, among them the anthropologists, the sociologists, the social planners, the psychologists, and the political scientists, have already begun to create within themselves movements of social concern. In the foreseeable future, these will show their effects in the educational policy-making of the universities. The members of these movements are part of an honorable tradition of university scholars, whose roots are in the history of liberal Western thought. Theodore Roszak in his essay on "Academic Delinquency," which begins the volume of essays on *The Dissenting Academy* by his colleagues in the social sciences, cites a passage from Nietzsche which serves as a ground for the development of just such movements.

> Now Pascal thinks that men pursue their business and their sciences with such single-mindedness in order to escape the most important questions which every moment of loneliness and true leisure would urge upon them—questions concerning the Why, the Whence, and Whither of life. But curiously enough, not even the most obvious question occurs to our scholars: what benefit their labor, their haste, and their painful ecstasies can possibly have? ... But if, as men of science, you go about science in the same manner in which workers go about tasks which life's daily necessities impose upon them, then what is to become of a culture condemned to await the hour of its birth and its salvation amidst this excited, breathless, aimless, fidgeting infatuation with science and learning? [4]

The most recent example to hand of the work of men of science in establishing a philosophy of social concern within the organized profession comes from a minority group in the American Political Science Association. At the annual Association meeting in 1968 they addressed themselves to the question of the proper function of those who are professional students of politics. They urged that their association encourage the development of research projects other than those of descriptive political science and, without loss of the objectivity of genuine scholarship in the field, turn the attention of the professional mind to issues which affect the present and future of organized society. Their action follows upon the organization of the New University Conference in March of 1968 in which a group of 350 intellectuals, both students and faculty, from 85 campuses, have combined forces to see what can be done on the university campuses to create what Richard Flacks calls a "counter-culture of humane concern." [5]

The center of effort for the reform of the universities is thus placed exactly where it should be, in the development of a new atmosphere of concern in which students and faculty members can exercise their talents as scholars and learners on issues and problems having to do with human welfare. The responsibility of the university is then defined by the actions of its constituent members as scholars, students, and educators with humane concerns, not merely as activists pledged to the use of the university as a tool for revolution.

If a revolution were to come, intellectual or otherwise, it would come from a constellation of forces, of which the scholar with an interest in such matters is a component, and not from a decision by the university to act as a center of the revolution. To those who wish to use it that way, the answer must be that the university respects both the concern and the integrity of the free intellect seeking a means of acting upon the society: the university as an institution does not act either as a tool of the status quo or as a political instrument for use by ideologists.

[IV]

Until now, the major argument of the universities about their involvement in public affairs has been that they are the centers of intellectual and social neutrality without which the society cannot sustain the necessary flow of creative ideas and criticism about its own values. As Richard Hofstadter has put it, "A university is firmly committed to certain basic values of freedom, rationality, inquiry, discussion, and to its own internal order; but it does not have corporate views on public questions." [6]

The fact is that the university does have corporate views on public questions, and, as has been the case ever since the university began to assume its position of social and political power at the beginning of this century, it expresses its corporate views by the actions it takes as well as by the views it proclaims. When it abolished the elective system after 1945, it made certain proclamations about education and the position of the university on the public question of how education can best be conducted. When it affects or neglects the lives of the poor in its own community by its corporate actions, it is expressing a corporate view on a public question and must make public statements in defense or explanation of the views it holds. When it takes corporate action to make policy on whether or not Communists should be allowed to teach, it makes public statements indicating why it holds the view it does.

When the president of the university speaks publicly, while it is true that he speaks in his own name, if he is talking about educational policy at his own university he is either expressing a subjective view out of keeping with the character of his institution and its corporate management, which he is very unlikely to do, or he is saying what the corporate view actually is. Something very close to a national corporate view of the function of the university was expressed by Clark Kerr in the Godkin lectures at Harvard [7] while he was president of the University of California in Berkeley. Although the regents and the faculty had nothing to do with writing the lectures, it was clear from the lectures that the policy of the University of California as a whole was reflected in the views of its president. In fact, that is what aroused many of the politically minded students when they analyzed the meaning of the policy as far as the education of students was concerned.

The university is not neutral, it is only in appearance disinterested—nor should it be. That is the whole point. We do not expect an American university in 1968 to proclaim that it has met in corporate session and now announces that it is against this

American war. But we do have a right to expect that in its policies it will reflect a fundamental corporate decision, that by their nature *all* universities are against *all* wars as a means of solving human problems.

The university exists to advance certain human values which constitute the best that is in man—of which the freedom of the mind and the spirit of free enquiry are at the center. In the case of Galileo's statement about the motions of planets, the freedom of the mind very quickly became involved in questions of religion, philosophy, and politics in which the church held both the power and the corporate view according to which truth was to be decided. Sooner or later, the university finds itself in the same position, that is to say, deeply involved in questions of politics and public policy, by reason of its support of the cause of free enquiry. To hold otherwise would be to deny the moral dimension of the human intellect.

It is possibly too obvious an example to cite the role of the German universities under Hitler, and the fact that because corporate policy lay in the hands of the state and was transferred intact into the universities, the application of truth to the operations of the society suffered a fatal blow. The obligations of the university extend beyond its protection of individual scholars from the denial of the right to express their honest conclusions, by the very fact that that obligation has been accepted as a prime necessity in the work of carrying out its mission. As the intellectual and moral conscience of mankind, the university can do no other. It is a question of where the university will throw the weight of its power and influence—on the side of an open, free, democratically organized, and peaceful world society, or on the side of whatever government is in power in the country it serves. We are dealing here with the whole of mankind and the obligations of the free intellect to create a free society. Otherwise, who speaks for freedom, for man, for the coming-together of peoples, for the compassionate virtues which deny the use of force and violence in the resolution of human conflict?

If the values of "freedom, inquiry, rationality, discussion" are to be celebrated only within the university's internal order, and its commitment in these matters is only to those in its employ, excluding the students, on the grounds, in Hofstadter's words, that "in ultimate reality the members of the faculty are the university," [8] then the university has established itself as a separate kingdom without responsibility of a moral *or* corporate kind to give intellectual and social leadership to a society badly in need of both. It has also asserted a kind of innocence in these matters which the facts deny.

The university also expresses its corporate views by the way it spends its money, in the social organizations with which it is most intimately connected—from schools and civil rights organizations to theater and dance companies—but above all, in the kind of people it appoints to its faculty and administration. If scholars with specific interest in public issues and social questions are appointed, rather than others whose interests are entirely in academic discourse and scholarship, a point of view is being expressed about what kind of internal community can best serve the external society. If scholars uninterested in teaching are appointed to carry out research assignments rather than scholars who are genuine teachers with a concern for students and educational policy, that is another kind of corporate statement which betrays the conception of neutrality.

It is here that one of the clearest solutions is to be found in the complicated question of deciding on a role for the university which *does* engage it in the solution of public problems and at the same time maintains its intellectual integrity as a center of disinterested thought. It is a solution being acted upon by a minority of members of the academic community. These men and women are working out ways in which, as scholars with a social conscience and a concern for social change, they can carry out their responsibilities both to the university and to the wider community, without betraying either their own scholarly integrity or the university's central purpose.

In general, this involves an extension of the ideas around which the scientists and scholars organized themselves to effect change in national policies on nuclear weapons and civil defense. It involves the deliberate organization of persons within the university community to create a new climate of opinion there. It involves the exercise of proper influence, in collaboration with students, in directing attention to specific issues of social importance. It involves teaching, with the inclusion of new areas of inquiry in the curriculum, and encouraging students to gain direct experience with the problems they are studying.

The university is not, as Mr. Hofstadter has asserted it to be, the members of the faculty. It is the faculty, the administration, the administrative faculty (its committees, chairmen, deans), the students, and the surrounding constituencies, but particularly the faculty, students, and administration. It has become customary to think of the university administrators as either the custodians of the buildings and grounds or the autocratic rulers of the university community. They are neither.

The truth is that the university administrator, although hemmed in by a network of hidden controls, has two major sources of power —the decisions about how to spend the money in his budget, and whom to appoint to do what he thinks needs to be done. His actual control over educational policy and the mission of the university, no matter what may be the persuasive power of his public statements, lies in what he sets in motion by the persons he appoints. Some of the most lively and invigorating programs of education in the country's colleges and universities have been set in motion by administrators, against the collective will of the faculty, simply by the use of the legitimate authority of the administrator to decide who should be appointed to the administration and faculty.

What has already happened in the student movement can happen in the academic profession. A critical mass can form itself within the university among those concerned with the role of the university in social change, and there is clear indication that the beginning coalition which has already been made between the activist students and liberal faculty members will increase in size and importance. Along with it will come a new definition of what it means to be radical, as more and more faculty members recognize that the issues the students are raising on all fronts are issues for which they have a responsibility at least equal to that of the students. What is now considered to be radical student protest will before long become liberal educational social policy. It is not necessary even now to identify oneself as a radical to be opposed to militarism, imperialism, social and economic injustice, racism, and bad education.

Nor is it necessary to lose one's objectivity as a scholar and scientist in order to act politically on public questions. The colleges and universities, having already become a base for a new political constituency actively cultivated by politicians running for office, are also a base for the development of a radical intellectual movement. Already the shades of opinion from conservative to moderate to liberal to radical are very much blurred at the edges of each by the moral urgency and relevance of the issues the radical students have introduced. Responsibility for serious treatment of the issues, both in the curriculum and in the community life of the campus, falls to the faculty and to the educators, whether or not as individuals they wish to commit themselves to any form of political action.

The universities and colleges must, in a word, accept the legitimacy of the radical tradition and accept the fact that it is part of the larger tradition of humanist scholarship. The intellect at work on philosophical, historical, or political subjects is bound to produce radical conclusions, simply by reason of the reinterpretation of historical fact and philosophical perspective made necessary by the introduction of new forms of knowledge. The present revisionist movement in American history, both in relation to the Cold War period and to the history of the Negro, is not necessarily part of a radical movement, but is the result of what happens when new emphases and interpretations are given to historical fact as the perspective is changed by contemporary history.

When students begin to find that what they are told in the texts of the regulation curricula does not square with the facts they have uncovered in their direct experience with the society or with the reports about society from the mass media, the center of gravity in conservative historical interpretation begins to shift, whether or not there are radicals at work in the academy. Since the dividing line between contemporary history and the history of the past has already shifted in the direction of the present, it is clear that much of the historical writing in the near future is going to merge with the general writing of social scientists and social critics.

It is also clear that the analysis and interpretation of American cultural history from now on will be more and more in the hands of the younger generation of scholars whose formative intellectual years have been spent on this side of the Cold War in the developing phase of the social revolution. More than this, the young generation of student activists, or rather, the older members of the young generation, those who came of intellectual age in the late 1950s and early 1960s, have been developing their own scholars and academics whose claims for appointment to college and university faculties are more than equal to the standards of conventional academic scholarship and the demands of teaching and research posts.

Many of the students involved in the reform movements in the early and middle 1960s have gone on to the graduate schools with no slackening in their enthusiasm for the causes with which they were identified as undergraduates. Others who have dropped out have come back, with a clear sense of purpose as to why they came, and with the deliberate intention of working within the academic profession in order to give full range to their interest in political and social change. They have retained their direct connection with those who did not come back and who are instead working in the communities as activists and reformers. Such persons on the outside are colleagues whose intellectual development continues, outside the university walls.

The academic credentials of these new graduate students are usually impeccable. They are among the best students, and their social views, especially on questions of race and poverty, are radical, and at the same time are becoming politically respectable.

Scholars of this kind are badly needed in the doubly expanded market for teachers who can deal intelligently with the social issues of a troubled society and for research-action scholars who can give direct help to the solution of problems in the disadvantaged communities. These intellectuals and activists have recruited themselves into the academic profession at exactly the time it needs them most. The fact that they have been or are radicals, and have worked at it, is the reason they know as much as they do and are so highly motivated toward knowing more and doing more. They have prepared themselves by practical experience as teachers and research scholars because they wanted to bring their talents to bear on the very problems with which the schools, colleges, and universities need the most help. The nature of their commitments then adds to their qualifications for appointment to the universities and colleges.

PART THREE

The Closed Curriculum: General Education Reconsidered

8: The Closed Curriculum

If the colleges and universities are to act as centers of intellectual and social energy and to have an effect on the lives of their students, they will have to be reorganized with that as their mission. The fastest route back to that mission is in the direction opposite to the road taken by the major universities over the past twenty-five years —the road to general education—and it might be useful to look at why the universities went that way and why everyone followed them down the road.

To me, the doctrine of general education is an administrative device, not a philosophical principle. The doctrine was originally stated in its most convincing form by the faculty committee on the Objectives of General Education in a Free Society at Harvard in 1945,[1] and the committee report, along with documents from Columbia University and the University of Chicago, set the pattern of discussion and reform for the American undergraduate college from that year to this. The Harvard committee took note of the expansion and fragmentation of all forms of knowledge and the subsequent splintering of the old elective curriculum into hundreds of unrelated and specialized courses through which the student could pick his way according to his purposes or whim. The committee then provided a rationale for a program of general education which, in combination with the Columbia and Chicago views, had an overwhelming effect on the subsequent organization of the American college.[2] The effect was to lock up the students of the country in a prison of requirements, standardize the undergraduate curriculum from coast to coast, take liberal learning out of the hands of the students, and strip them of a role in their own education, thus stopping most serious and deep-going experiment in undergraduate education for nearly twenty-five years.

Only now, by the series of student revolts and non-revolts—that is, non-revolt considered as sustained apathy by those not yet sensitive enough to revolt—are the experiments beginning to move again and the grip of the all-required curriculum being broken. What the general education movement did in the power structure of organized learning was to remove the only defense the student had against bad teaching, the elective principle, which gave him the inalienable right to choose his own teachers. With the removal of the principle, teaching became a task engaged in by persons with other interests who, by reason of the requirements, were safe from the possibility of being deserted by the students who had been assigned to them.

The theory of general education is merely part of a broader theory which defines education as the coverage of subjects and not the development of lives, and defines the student's mind either as a muscle to be trained or as a clean slate on which the academic profession can write its messages. The reason the general education movement has had so powerful an effect on educational theory and practice is not only that its rationale was the product of ideas from the prestigious institutions, but that it and the proposals for reform stemming from it went to the center of major weaknesses in much that was being done in the colleges up to that point, the point reached at approximately the period of World War II.

The undergraduate colleges at that time had simply lost their mission. Having been founded to provide a liberal education for a relatively few students, in the post-war years the colleges found themselves in a mass democracy requiring mass education. They were also in a society which had just finished mobilizing its entire educational system to fight the biggest and most complex war in history. In doing so, it had used the colleges and universities as the major resource for the supply of manpower in a military victory which depended for its success on the sophisticated power of the organized intellect.

Even the liberal arts and sciences were mobilized. They formed the basis of a five-semester set of courses in the Army Specialized Training Program, the Navy, the Air Corps, and the Marine Corps, as a combination educational introduction, prerequisite for Officer Training Corps, and manpower reserve pool for military personnel. It was the beginning of the organizational pattern of general education. Its virtues were that it provided a screening device to locate those able to handle later training programs in the officers' training schools, it gave some general education to intelligent high school and college students, and it isolated into manageable groups those who were to be given responsibilities in the managerial and executive sections of the war society. The military-industrial-educational-social complex had thus been established, and the forerunner of the general education movement was set in motion. Once that complex had been organized and put to use, close links between the government and the universities had been irrevocably established. The universities were in control of the resources for developing the country's manpower on a mass scale.

[II]

What then was left to the colleges? The colleges which were separate from the universities could not compete with the big institutions in offering preparation for professional work, since they had no graduate schools of their own. At the same time, so many students were coming to college in order to prepare themselves for entering the professions and vocations that the curriculum had to take that into account unless it were to continue with a mission that had become obsolete.

Under the old elective system, if students in the undergraduate college simply took the courses offered by the college departments, from introductory to advanced work, and chose other courses at random which had little to do with any integrated form of knowledge, either professional or humanistic, what the students had when they emerged from their four years was a tattered set of academic credits on a transcript and an education lacking in unity of purpose or of content. It was neither liberal nor adequately professional. In the meantime, the courses in the liberal arts and sciences had become vocational, in the sense that they prepared students for further work in a field, or they did little more than to introduce nonspecialist students to the subject matter of a field they never expected to enter.

The liberal element in liberal education had accordingly either disappeared or become irrelevant to the student's purposes. The colleges had, without conscious choice, been assigned two major functions: to serve the expanding population as instruments of social and economic mobility, and to teach the young to be Americans and Western men in the post-industrial society. If a college education were to mean anything as far as the liberal arts were concerned, the argument went, something would have to be done to unify the curriculum and the experience of the student around an educational philosophy.

The doctrine of general education was then invoked to fill the vacuum. It was a doctrine which meant, in practice, a new ordering of subjects rather than a new infusion of purpose. If students were to learn the meaning of their own cultural and historical tradition, and to establish within themselves a sense of continuity with the ethical and aesthetic content of their own civilization, it was argued, new courses in the humanities and Western civilization would have to be devised for all of them to take. In the words of the report of the Harvard committee, ". . . the tradition which has come down to us regarding the nature of man and the good society must inevitably provide our standard of the good." [3]

Whether or not this is true, courses based on the idea were arranged on a national scale, and were of two general kinds. The first were courses similar to those started at Columbia beginning in 1929 in the sequence entitled Contemporary Civilization, and later, in 1937 in the humanities sequence. These dealt with the major literary, philosophical, and aesthetic documents and objects of the Western tradition. The second were the survey courses developed at the College of the University of Chicago in the natural and social sciences and the humanities for all students. Other courses in the social sciences and the natural sciences were started, at Harvard, Chicago, Wisconsin, and elsewhere, to make an over-all undergraduate curriculum which would avoid the fragmentation of disparate offerings and express in curricular form the concept of the unity and breadth of all knowledge.

The negative definition of the theory betrays some of the weaknesses in the original Harvard conception—it was to be two years of nonvocational, nonprofessional, nonspecialist education. In practice this meant that it was to be nondepartmental, that is, an education designed by members of the academic departments for purposes of the liberal education one would have assumed to be in the forefront of the departmental mind in planning the courses the departments were already offering. The separation of "general" education from "liberal" and "specialist" education meant that it was perfectly possible by the negative definition to have an education whose purpose was in fact nonvocational, nonprofessional, and nonspecialist, but with no other purpose than that it was to be general instead of liberal. The theory was flawed at the start by opposing general to special, as if the liberalizing effects of work in depth in a chosen field of knowledge were not operative, while breadth in the range of coverage of subjects automatically conferred a liberal outcome.

Fortunately, the distinction did not seriously affect the curriculum at Harvard, where "liberal" and "general" were used as identical terms "as that which befits or helps to make free men." [4] Those who taught the courses in the general education sections of the Harvard curriculum were usually distinguished scholars and teachers interested in teaching courses which drew upon their own depth and breadth of scholarship without any academic constrictions. At their best, these courses were the intellectual inventions of scholars who let their minds run free on the problem of teaching freshmen and sophomores.

But it did raise the question as to why such courses could not be given equally well by gifted teachers working within the regular departmental system by the simple device of making the introductory courses there into something more relevant and less academic than those already offered. There is no need to sacrifice the quality of intellectual content and its liberating effect on the mind simply because one is *introducing* a student to a given area of knowledge. The question has been answered at Harvard, and in the sciences at Columbia, by the development of new kinds of introductory courses among which nonspecialist and specialist students can choose in fulfillment of the curricular requirement that they become generally educated. Presumably their liberal education has not been damaged in the process.

On the other hand, the reasoning of the Harvard committee and their counterparts at Columbia and elsewhere did not extend to any questions about the method by which liberal or nonvocational learning can best take place, or about the apparatus of lectures, academic credit, examinations, and grading by which liberal learning is administered. If its purposes were nonvocational, some other purpose beyond a rhetorical statement about coming into one's heritage in the tradition of Western man would have to be established in the minds and motivations of the student.

That is what seldom becomes clear as far as the student is concerned. He usually does what he is told, accepting the rhetorical purpose but not understanding it or committing himself to it. The planning for general education simply omitted the live student as an element in the educational process, assuming that if the student read the books and looked at the objects, discussed them, wrote papers about them and what they contained, and passed examinations on them, he would be committed to the values of Western civilization in such a way that these would show themselves in his political, social, and aesthetic behavior.

In effect, general education was defined as a series of required courses taught within the same lecture-examination-credit-grade system, with books, classrooms, libraries, and academic study as the prime educational instruments. For the Harvard student, this meant that the tutorial system was abolished, and that for the student's first two years his time was spent in large lecture courses with the usual discussion sections and personal work carried out by graduate assistants. It was all a matter of the subject matter of the courses, not the total experience of the student; it was the organization and distribution of specific sets of requirements in general areas of knowledge, not the liberation of the student's mind and imagination by experience in the creative arts, in society, or by critical analysis of contemporary culture.

The result was that when the general education doctrine and program were taken over by the colleges and universities across the country, the pattern of instruction was stabilized at the low level of the lecture system accompanied by the usual discussion sessions led by graduate students. The courses in general education in the natural sciences, the social sciences, and the humanities were either the usual introductory courses of the departments, with slight modifications to adapt them to the general education idea, or they were courses which drew upon materials and personnel from several fields—social science courses with units of anthropology, sociology, psychology; humanities courses with units of philosophy, history, literature, art history; and surveys of material from the natural sciences.

The practical effect was that those who taught the courses either came from the regular departments and were asked to teach courses in which many of them did not believe, or were appointed to teach in the general education curriculum and had no home in the departments. Since that is where the academic career lies, another hierarchy was raised, with the teachers of the general education courses in an echelon lower than those moving upwards in the departments. In the long run, this has meant that the younger, more inexperienced teachers, usually with career aspirations which can not be fulfilled by teaching packaged courses to the least experienced students, are the ones who staff the general education programs. Those who, although young and inexperienced, are most interested in teaching undergraduates and have the most talent for doing so feel inhibited and constricted by the *a priori* curriculum into which they are fitted by the doctrine of replaceable parts for a going machine.

But more than this, a theoretical effect with wide practical consequences took hold. The theory of general education was encapsulated within the boundaries of the academic mind. In trying to establish a unity in knowledge, the theory remained at the superficial level of considering what bodies of knowledge from the available store should be put together and taught to all students in order that they should possess a common heritage and share a common intellectual experience.

Since the intellectual experience was not deep, it produced a unity which was spurious. The unity of knowledge does not come from the coverage of academic materials, no matter how broadly spread, but through the unity in consciousness reached by the student who learns to see the connections between one idea or set of ideas and another. He learns to do so by becoming immersed in materials of study and experience whose intrinsic interest to him is such that his mind is drawn toward the connection between what he knows and what he does not know but wants to find out. When his teachers assemble the materials with all the connections made, and then point to the connections between ideas, all the work of unifying is being done by the teacher, with almost nothing left for the student to do.

[III]

The fact that an undergraduate curriculum of this kind could be accepted as the answer to the major educational question of what to do with the colleges is a tribute to the respect shown to the university scholars who created it and the weight of reputation of the universities where their curriculum reports were written. But it is a certification of respectability rather than of educational wisdom. The method by which the curriculum was put together works against that, and against the educational imagination.

It is a method based on the premise that educational policy in a university or college is the sole responsibility of the collective faculty. It develops from there into a way of applying the regular practices of the faculty committee system to express the will of the collective faculty about how education should be conducted. This, in spite of the fact that most members of the collective faculty have a demonstrated disinterest in teaching and in education, know little about it, and think of education as something which people in colleges of education do against the interests of intellectuals.

To carry out educational reforms, a committee of faculty members is assembled to represent a cross section of the academic departments and divisions of the university, and is charged with responsibility for making the undergraduate curriculum. Granted the present system of organization of the collective faculty, it is almost impossible for such a committee not to reflect the educational biases of the academic mind and the internal political interests of the section of the university represented by the individual members. There is a difference between persons trained in the skills of the academy and persons who have spent a great deal of time thinking about and working on problems in teaching, learning, and education. It is not enough to walk into curriculum committee meetings with a preparation for educational thinking which rests on the merits of a successful academic career. The difference here between an academic professional and an educator is crucial.

Usually without benefit of either empirical research or philosophical analysis of its own premises, isolated from the judgments and ideas of informed students and from the reality of educational needs in the society outside the university, the educational policy committees operate by discussion and writing reports. The content of the discussion is drawn mainly from other faculty reports and documents from other universities, with the greatest weight given to those prepared in well-known institutions.[5]

The educational plans which result have a sameness about them no matter where they are written, since they tend to accept the same premises and are written by the same kind of people. The curriculum for undergraduates is most often a composite of what each section of the university departments wants to have included in the course material, and the fact of sameness is then interpreted as a kind of universal wisdom among informed scholars as to what constitutes a proper education for all undergraduates. What is actually a consensus of the academic profession as to how its subject matter can be distributed and administered effectively in fairness to themselves is mistaken for a universal educational truth.

The point is that the Harvard, Columbia, or University of Chicago programs, those most widely influential during these past twenty years, work well or badly in their local setting to the degree that they do what needs to be done to educate the students according to the purposes and aims of the institution. Because the curricula work well, when they do, or because the local purposes are of a specified kind to which the curriculum is a response, it does not follow that what is done in these institutions is applicable to what could be done elsewhere with a different student body and a different set of purposes. Yet the academic profession, organized on a national scale, whether or not it intends to do so, exerts a controlling influence on the national planning of education whenever it develops individual programs for its own institutional use. This flows from the acceptance of the colleges of the national hierarchy in the academic profession whose members are distributed nationally from a base in the centers of graduate education high up in the hierarchy. Not only do the ideas in the educational documents carry their influence by prestige into the formation of undergraduate programs elsewhere, but the graduates of the major graduate schools carry them personally into the undergraduate colleges. The colleges, in their efforts to become "centers of excellence" by becoming feeders to the prestigious graduate schools, do everything they can to appoint the graduates of those schools to their faculties.

The result has been that for students in college after college, the general education courses are simply a block of necessary material to be covered before going on to other subjects. For students who already know what they want to do and are ready to do it, this is one of the most frustrating experiences with which they could be faced. For those who do not know what they want to do, it provides little help in finding out, either as a road to self-discovery or as an inspiration to serious intellectual effort in the pursuit of a liberal education.

Evidence of the theoretical as well as practical failure of the general education idea from the student point of view comes from the University of Guatemala, where it was not until a student strike in August of 1968 that the General Studies program, installed in 1964 with the help of the U.S. Agency for International Development and Michigan State University, was abolished as a requirement for all students at the university. An additional impetus for getting rid of the program came from politically minded students who read into it an American CIA way of keeping Guatemalan students out of politics for two years, although fundamentally it was the educational issue which caused the controversy and the student action.

Before the general education program was installed in Guatemala, the student, without an entrance examination, went directly into the professional studies in the area in which he wished to make a career. The general education program not only delayed his professional work for two years, but faced him with courses in mathematics and other fields for which he had had inadequate preparation and whose relevance to the career and further studies he was obliged to carry out in connection with it was very difficult for him to see.[6] It is equally difficult for those students in the United States who have not yet understood as clearly as the Guatemalans what it is about their education that they find so irrelevant.

Another flaw in the theory appears when an analysis is made of the difference between specialist courses and nonspecialist ones. The specialist course is wrongly defined to begin with. If it is taught merely as technical preparation to take another specialist course in a sequence leading toward graduate school professional studies, it does not belong in the liberal arts curriculum in the first place. No matter how valuable it may be as technical preparation, it lacks the fundamental attribute of scientific, humanist, or social study—that is, the attribute of intrinsic intellectual interest or humane concern which impels the student to think his way through the ideas, issues, and questions by an inner drive toward knowing. That is what education in the liberal arts and sciences means, and the degree to which it is successful is measured by the degree of intellectual investment and conscious acquisition shown by the student. The instruction, whether specialist or nonspecialist, depends for its success on this, not on whether the student is compulsorily exposed to a broad range of subject matter or a narrow range broadly conceived.

"Compulsory exposure" is the key concept in the psychology of general education, and its use as an educational term gives away the defect in its psychology and strategy. Further evidence of its defect is provided by the fact that at Harvard and elsewhere students are excused from taking the general education courses. They may go straight to the special studies in which they are interested if they can show on advanced placement tests that their "general" or "liberal" education has already been accomplished by something they have done in high school which is a replica of what they would have done in college. Rather than offering such students the opportunity as freshmen to work in a field to which they are naturally drawn, in courses which are both liberal and special at the same time, they are encouraged to jump over the very things which, in theory, have been designed to deepen their minds and broaden their knowledge.

[IV]

In the case of the Columbia and University of Chicago ideas, the conception of general education is much more rigorously argued and rigorously applied than at Harvard, although in my judgment no less fallacious in theory. The conception rests on a theory of knowledge and of education which defines the educational process purely in terms of classroom instruction appropriate for developing the qualities of the academic intelligence. That the academic mind at its best, with its analytic, critical, organizing, conceptualizing attributes and a wide range of information, is usually a good one for general intellectual use is not at issue. But the academic mind is one which is trained to do particular things very well, and is not necessarily the model for the mind and character of the liberally educated person, or even of the intellectual who intends using his mind outside the academy.

In the original Chicago plan, the student who had spent two years in acquiring a body of knowledge and in learning how it is organized into its disciplines and concepts, and who could demonstrate by examination that he had acquired and could manage the content of the curriculum, was declared to have a liberal education. That is what liberal education was said to be. If a student, of whatever age, could demonstrate by examination that he had already acquired parts of the knowledge, or even the whole of it, he was exempt from having to become any more liberally educated than he already was, at least in that part of his young life covered by the examination.

Liberal education is thus once more defined in negative terms. It is nonprofessional, nonvocational, nonspecialist. Or, in its positive definition, it is a program to put the student in touch with his own heritage of the past and to acquaint him with the outline of certifiable knowledge of the present. It is designed for man the rational animal, to teach him how to engage in rational activity.

That seems to me to be what is fundamentally wrong with the idea of general education and what was fundamentally wrong with the college at the University of Chicago when, from 1943 on, this was its program. I do not mean that a college has failed if it does not go on doing whatever it started out to do, or if its program is modified by continuing experiment. That the present college at the University of Chicago has stopped doing many of the things I am describing is an indication of the failure of the idea, not the failure of the college, either now or as it existed more than twenty years ago. I mean that the Chicago idea was wrong from the start, that it exerted a regressive influence on undergraduate education across the country, and that it did so because it gave a clear-cut solution, based on false premises, to the problem of how to define the undergraduate college and what to do with its curriculum.

The failure of the idea rests on the fact that the social and educational philosophy on which it rests is a form of eighteenth-century rationalism with traces of the original Aristotelian faculty psychology, and is false to the social and psychological reality of the twentieth century. It proceeds from the proposition that human nature is everywhere the same, that man is defined by the fact that he possesses the faculty of reason, and goes from there to distinguish the liberal arts college from any other kind of institution as the place where the rational faculties are to be cultivated by a common intellectual experience for all students in a common body of knowledge. The origin of the idea in Western thought is obvious. What is less obvious is how so complete an expression of the élitism inherent in its theory of knowledge and of society found itself transplanted into an energetic, democratically oriented American college in the American Midwest.

There are many reasons. Among them is the fact that Alexander Meiklejohn, with his extraordinary gifts as a teacher, his love of the Greeks, his conception of the state, his passion for absolute first principles, and his knowledge of education, had put them to work on developing an educational philosophy which appealed to the national community of humanist scholars and their educational representatives. Meiklejohn gave a clear and convincing rationale for the occupational biases of professors in the humanities. His ideas found their practical expression in the all-required program of the two-year Experimental College at the University of Wisconsin in the 1920s and 1930s, and later in the Great Books program at St. John's College in Annapolis. The ideas received independent support in the humanities curriculum at Columbia and at Chicago, in the latter case through the work of Robert Hutchins in stating his own variation of the Meiklejohn rationalism and the Mortimer Adler views about liberal education, and in organizing a college to suit.

The effect of Hutchins' public statements, beginning in 1936 with a series of lectures, "The Higher Learning in America," [7] gained strength from the position he occupied as president, and later chancellor, of the University of Chicago, at a time when few university presidents or educators had so well-developed a style of public expression and the daring to use it so forcefully on educational issues. Wide circulation was given to a set of ideas which gained in public influence by the clarity with which they were expressed. They were clear because they reduced the complexity of education to a few basic and understandable propositions which bore the weight of ancient authority but were in fact little more than slogans.

Having carried the art of the sweeping statement to one of the highest levels it ever reached in the public discussion of cultural issues in America, Hutchins was able by reason of his gifts in exposition and command of the public media to create what amounted to a national polarity in popular thought between the progressive philosophy and educational theory of John Dewey and the classical views of the Western tradition. His achievement was to make a kind of rousing public wrestling match between Dewey, the common man's friend and everybody's intellectual, and Aristotle, the all-time heavyweight champion of Western thought. Once the issues had been put in these terms, the rest was comparatively easy.

The situation in the schools, the colleges, and the universities was in many ways exactly as Hutchins first described it. The curriculum had formed itself in the universities by accretion rather than by planning, by meeting whatever needs came along rather than by making priorities among them; and education in the schools was on the way to becoming a social enterprise with a few intellectual attachments. Almost anything one wished to say about what was wrong with the schools and colleges could be shown to be true, and any rigorous analysis of the relation of the educational system to the broad-ranging intellectual needs of a developing society would confirm the Hutchins criticisms. Although Dewey's criticisms of the same situation were much more deep-going and were based on a much more accurate and fundamental view of the nature of contemporary American society in a state of post-industrial change, the way in which the educational issues were stated for public debate made it very difficult to see that this was the case.

In the Hutchins exposition, which came to be a generic type, there was, on the one hand, practical, vocational, empirical education as urged by Dewey and the progressives, which led to child-centered, adaptive, socially oriented, and intellectually shallow curricula and teaching, as well as to the corruption of education into a form of service to the psychological and social needs of students and society. On the other hand, there was liberal education which developed the rational faculties and the disinterested intellect, and maintained the values of Western civilization through a knowledge of the Western tradition and the body of truth the tradition has handed down. The education of all citizens in a democracy must be liberal and nonvocational in this sense if the principles of rational thought are to survive. Rational thought is the antidote to the practical world of materially minded, achievement-oriented vocationalists more anxious to get ahead and get things done than to think about what should be done for the ultimate benefit of mankind. Since human nature is everywhere the same, education should be everywhere the same—the content was ready at hand in the proven wisdom of the texts of the great books of the past.

When this view is applied to the operation of a college, the classical disjunctions immediately appear, and the class basis of classical education is introduced into the system of democratic culture. The humanities, considered as the body of philosophy and literature from the past, are the source of moral and cultural values. Science is the accumulation and organization of fact, and is morally and ethically neutral. The body is separated from the mind, and the mind is what is to be educated; intellect is separated from emotions, liberal from vocational, social from intellectual, art from life, fact from value, science from the humanities, students from society.

There would be no more reason to include or take account of students in the planning of education than there would be to include plumbers, morticians, fly-fishermen, or farmers. Nor would there be any reason for taking account of the emotional or social life of the students in planning the college or its curriculum. That is custodial work, as Hutchins was fond of repeating year after year—child care, having nothing to do with liberal education or the intellect, a matter for the Boy Scouts, the churches, the sports programs, the YMCA, the landladies. No matter how big a factor they might be in the internal morale of the college and university, or how much the students might enjoy them, organized athletics have no place on the campus, since they have to do with cheap emotion, social celebration, and popular nonintellectual pursuits.

Anyone interested in that kind of thing does not belong in a college, and there is no need to replace intercollegiate athletics by any other kind of social device for collective celebration in the community: the college community, being a society of young intellectuals, can form its loyalties and social forms around pursuits less vulgar. Nor is there any need to link the college or the university to the society outside the campus, no matter how desperate the society may be for the help of scholars and intellectuals to solve its social, economic, and political problems. The function of the college is to make its students able to understand justice as a concept, not to apply it in the situations of actual injustice around the corner. That is for the YMCA again, or for the social workers. The business of the college is with the student's intellect and the business of the faculty is to decide what the curriculum should be for all of them.

The success of the early years of the Chicago college, as it evolved from 1937 onwards, lay in the fact that it brought together a first-rate group of young faculty members and administrators who were seriously interested in building a new curriculum, with bright young students for whom the curriculum and the quality of intellectual life of the college were a new and stimulating experience. But the fatal disease of all fixed curricula, and the Chicago one was the most completely fixed of all, is that once the experimental work of putting it together is complete and other teachers join the college, the zest for curriculum-building cannot continue among those who are asked to teach someone else's courses and administer someone else's examinations.

Another part of the same disease attacks the system when students with different conceptions of what their education should contain, and a greater maturity in what they know and want to know, find that fixed general education requirements prevent exploration of areas of knowledge of interest to them. They also find that the separation of liberal education from the practical concerns of politics, social change, the arts, and contemporary life turns it into a series of academic exercises. In a system of this kind, the critical habit of mind outweighs the creative, the ancients are given precedence over the modern, the theoretical over the practical, the abstract over the concrete, argument over problem-solving, and, finally, intellectual authority over educational freedom.

The effect of the Chicago college idea on American educational planning in the 1940s and 1950s was to confirm and strengthen the idea that (a) the college was the in-between institution, after high school and before graduate school, where a liberal education unobtained and unobtainable in high school should be provided; (b) the college should put together a common body of knowledge for all students; (c) that this need not take into account the reality of the student, his potential contribution to the curriculum, or the diversity of his purposes and needs; (d) that the purpose of the student and the purpose of the academic college coincide, and that what is taught in the academy by the academic faculty is what is most useful and intellectually enhancing in life.

9: The Academic College

In general, the ideas of the college at the University of Chicago were also basic to the planning of the Columbia College curriculum in contemporary civilization and the humanities, which designates a set of assigned readings required of all freshmen and sophomores; the content of the courses has been refined and developed over the years since 1929, and from 1937 when the program first began. In 1945, a second year of the humanities sequence was added at Columbia to include studies of the masterpieces of music and the plastic arts. Although efforts were made to form a similar sequence in the natural sciences, they were not successful, and that requirement is absolved in the conventional way by choosing among the science offerings in a broad range of courses.

There is considerable testimony that in the years when the Columbia contemporary civilization and humanities courses were taught by some of the best teachers in the college, they had an important and lasting effect on Columbia students. Daniel Bell refers to a conversion experience among many of them, "a shock of ideas that gave them a new appreciation of the dimensions of thought and feeling—a conversion, so to speak, to culture." [1]

But the question is, conversion to what culture?

The answer which forces its way into a generalization is, the conventional culture, the culture of those who have taken hold of the masterpieces of Western literature, philosophy, music, and the plastic arts, have learned to understand them, talk about them, and

148

admire them, and thus to change their way of life to one in keeping with the idea of the educated man of culture, at home at Lincoln Center, the Metropolitan Museum, and among the enlightened industrialists, bankers, and professional men who support them. Another answer is that it provides a comprehensive introduction to the tradition of civilization to which America and the West are joined, and serves for those among the young who represent, in Lionel Trilling's perceptive phrase, the adversary culture, as a testing point for the tradition of the new and as a place for examining the full range of values around which Western civilization has formed itself. In the strange and complicated educational career of Allen Ginsberg at Columbia College, the curriculum was that kind of testing point. It was, he now says, an example of how "the whole syndrome of shutdown and provincialism extended to the academy. . . . Almost anything of importance was not taught. . . ." [2]

Columbia University locates the center of effort and the majority of its students in its graduate and professional schools. The college, in its university setting, while sharing a common cultural aim with the university, is not a major source of cultural or educational influence in the university community at large. The college inherits its culture from the parent body rather than creating it from the student body. Not only is the internal life of the university organized, as at Berkeley, for the benefit of the faculty and its interests, under a tightly held baronial system of departments and professional schools, but the university has accepted the idea that its own greatness lies in its age, its prestige, its important alumni, its important faculty members, and its place in the national and international power structure. It also assumes that its educational aim should be to provide the highest kind of academic education for the brightest academic students the university is able to recruit to its classrooms.

At Harvard, a broader conception of educational achievement has always been taken for granted, and the more mellow atmosphere there and the more diverse and interesting student body has always made the Harvard snobbery more bearable, since it is exercised with a certain flair. There is less competition and more scepticism in the air; the undergraduate college is the central place from which the Harvard mystique emanates. The attitude to intellectual and curricular freedom, reflected in the eclecticism and flexibility of the Harvard general education program as it has developed, allows in practice the contradiction of the theory of general education on which it is based without inducing any sense of theoretical failure among its sponsors. The contradiction is accepted as a natural irony to be found in all efforts at making educational theory work in practical situations.

The Columbia aim is, like that of the earlier college at the University of Chicago, more precise and more intellectually militant. Testimony to its success in the past comes from many sources, including one most immediately to hand in what Norman Podhoretz has to say in his autobiography, *Making It,* about how he crossed from Brooklyn to success and fame in Manhattan by way of Columbia, and how he learned to be openly in love with success later on in life. "To wean me away from Brownsville," says Podhoretz, "all Columbia had to do was to give me the superior liberal education it did: in giving me such an education it was working a radical change in my tastes, and in changing my tastes it was ensuring that I would no longer be comfortable in the world from which I had come." [3]

What Podhoretz does not seem to have noticed, in developing his overblown theory that the refusal to admit one's own passion for success has replaced sex as the dirty little secret one can never talk about, is that the Columbia aim, in making success possible by civilizing the socially and culturally disadvantaged, was merely adding one more upper-class trait, modesty, to the cluster of attributes with which it was trying to endow him. The upper classes had long discovered that you could do a great deal more with sex, and private success of all kinds, if you did not talk about it publicly.

A further question is raised by the Podhoretz testimony when we ask about the nature of cultural disadvantage. In one sense it is a genuine cultural disadvantage to be absorbed into an élitist Western culture whose boundaries are closely set by Western conceptions of the nature of man and his place in the world and established views about the nature of the institutions which support that world. If the American college and its curriculum deliberately sets out to make cultivated Western men out of bright poor boys along with the other bright ones who can pay their own tuition, it has produced a stunted philosophy which leads to a major cultural disadvantage in its educational purpose. The mind, conceived as a sensitive instrument for exploring the world of fact and imagination, is confined to an intellectual and cultural territory which excludes the raw material of the world's total reality.

Reduced to practical terms, this means that the admissions policy of the college, in seeking out a certain kind of academic aptitude, is seeking candidates for its own curriculum. Those who do not possess an academic intelligence but who have other and more fascinating human qualities are automatically excluded, thus depriving the college of a bigger range of talent and a larger source of ideas for the curriculum and its surrounding college community.

Evidence of a kind opposite to that given by Podhoretz comes from another writer, Pete Hamill, a talented journalist whose career also started in Brooklyn but who did not have a Podhoretz scholastic mentor in his school who could steer him through to the Columbia program and into the literary world of Manhattan. Hamill had "quit high school at 16, worked as a sheet-metal worker in the Brooklyn Navy Yard, joined the Navy at 17, read and studied to make up the missing years of high school. He had received high scores on the equivalency examination. He had read Fitzgerald and Hemingway and Conrad in the Navy and he wanted to be a writer. He was prepared to work as hard as anyone at Columbia." [4]

Hamill was refused admission to Columbia by an admissions officer who, according to Hamill, told him that the Columbia choices were made on academic qualifications, and that he would do well to look into the community colleges, since they were more suited to his kind of educational record. "All right," Hamill reports himself as saying under his breath as he left the campus, "I'll do it some other way. You hard Protestant bastards. There are other ways to an education." [5]

There are other ways, and Hamill took them. It is clear from what he has done since then that Columbia missed a good contributor to its own culture, although from Hamill's point of view he is well off in having taken his alternative. His education did not make it necessary for him to be converted to "culture." He simply expanded the one he was born into and has been writing about that expansion ever since.

My point is not that Ivy League colleges in the United States should take in sheet-metal workers who have been in the Navy and want to write, while excluding academically talented boys ambitious for social and literary success. It is that without taking account of the ideas as well as the people excluded by the curriculum, it is not possible to design a self-regenerating curriculum or an imaginative educational policy. The culture of the college should be created by the members of its community with the help of the curriculum, not imposed on the members as a high or middle form of culture.

One of the basic reasons for the success of the student militants in closing down Columbia University in 1968 was the disciplined action of the black students in organizing their own occupation of a university building. It would have been possible for the university immediately at the beginning of an occupation by white students of the same building to have given the orders and taken the action necessary to clear out the white students. In the case of the black students, there was a power base just around the corner in the citizens of Harlem, and direct action against black students would have involved the university with the possibility of violent action by the community.

In other words, the black students were already introducing a new culture into the intellectually and socially restricted environment of the university, with a new set of ground rules as to how the decisions of the university on cultural and social policy should be made. A required program of studies in the humanities, dealing with abstract issues of justice, philosophy, and polity, is simply an inadequate instrument for dealing with the black representatives of a new culture which does not wish to adapt itself to the old, and possesses within itself qualities, ideas, values, and styles of thinking which are of high importance to the total university community into which it has come.

[II]

What becomes clear about the theory and practice of general education at Columbia University and elsewhere in Daniel Bell's brilliantly argued book about general education and the reform of the curriculum at Columbia becomes even clearer when it is seen in the light of the 1968 student revolt.[6] In Bell's case, the method of approach to educational reform was deliberately designed not to be a committee report, and not to be directly a part of the Columbia apparatus of decision-making by faculty committees. As the author of a major educational study, Bell was referred to by his sponsors at the university as a one-man committee, working at a task largely self-defined whose results were to be spread before the Columbia faculty and the academic profession for what use they might be in the process of reaching conclusions about curriculum change. Until the student revolt, little interest was shown by the Columbia faculty either in the issues raised by Bell or in radical change in the structure of the curriculum. The curriculum has been treated as a matter of the content of courses, not as part of the development of student life.

One instance of faculty interest at Columbia in the issues of general education is cited by Robert Friedman in the student book on the revolt at Columbia, *Up Against the Ivy Wall*.[7] Robert Friedman begins his introduction to the book with the following remarks:

> The weekend before the revolution at Columbia had its Bastille Day, a group of faculty members who teach the course that is the symbol of the *ancien régime* gathered at the former estate of Averell Harriman to plot quietly the overthrow of a Columbia College tradition. With the help of four students who conveyed the disillusionment of many undergraduates, the thirty professors summarily did away with the survey approach to "Contemporary Civilization" (CC), a course required of all freshmen since 1919. They guillotined the works of Plato, Aristotle and Aquinas which had for so long been required reading and decided that they would begin the study of Western civilization with the Reformation.
>
> What was perhaps most significant about the new CC course developed that weekend at Arden House was that almost an entire semester would be devoted to a topical study of revolutions. As the CC reformers discussed which revolutions should be studied, between meals served on delicate china and walks along wood-lined paths fifty miles north of New York City, the newest revolution, which might be included on next year's reading list, was spreading its vague fingers across a thawing campus.
>
> Educational reform was once again a step behind reality.

> Studying old revolutions in the classroom while new ones were
> taking place on the Harlem streets just ten blocks away is
> typical of the University's relation to society. In recent years
> students had come to discover that mass urban study programs
> and courses on revolution were not enough; the University was
> a social as well as an academic institution and would have to
> play an active role in the society it once attempted to avoid.
> Columbia—on the shores of one of the nation's largest black
> ghettos and adrift in a society sick with war, manipulating the
> lives of its young people for misguided crusades—was tottering
> along with the old order it had served so well.

It seems to me that Friedman has described the situation accurately and that the thirty teachers of the Contemporary Civilization course could very well hold a series of further meetings to
examine the entire theory on which the present course is based.

It is a theory which finds strong support in Daniel Bell. Since
Bell is one of the most distinguished and able social scientists in
the field of contemporary scholarship, and since his range of experience in the academic, intellectual, and government community
is unusually broad, he represents in what amounts to a pure state
the idea of the contemporary academic man, at home in his own
profession and in close touch with the reality of the post-industrial
society about which he has written so extensively. In more senses
than one he is a one-man committee, since he speaks for the
thinking of a special kind that the academic profession is capable
of doing in the matter of educational reform. His ideas must be
taken with the seriousness they deserve, especially by those who,
like myself, disagree so completely with his concepts and conclusions. Behind him everywhere in the country stand the academic
men, ready to refer to him in their curriculum committees, and
quite possibly to take his concepts whole. It is for this reason that
in choosing to come to grips with him one can come to grips with
some of the central educational problems now under national discussion in the wake of the student protest movement.

"In this day and age," says Bell, "and even more in the coming
day and age, the distinctive function of the college must be to
teach modes of conceptualization, explanation and verification of
knowledge. As between the secondary school, with its emphasis on
primary skills and factual data, and the graduate or professional

school, whose necessary concern is with specialization and technique, the distinctive function of the college is to deal with the grounds of knowledge: not *what* one knows but *how* one knows. The colleges can be the unique place where students acquire self-consciousness, historical consciousness and methodological consciousness." [8]

Here we have the doctrine of the academy plain and straight. Education is the process by which students become academic intellectuals. The secondary school is a preparation for college—it deals with the primary academic skills and factual data—the graduate school deals with specialization and the technique of knowledge production. The college is the place in between where students learn how to get ready to produce knowledge, while locating themselves in history and finding a psyche of their own.

This furnishes the ground on which the system of educational manipulation rests, with the university as the Grand Manipulator. The student is cast in the role of providing mental and social material out of which intellectual manpower is produced to supply the society and its institutions. In the meantime, life is to be lived in ways congenial to the purposes of the institutions and the ends they serve. Changes in the university as an institution, when made, are to be made in ways which improve the means through which its established ends are served. Bell points out in defense of the limited way he has conceived his task of educational analysis that he is of course aware that changes in the organization of any institution affect human behavior "by the structures in and through which an individual lives and works," and that in the case of the university, one factor in organizational planning must consist of "the changing concerns of the student body and the character of their demands."

"Equally," says Bell (that is, equally with the factor of structural change), "any discussion of curriculum must take into account not only what students should learn, but how the students' own needs and puzzlements affect them. The events at the University of California at Berkeley in 1964–65, and the nascent radicalism of a small but articulate group at Columbia, have made us all aware of the dissatisfactions and disorientations of the students about the character of their educational experience. Any judgment about a curriculum is a judgment of what a student's

intellectual experience ought to be; . . . But a student's world is
more than an intellectual one, for it involves the relationship of
intellectual study to other commitments—political, moral, aesthetic, and religious. I have tried to keep this in mind."

Having said this, Bell then puts the students out of his mind and
does not return to them throughout his entire study. ". . . Within
the confines of my time and task, I have undertaken only to deal
with the intellectual problem—the content of the curriculum—and
to eschew analysis of institutional structure and the character of
student life. The redefinition of general education is what I have
set as the agenda of debate." [9]

Once more we are face to face with the bare doctrine of the
professional academy, the doctrine of education without students,
although this time in a confrontation which begs the entire question of what is reform and what is education. The intellectual
problem in the reform of education is *not* simply the academic
content of the curriculum. It is *not* simply a matter of developing
a rationale for the sequence of a particular kind of course while
keeping in mind that students with a variety of commitments will
be taking them. To redefine general education is an intellectual
problem of the broadest possible scope, and the range of enquiry
must go on to questions about the nature of man and his purposes and to the varieties of intellectual and personal fulfillment,
which are obviously not exhausted by reaching facility in the "conceptualization, explanation, and verification of knowledge."

What, for example, is conceptualization good for, other than for
the ordering of perceptions and experience into manageable, usable,
and marketable forms? Is it enough to conceptualize an object,
an idea, a feeling, a sentiment, or a value to exhaust either its
meaning, its importance, or its motive force in a life or in a culture? Do we want to use our colleges to produce hundreds of busy
little conceptualizers, explainers and verifiers, talkers and analysis-
makers at a time when the conceptualizing and analytic mind has
been running wild through the world, having detached itself from
the simple human virtues of love, compassion, tenderness, and
empathy which it is the task of any education in sensibility to foster?

The content of the college curriculum is the student's whole
life, his life in the context of his commitments, and it is the responsibility of the college, through whatever it does, to give him the

means of creating some kind of order among his commitments. In the process of making that order, he will find it necessary to place a high value on the use of creative intelligence, since that is one of the major instruments he is being taught to use. He will also come to rely on poets, writers, artists, philosophers, scientists, scholars, and his teachers, whose books and ideas are available in the formal curriculum, to give him a sense of identity with the world of the intellectual. Which of the books and ideas, which other kinds of experience are the most likely to help him in his work of discovering and creating a body of his own knowledge will depend on the nature of his existing commitments and the kind of experience, intellectual or otherwise, which has led him to make them. Since there is a certain body of knowledge and experience which most students share on coming to college, it is possible to put together book lists, readings, topics, issues for exploration, discussion, and research which build upon that body of knowledge and are relevant both to the student's experience and to the historical tradition which, in one way or another, he is joining.

But this or some alternate way of inducting the student into the world of sensitive, thinking, acting men is ruled out by definition in the general education concept. Some of the most promising and creative alternatives, including those in effect at the experimental colleges, at San Francisco State College, in the Peace Corps, the National Teacher Corps, the University of Michigan, are not even mentioned in the Bell study, presumably because they are outside the sphere of interest of the academic profession. The circuit of thought about education is complete when it has moved from Chicago to Harvard to Columbia and around again. As Bell puts it, the intellectual problem is the content of the curriculum, and it is the set of books and objects inside the structure, not the structure itself, which sets the agenda of debate.

[III]

Since the student is not part of the debate, this does not seem to me to be the real debate or its proper agenda. It is merely a debate among members of the academic profession, closed to the public, about the best means of pursuing the profession's goals.

The true debate is in the real world in which students and ideas exist in their own right, where institutions of all kinds, including the universities, are continually brought under critical examination on the relevance of their aims and practices to the welfare of the wider community.

Mr. Bell comes to that debate only once in passing and again at the close of a book rich in educational and social fact and fertile in educational suggestion. The study has achieved what Bell set out to do, to make his own rationale for general education, "to undercut the distinction between general education and specialism," [10] and to win a running argument, which seems to have set the terms of reference of the study, against Jacques Barzun and his notion that the American liberal arts tradition is dead or dying and that the liberal arts college cannot survive the invasion of its curriculum by the high school at one end and the graduate school at the other.

In achieving that aim Bell has made clear some issues and ideas which have long been muddied by scholars and educators less gifted in analysis and exposition. His key terms throughout are "conceptualization" and "coherence": the nature of college education is a series of logical steps toward higher forms of conceptualization in which "first comes the acquisition of a general background, second the training in a discipline, third the application of this discipline to a number of relevant subjects, and fourth the effort to link the disciplines in dealing with human problems. It is this progression, involving at each step of the way an awareness of conceptual innovation and method, that is the heart of ordering a curriculum." [11]

When Bell faces the bigger issue of debate, on philosophical presuppositions, although not equally clear, he is equally concerned for coherence. In education, he says, there are no eternal verities, no single quadrivium; there are "tasks appropriate to the elucidation of tradition, the identification of societal values (which can be rejected as well as accepted) and the testing of knowledge." [12] But in the modern university, says Bell, there is a new problem, its most perplexing challenge, to conserve the past and reinterpret the present while at the same time testing the new— not the new in science and sociology, but the new in sensibility.

Bell has looked at this new problem, conceptualized it, and is both offended and alarmed by it. "This fact of modernity," he says, "emphasizing will and passion, subverts established order not because it reshapes experience (as any positive enquiry must), but because it taps an energy, demonic at its source, that overflows the containing vessels of art and because it insists on its own subjective experience and desires as the standard not only of the esthetic but of moral truth as well." In its most recent stages, moving from the early Camus to the anti-novel with its anti-heroes, to Burroughs and Genet, the post-moderns have reached a state of rejection of the moral order. "The result is either nihilism or gnosticism—forms of private knowledge and belief which in their moral radicalism are subversive of society itself." [13]

But surely, with the forces of stability gathered together so systematically and powerfully in the social and economic institutions which control post-industrial society, the danger is not that the social order will be subverted by a new sensibility. The danger is that the social order will crush or corrupt the development of a new sensibility. Nihilism is of many kinds, including the nihilism of Descartes, who dismissed everything self-evident to examine the grounds for the evident, or of Hume, who rejected the logical assumptions of rationality to find new grounds for empirical philosophy.

Have we not had enough of moral dogmatism? Can we not at least entertain the view that subjective experience and desire can furnish the standard for moral truth, or that all moral truth is a fraud created by societies against the true interest of humans? Was it not the very subjectivism of the student philosophy in the French student revolt of 1968 which went to the heart of the problems of social and political change in France? Is not radical subjectivism, that is to say, the judgments of the private self confronting public truth, a mode of thought which validates itself when it demonstrates contradictions and inequities in the moral system? If civilization is on trial, it is the civilization of those whose values are ultimately social and political, and therefore not only anti-subjective but anti-human. If the youth are drawn toward those who proclaim a doctrine of will and desire, what living proof do the educators and the social managers have that their own doctrines and systems are rational and not themselves the subjective product of a different kind of will and a different set of desires?

For what seems to be his own answer, Bell turns to Lionel Trilling's sensitive analysis of the modern sensibility and Trilling's use of the concept of "the adversary culture" [14] to describe the thrust of radical subjectivism into the society. Bell concludes that what has been happening among the post-modern artists and writers has become "an assault against the final taboos of cultural and psychic life itself." Trilling's answer to that, and one which seems to me to be entirely sensible, is to urge that the assault be met in a way which can help to preserve the insights which invoked it. "It must be confronted," says Trilling, "with the mind that insists that . . . the world is intractable as well as malleable. And such a countervailing force must, I believe, be specifically offered to the radical subjectivity of our students, else they will never develop their powers of intellectual mastery; they will fall into inertness and the weariest of all conventionalities, the conventionality of an outworn radical mode." [15] In other words, we enter the area of a major educational problem.

All this and more is involved in thinking about the reform of general education, and it is at this point that one looks for a sign that Bell's conception of man and of the nature of the university as a factor in the development of a humane social order will come to light. Instead, Bell turns to other scholars, this time to Bernard Berelson and Gary Steiner, authors of a definitive account of what scientists of human behavior have to say about the nature of man.[16] Bell concludes from their testimony that "behavioral man" is a social product, social producer, and social seeker, who manipulates his environment in such a way that he becomes incapable of seeing it as it really is. He has developed to a high capacity the art of self-deception. When he hears something with which he disagrees he creates psychological defenses against it. He has little tolerance for the bare and personal truth, little impulse toward full disclosure of himself to anyone, including himself.

If this too can be the reality of man, then a central problem is raised for education, a problem which should be treated *somewhere* in the college curriculum or in the construction of an educational philosophy strong enough to deal with it. But again, the issue is not joined. Both these modes of sensibility—of radical subjectivism and of total social adaptation—are dangerous, for different reasons. The university cannot remake a world, says Bell, although it can hold up standards by which it might be remade. Nor can it remake men. "But it can liberate young people by making them aware of the forces that impel them from within and constrict them from without." [17]

But is not this kind of awareness a way in which man is remade? If education can liberate young people in this way, then is it not here that the enquiry into general education should begin, not with the subjects and disciplines of the curriculum? Isn't this the intellectual problem? An education in the colleges which began with the realities of student life and went from there to the process of liberation into free and active thought about the nature of oneself, of truth, of society, of education, and of personal commitment, would very quickly transcend the boundaries now set by the curriculum-makers of the academy, and would pick up where the experimental colleges and the student movement have left off, pressing forward on new ground to make curricula which grow out of the active efforts by students to find their way to an education.

[IV]

There is one more issue in the agenda of the real debate, the biggest issue of all, and one to which Mr. Bell addresses himself only casually, almost inadvertently, in the closing pages of a study which has assumed the answers to questions until then unasked. At a time when the kind of sustained analysis of which Daniel Bell is capable is exactly what the subject most needs if the universities are to invent their own imaginative reconstruction, it is a matter for great regret that his attention was diverted into other considerations. The issue is, in his words, "the radical disjunction between social structure and culture, a disjunction expressed most directly in two major orientations towards the future that divide the intelligentsia today—the technocratic and the apocalyptic. This issue, I submit, will be the source of a serious intellectual crisis in the university." [18]

If it will be the source of a serious intellectual crisis in the university, as the evidence shows that it has already become, then why is not *that* the educational problem with which all curriculum-makers must begin? The technocratic view, as Bell describes it, distrusts ideology, uses the discipline of the mind and techniques of rational problem-solving, sharpens definitions, and has created a breed of professionals who form a new community with access to certified knowledge and intellectual competence which cannot be denied or thrust aside. Among those who distrust and are alienated from the technocratic professional are the dispossessed young intellectuals who abhor the idea of social engineering and have formed their own communities within the society, with their own political ideas in a new kind of adversary culture. "In the end, however," says Bell, "they lack the technical knowledge, or even the willingness to acquire it, that could test their abstractions against a social reality. . . . They live, sadly, in a half-way house." [19]

These are the students I am writing about. They are living, but not in the least sadly, in a half-way house. That is, they have not yet taken up residence in a controlling position in their society. They do not lack technical knowledge or the willingness to acquire it. They are acquiring it precisely by testing their abstractions against a social reality, and the place they are doing the testing is in the reality of the ghetto, in the rural society, and in the life of the colleges and universities. That is why their educational and social ideas have become at the same time more mature and more effective than those of the academic professionals, who have remained with the technocratic view of social change by manipulation.

The universities, as Bell says in his concluding statements, are increasingly committed to a technocratic orientation, and most of what he says about the role of general education indicates that is what Bell thinks should be its commitment. It is a scenario of education by Daniel Bell for living in a world of Herman Kahn. The closest that Bell and the university professionals are prepared to come to a confrontation with the apocalyptic, if that is the proper word for those who are radical in their views about the technocratic society and the norms of culture and psyche, is to say that this is the most urgent cultural problem for the university in the future. Since it is a problem which by its nature can not be solved by technocrats, unless they increase their present power over all curricular matters and simply shut down the apocalyptics, it will have to become a central factor in the educational planning of the universities and colleges. That means that the curriculum will have to start with an examination of the culture, the philosophy of the social order, the obligation of the university to the liberation of its students into political and social consciousness. In other words, it will have to start with the students. That is the intellectual problem.

PART FOUR

The Reform of
Mass Education

10: The Return to Progressive Thought

After forty years we have now come full circle. The unsettled problems of the 1930s are back with us, this time in fuller force. But now, in the 1960s, the test of social and educational theory is back where it ought to be, and where it was during the progressive era. The test lies not in whether the theory works well for those in charge of the system and who occupy a privileged position in it, either as teachers, students, administrators, or citizens. It lies in the answer to the beautiful clarity of John Dewey's question: What sort of individuals are created?

When the test is put that way, there are some further questions. How does current educational theory and its application in practice help to deal with the problems of a society in a state of revolution? Does it minister to all American children? How does it help to create the conditions in which the citizens, their children, the teachers, the schools, and the colleges can work together to raise the quality of life in the American community? When these questions are answered, it becomes clear that conservative theory is bankrupt and its practices are counterproductive. It is not working well, even for the privileged, whose activist sons and daughters have turned against it.

There is more clarity now, at last, about why it isn't working. Conservative theory calls for an orderly national structure of similar, if not identical curricula and educational organization. It calls for changes in education which concentrate on revisions of subject matter. It calls for an education for teachers which stresses their preparation in academic subject matter and their skill in teaching the conventional curriculum in conventional ways, and by the use of additional skills with technological devices which save time and increase the rate and degree of absorption of the subject matter. It calls for more discipline, more testing, more competition, more standardization and control over the curriculum by the faculty, the textbooks, and the test-makers. It asserts the authority of the institution over the curriculum and of the teacher over the learner. It teaches adaptation to the society, not creative thinking about its character and future.

When its methods are successful, it moves the college student out of the environment and the sector of the society where he is most needed and into a favored position in the economic and social system. It has no philosophy of social change, it has only a method for keeping the society going. As a result, it has frozen itself into a system of education which has generated inadequacies so scandalous and widespread in their effects as to have damaged the lives of generations of children in the rural and urban slums. It is presently in the process of damaging more of them before it accepts defeat at the hands of its victims.

In place of the ideal of a community with the school and college at the center, we have in the major cities and towns of the United States a situation in which parents and students have to fight, storm, and struggle even to be recognized as interested and intelligent parties, capable of taking their part in reaching decisions about the conduct of school and college affairs. In place of creating situations in which the child or the college student can find his way through to himself and his world, the theory has been one which, having on principle neglected the individual and his environment as factors in his education, places the blame for educational failure not on the character of the schools and the colleges, but on the individual and his environment.

This generation has the great good fortune to be born at a time when the society has finally caught up to the theory and practice of the conservatives and has begun to change them by the sheer force of social reality. Education is becoming progressive in spite of itself, having gone to school to society. The irony is that society and the students are now doing for education what the progressive educators were not able to do for the students or for the society. The social and educational legislation of the Eighty-eighth and Eighty-ninth Congress released the possibility of forming a parallel educational system, outside the formal institutions yet linked directly to them. Although the philosophy within the legislation was not defined in such explicit terms, it was in fact a philosophy which conceived education as an instrument of democratic social change.

It spoke to the concerns of thousands of persons in the American community by calling upon them to volunteer to join a movement of social change and by providing the funds and programs through which their efforts could be mobilized on a national scale. The students, with new opportunities for service to the community, through the invention of new social institutions, from Head Start and VISTA programs to street academies, are creating their own image of what a college should be. It is turning out to be the kind of college the progressives hoped would some day exist in profusion—a college for students, for teaching, for action in cultural and social issues, for liberating minds and lives, for learning about the world, for learning to judge it and to act in it, for engaging in the arts, for finding ways of thinking and acting which honor the tradition of humane learning by giving to each the fullest chance to do something important of his own.

The progressives in education of the 1920s and 1930s spoke constantly of the necessity of placing the context of education at the advancing edge of social movement, so that what was done in the schools and colleges could not only anticipate changes in the movement but, by staying close to the reality of social need, could help give direction to the change. That was why, rather than excluding parents from a share in the work and policies of the school, the progressives wanted the parents and the community involved, knowing that no matter what was done to give the children new insights, new ideas, and a feeling for democratic life, it could be defeated by parents and a misinformed community, since in so many ways, the parents *were* the community. The school must act, in the progressive view, as a center of moral and social energy, where the principles of democracy could be seen at work, not only by the way the children were taught, but by the way in which the community became responsible for meeting its own problems. The link between the society and its educational system was made through the lives of the children. They were the living tissue which joined the teachers and the community in a social organism. Around questions having to do with the education of children the live issues of American democracy turned—questions of race, of economic justice, of freedom. What was taught in the schools could become what was believed in the society.

Students who have volunteered to tutor children in the ghettos of the 1960s have discovered these connections for themselves, and their work with children has given them an education in the problems of society. They are now applying what they have learned to their own education; what they want is a progressive college.

[II]

There are other links with the movements of the 1930s. The progressives then spoke constantly of the education of the individual, of the relation of his actions to his thought, of his involvement in his environment, and their educational plans developed from the context of that environment. They wanted a curriculum which could arouse the child's intellectual interests and satisfy his natural wish to make something of his own. They wanted him to learn to make his own choices, to take part in the government of his own community, and to create a body of knowledge out of the materials of his own experience and by reason of his own efforts. They argued the case for abolishing the system of competition—competition for social superiority, popularity, external rewards—and they wanted an educational environment in which each person had his own place and was cherished in it.

They wanted each person to learn to judge the other by the quality of his acts and the integrity of his personal values, not by his color, his social position, his money, or his external achievements. They wanted the emotional life of the child and the young adult to be taken into account in his education, and the qualities of warmth, sympathy, empathy, generosity, and affection to provide the atmosphere for his emotional growth. They wanted the authoritarian environment of the conventional school and college replaced by one in which the student could learn what it meant to be democratic by acting within the structure of a democracy in his life in the school and on the campus. They wanted the student to develop independence of mind and character by thinking and acting independently, by entering the reality of social, political, and intellectual experience, not by being told about it at second hand. They wanted students to gain a sensibility in the arts and life by engaging directly in the experiences of the arts and of life.

They wanted all this and a great deal more, and they didn't get it. That is, they did not get it except in special cases and for a limited time when the early years of their movement began and those whose educational ideas had grown from experience in teaching put their ideas to work in a political and social environment responsive to their value. The American society of the 1930s was one in which progressive ideas were basic to the solution of the American problem.

The problem was the reconstruction of an economic and social system which had been wrecked by the ideology of a capitalist democracy where the concept of economic and social competition and the survival of the fittest had been raised to the level of a religious principle. Poverty, the great leveller, and hunger, deprivation, unemployment, and a sense of social injustice—the great activators—formed the basis for a new idea of social democracy in which education was the central pivot around which the society turned. Education was a way of coming together again; it was the means through which the country could learn to believe in itself once more and could find ways in which the competition of man against man for the necessities of life could be replaced by a spirit of cooperation in sharing the benefits of a reconstructed society. The society itself could look to the universities and schools as community centers, friendly places where the teachers accepted you as you were and did the most they could.

The teacher, the parent, the child, the college student, the citizen, shared together in the reality of a form of classless society—classless in the sense that there was, in effect, only one big class, the poor, with a separate set of the rich, and a government which by necessity was on the side of the poor. Education could then be seen, literally, as an instrument of social change. Government and education combined forces and went to work together, as partners in the progressive movement, through the National Youth Administration, the Civilian Conservation Corps, the WPA, and, in a different dimension of education, the TVA, and all the newly formed agencies of reform, to give to youth and the citizens a sense of purpose and a place within the society.

Those problems for which that partnership was designed were never solved. They simply lay dormant while we mobilized for a war, won it, then busied ourselves with arranging the benefits of a military, industrial, government-subsidized economy in the 1950s, shooting off our rockets, our bombs, our propaganda messages, and organizing education, not for the solution of the social problems, but for supporting the economic and social system we were so busy constructing on behalf of a white middle-class society and its managers. We owe to the social revolution of the 1960s, and the part the students, black and white, have played in generating its internal energies, the fact that we have now been forced to come to our senses and to return once more to the unfinished business of the 1930s and to the aborted revolution in education which showed so great a promise for making democracy grow.

We owe to the students the fact that they are supplying the brains, the idealism, and the social energy for making the present government programs work, just as they did in the 1930s in a different context. The partnership between the government and the schools and colleges has been resumed, with the students and other volunteers as the intermediaries, extending the meaning of education into its social and cultural dimension. In doing so, we are finding our way back to the progressive tradition, not by having argued our way into it, but by discovering that the ideas contained in it are essential to the solution of problems which threaten to overwhelm the society. There is no point in insisting on an academic style of teaching and learning in the schools and colleges when so many of those who need education the most are not equipped to respond to the kind of education offered.

[III]

We are now entering an era of educational decision comparable to the time in the nineteenth century when the land-grant concept of the university produced the greatest single idea for the development of higher education that the world has ever seen. I put the proposition as extravagantly as this because the land-grant concept of education as service to citizens is much more original and extravagant in its implications than is commonly recognized, and at a time when the concept is either misunderstood or taken for granted. The genius of the idea lies in the fact that throughout the entire sweep of education, the quality of what is done in all its institutions is to be measured by the degree to which they nourish the life and minds of the students and the citizens.

It is this idea which lies at the heart of the philosophy of the experimental colleges. Those who were concerned in the 1920s and 1930s to build colleges on new principles, at Antioch, Bennington, Black Mountain, Sarah Lawrence, Goddard, and elsewhere, placed the student at the center of education and placed education in the context of the wider world. The advocates of the experimental colleges were part of an intellectual and social movement which had its roots in contemporary radical thought and in the modern sensibility. They were linked to the new movements in the arts, in psychology, psychoanalytic theory, literature, and social change. In one sense, theirs was an effort to extend into higher education some of the ideas native to the progressive movement in the schools. They wanted to make a connection between what was done in the schools and what could be done to reform a college system which contained most of the same characteristics as the school system against which the progressive movement was rebelling. In another sense, it was an effort to redefine the college itself, and to make a new kind of institution which was free from all constrictions, whether from the conventions and controls of university education or, by influence, from the habits of thought and traditional conceptions of what a college should be.

The experimental colleges never became a movement to reform colleges in general.[1] They simply started. They brought together people who wanted to come—educators, scholars, scientists, artists, teachers, and students—to make education in one college. There were no problems in the denial of student rights in making educational and social policy; the students were an essential and integral part of the governance and educational policy-making from the beginning. There were no problems of dealing with a huge mechanical system, with highly organized subject-matter departments, lectures, examinations, credits, grades; since the colleges were small, there were no formal departments, required courses, or testing devices; students worked together and with their teachers in a variety of ways, according to their talents and interests, in a community devoted to the arts, the sciences, the humanities, the study of society.

Some students stayed for one year, others two, three, or four. But since the purpose in being in college was for the satisfaction of learning and living in a community of interested persons, it was not possible to *fail,* or to be a drop-out. Occasionally there were students whose behavior, either social or intellectual, made it use-less for the association with the college to continue, but in a vol-untary community, those who left and those who stayed were on equal terms. Being away from the college and at work on some-thing else was one of the ideas for education which was built into the structure of the curriculum. Students who remained for four years and had satisfied their teachers that their time had been usefully spent in most cases received a bachelor of arts degree, al-though its award merely recognized the mutual agreement of the student and the college that the four years had been a satisfactory period of intellectual and personal growth.

Over the years since the experimental colleges began, the influ-ence they have had on educational theory and practice has been considerable, but mainly in proving to sceptics in other colleges that some of the progressive ideas could be transferred into the regular college system—courses in modern dance, theater, inde-pendent study, student research, off-campus periods, non-graded courses and examinations—and that these would work well in a conventional setting. There has never been a serious consideration among university educators of the philosophy on which the experi-mental colleges were founded. They were classified, for example, by the authors of the Harvard Report as colleges which used indi-vidual guidance as their means of assigning a curriculum. In gen-eral they have been dealt with in the history of education as Christopher Jencks and David Riesman dealt with them in *The Academic Revolution,* or as Daniel Bell dealt with them in *The Reforming of General Education,* as oddities, special institu-tions to be mentioned in footnotes or a short paragraph, not as experimental institutions for testing out a radical conception of education whose time has now come.[2]

Because they were small, never more than five to six hundred in size, it was assumed that the methods—small classes, individual conferences, tutorial work, field work, and so on—while obviously valuable if a college could afford them, had nothing to recommend for solving the problem of the big university and the larger liberal arts colleges. In the case of Sarah Lawrence and Bennington, because the students were women, it was assumed that colleges of this kind could work as well as they did in creating serious intellectual and cultural interests because the women were under less pressure than men students would be to do the kind of college work which would lead directly to a career. The general attitude of educators who were sympathetic to the ideas and the programs of the experimental colleges was that, while this might be an ideal way to organize a college, you could not do it without such a high tuition that it would keep out the students whom it would profit most, that it would not work unless you had students who were already highly motivated and mature, that you could never get the graduate schools to recognize a degree from an institution like that, and that the whole idea was too impractical to serve as a model for broad-scale reform.

The fact that none of this was true, and in large part irrelevant, did not deflect the criticism or change the preconception. There is no philosophy of education better adapted to raising the level of learning throughout the entire culture than this one, and a progressive admissions policy by which a college accepted the first 500 students who applied, or, in the manner of the new Federal College in Washington, D.C., accepted 2,000 students by lottery, would have a radical effect on improving the character and quality of the national undergraduate curriculum. Some of the same sympathetic educators were among the first to denounce the practices of the conventional colleges, and to inveigh against tests, lectures, grades, impersonal instruction, and the control of the college curriculum by the graduate schools, but they did not turn their minds toward forming an opposition movement to the practices they denounced.

Among those in former years who were unsympathetic or hostile to the experimental point of view—that is, most of the university educators—the attitudes displayed began with the notion that these were "off-beat" colleges, and went on to criticize Deweyism, scientism, presentism, spoon-feeding and pandering to students, permissive atmospheres, bohemianism, having students meddle in college affairs, and intellectual dilettantism which encouraged students to avoid hard subjects and the true disciplines of learning. The view expressed most consistently about students was that they were *students,* ill-prepared to render judgments of any kind in educational policy, especially in the matter of their own education. They were in college to get an education; the faculty knew what that was; the students were its recipients, transients who came and went, incapable of learning enough about education or anything else to be of any help to the educational planning.

It is true, therefore, that although the infusion of modern ideas, Dewey's among them, had formed the basis for educational change in the schools and in the society in the 1930s, they did not penetrate the system of higher education. Except for isolated instances, in the General College at the University of Minnesota, for example, the ideas were never taken with the seriousness they deserved. The reason for that, going beneath all the other reasons, lay in the fact that the system of higher education was already in the hands of the academic profession and the university had already become so highly organized on the corporate model, both in its administration and in its departmental system, that it had made itself almost impervious to new educational thought and radical ideas for reform. The university was much more susceptible to the influence of any ideas which advanced the cause of the organization, with its preference for building manageable bodies of knowledge and assembling academic professionals in the departments. When the opportunity presented itself, in the form of the general education movement, to strengthen the existing system, to cope with the radical expansion in the number of students while keeping the organization intact, the universities seized on the movement and went on from there.

[IV]

Here in general education was a plan made to order for efficiency in administration. The obligations toward the education of freshmen and sophomores in a common culture could be met by requiring them to take standard courses for two years. The obligations toward the departments could be met by providing generally educated students in the junior year to fit into the requirements of the academic majors who would become the educational consumers needed for the graduate schools.

The academic control was further strengthened by the power of the lecture–academic-credit–examination–grading system, which not only standardized all knowledge into units of credit and numerical judgments of academic achievement. It turned what had been a device for making it simpler for students to move from one university to another into a universal but mindless principle of higher education. When control could also be extended by the same method over the curriculum of the high school through academic credits and subject-matter requirements for admission to college, and over the curriculum of the college by the requirements for graduate school, the system was complete and inexorable. With a system which worked so elegantly on behalf of its own purposes, what madness in educational theory would advocate a change?

In the process of ordering both knowledge and the learner into one gigantic rationalized system, the university had done something else. It had separated the student into two distinct parts: his obligatory academic life as set down in the formal curriculum, and his other life, which it then set out to control—politically, emotionally, socially, and personally. It did so by an administrative system of rules, deans, sub-deans, mental-health experts, psychological advisers, house mothers and other supervisors installed in row after row of body-containers which segregated the "dorm" students, the proletariat of the academy, from the more stylish well-to-do of the fraternities and sororities, from the poor and bohemian of the boarding-house set, and the commuters.

The training for service in the administrative side of student affairs (or, in the phrase which gives it away, "student personnel work") is carried on in programs separate from those which prepare the scholar-teacher. The potential dean of students is a professional student adviser or personnel worker, and the body of knowledge in the education of personnel workers is drawn mainly from psychology, the social sciences, and administration. The norms of student behavior, however, are drawn, not from a deep-going analysis of the causes and possibilities of deviant and idiosyncratic character traits, the kind of psycho-social investigations begun by Freud in *Civilization and Its Discontents* or later in the work of Erikson or R. D. Laing, but from the norms of behavior in regular middle-class society, transposed into the college community. The concept of mental health most often found among the student personnel professionals is drawn from the psychology of adjustment, and the effort of most advisers is in the direction of developing well-adjusted students who will do their academic work properly and succed within the university culture. In fact, a majority of the cases seen by the psychological advisers are those of students with "bad grades" who "can't concentrate," can't do the work, can't get hold of themselves. The influence of Carl Rogers in establishing a philosophy of nondirective psychological counselling has been considerable, although what is taken from Rogers is not the full range of his psychological and social insight but mainly the technique of conducting interviews.

The consequence of the administrative separation of the student's life into academic and mental health or social sections is to drive deeper the separation between teaching and learning, the professor and the student. The possibilities for a renewed relation of teacher and student are removed by referring cases of bad grades or educational failure to the counselling service instead of dealing with whatever might be the learning problem of the student as a matter for discussion with the person who is teaching him. At least in a badly working elective system there were advisers to students among the teachers, and a possibility that the teacher would learn where his own failures lay by a confrontation with students who were doing the failing. Under the present system, with graduate students leading the discussions with students, and the university counsellors advising students about how to succeed in spite of the system, the professor is removed farther than ever from the possibility of personal knowledge either of individuals or of his students as a whole. He is denied access by the system to knowledge which is properly his.

The administrators and counsellors are therefore seen by the student activists, and by many who are not activists but are perceptive about the nature of the system, as persons employed by the university to help adjust them to a situation against which they have an implicit or explicit antagonism. The deans and student personnel staff are seen as persons who administer rules made by university officials for the management of student lives. Combined with the fact that the deans and counsellors are not part of the academic faculty, usually do not teach or, if they do, teach courses in counselling to those who will occupy a role similar to theirs, this means for many of the new breed of students that the whole administrative apparatus of the student personnel section is perceived as an authoritarian device disguised as organized benevolence. It is the instrument of paternalism.

Now that questions of sexual promiscuity, drug-taking, and deviant political behavior are becoming more prominent in the experience of the campus authorities, many of the students most in need of help in gaining some direction for their lives and personal values avoid any contact with the university counselling system on the grounds that what is said in private may turn up in a public hearing or a court case having to do with marihuana. The absence of the free community of scholars and learners has already resulted in turning some college officials into informers, with the release of university files to those who demand them under the threat of a contempt-of-court citation.

In making these generalizations, I am of course referring to the massive tendencies and organizational patterns rather than to individual programs and institutions where the generalizations do not cover the work going on. It will be obvious that *because* the work of the student personnel profession is carried on outside the academic system, there are opportunities for working with students directly and supporting their efforts in educational reform, just as there are further opportunities for the social action programs of the religious associations and their chaplains and staff to start some fresh thinking and educational projects on campuses where students are neglected. It is also true that any faculty member with an interest in breaking through the pattern to reach his own students and applying his own ideas in his teaching is free to do so, and many university teachers have done it.

The system can be beaten. It must be, until it is rearranged. There are many ways in which it can be rearranged if it can't be overthrown. In the past I have found myself in the position of arguing that it be overthrown, not by force but by radical internal reconstruction. But the possibility of that kind of overthrow, even with the new energies released into the task by the student movement, seems so remote, in view of the strength and institutional advantages of the present system, that I have come around to the view that it must be undermined by an infusion of virtue, subverted by better ways of using the system, which will then fall by its own weight. The strategy for undermining is to use the resources of the students to do everything in their power to teach themselves, and to apply the strategies of learning which they have developed in the student movement to reconstruct the basic pattern of instruction.

11: Styles of Teaching

The ideas of the experimental colleges of the 1920s and 1930s went counter to most of the tendencies and developments in the conventional institutions. They were not academic colleges. They started with the idea that the college was a community of persons joined together by interests they held in common, free to pursue these interests in cooperation with each other in ways they would devise as they went along. The conception is not unlike Charles W. Eliot's view of the community he wanted to see at Harvard in 1863, "a cooperative association of highly individualistic persons," except that for most of us in the experimental colleges, we wanted a cooperative association of individuals who were not *necessarily* highly individualistic, since that too would be demanding conformity to a type to which some, but not all, might wish to aspire.

We wanted a community in which the talent and individual character of each person who entered it—teacher, student, administrator—would have a full chance to grow in its own terms. We wanted an open-handed style of life and learning which would grow and change through the plans made by the members of the community working together. There would be joy there, and a sense of easy comradeship. That it is not impossible to build such a community, whether in a large university or in a small experimental college, is one of the basic beliefs on which this book rests. The tragedy in the educational developments of these past thirty years lies in the fact that, for some of the reasons already given, this vision of what the university could be has never been considered a live possibility. Instead, the history of the colleges and universities has proceeded in accordance with a set of institutional practices conditioned by their own internal order, responding to a wild variety of external pressures from the society, without taking thought of what could exist if the intelligence and good will of students and teachers working together were set to work to build that kind of community.

I have said continually, and with a feeling of urgency which stems not merely from the events of these past five years of student discontent, that the colleges and universities should be built around the students and their lives. In saying this I mean that a number of specific things can and should be done and that they should be done as soon as possible. The ideas I propose have been around for a long time, longer, in fact, than those presently in use by the other side. By the other side I mean the educational ideas of the academic profession, which, from the point of view which I am arguing, form a counter-culture against the culture of the ideal community for learning.

What is meant by a theory which says that education must be built around the student and that the student must be involved in planning it, making it, and doing it, is that knowledge is not a thing but a psychic state. Until the one who seeks it acts within his own consciousness and makes an idea or a fact or an experience part of his own psychic development, he has not gained knowledge. When the traditional method calls for building education around the subject matter and presenting it to the student in lectures and reading assignments, it is seizing upon an obvious and, in limited ways, a valuable device for bringing the student in touch with the accredited body of knowledge. It is also, in a limited way, bringing the student in touch with the teacher. Sometimes, and more often than not, this is a negative experience for the student, since so few teachers are gifted as lecturers.

But that way of conducting education has very limited practical value. It does one kind of thing which is comparatively easy to do. It is absurd to build a system around it.

The temptation of the educator under such a system is not to let ideas or books alone, not to let the writer of the book or the creator of the idea speak to the student himself, but always to intervene nervously, to describe, to explain, to organize the knowledge for the student, leaving the student with little to do of his own. In this way the system of college instruction empties books of their content, empties art objects of their true meaning, and addicts the students to habits of thought that often last for the rest of their lives. Everything must be placed in summary. Ideas are topic sentences. To read is not really to read, it is to prepare for a distant question. That is why so relatively few college graduates have learned how to read or to write. They have been taught to turn books and ideas into items of information. When they were students they learned to get rid of their books at the close of each semester, a perfectly natural response to the system. Having been used for the purposes of a course, books, like paper cups, are disposable.

"Examine for a moment an ordinary mind on an ordinary day," says Virginia Woolf. "The mind receives myriad impressions, trivial, fantastic, evanescent, or engraved with the sharpness of steel. From all sides they come, an incessant shower of innumerable atoms, and as they fall, as they shape themselves into the life of Monday or Tuesday, the accent falls differently from of old; the moment of importance came not here but there; so that if the writer were a free man and not a slave, if he could write what he chose, not what he must, if he could base his work upon his own feeling and not upon convention, there would be no plot, no comedy, no tragedy, no love interest or catastrophe in accepted style." [1]

If the teacher were a free man, if he could teach what he chose and not what he must, if he could base his work upon his own feeling and not upon convention, there would be no formal syllabus, no required curriculum, nothing but his continuing response to the students who came to him for instruction. It is only when learning has to be organized into institutional forms that the teacher's response becomes inhibited. Whatever the structure of organization for teaching, it must be arranged to guarantee that there will be the least possible violation of the freedom of the teacher's work with his students. Even in the largest universities, what it finally comes down to is one student and one teacher, no matter how many others are in the community surrounding both persons. The best arrangements for teaching and learning are those which are most open, allow the greatest amount of room for individual spontaneous choice, and the greatest amount of encouragement to the teacher to work out his own ways of teaching his own students.

[II]

Consider the basic matter of books and their use as educational instruments. Nearly all college learning is done by means of books and their assignment week by week, usually through a basic text for the course with assigned collateral reading, the whole of the reading to be discussed in sessions with graduate students once a week in each course. The heart of education where books are concerned is to get the student alone with a book in the right state of mind, that is to say, receptive, interested, curious, involved, or, if possible, *possessed* by the book.

I have never been able to understand why educators do not seize on this simple fact and make it the center of their planning, especially in the humanities, the social sciences, and the arts. Why do they not make one full life from the double life which students lead, rather than ignoring their intellectual and personal interests outside the organized curriculum? Students are too often made to read more than they can handle, or less than they are able, or nothing they can enjoy, or too little of too many things, in a way calculated to destroy their possible involvement with the writer.

In the case of textbooks, it is impossible to find the writer. He is hidden beneath the prose, and expresses what is known by countless other academic minds whose ideas and facts are screened through his. The textbook has its use in putting down for reference what is generally asserted by the academic profession in a given field, and has the function of holding the curriculum together in the absence of good teachers who can present their own knowledge with the help of original texts. Those who argue for the use of required courses and their equivalent required textbooks say that without the textbooks and the requirements both the teaching and the learning would fall apart. A textbook is a way of making knowledge safe from the vagaries of teachers; the required course is designed to make it safe from the initiatives of students.

As a result of the preconception that learning is reading, another factor enters in the case of students who are already good readers and have gone through a great many books in high school outside the curriculum—with paperbacks covering European and American literature, for example, in a way in which none of us when we were in high school or college could have done, since the books were not available, and when they were, they were locked up in libraries we were not accustomed to using. As the literary intelligence and the reading knowledge of incoming freshmen has risen in many of the highly selective colleges and universities, some of them have outrun the capacity of the faculty to adapt to them. The response of many university teachers has been to make longer and fuller reading assignments simply because the capacity of the students to read faster and absorb more has grown, in some cases spectacularly. The brightest of them are kept so busy with the reading that they have no time to think seriously about what their reading contains. Some students, not confined to the prestigious institutions but straight across the country, have developed prodigious skills in reading fast and cleverly, and can sprinkle their papers with quotations which advertise the wealth of their coverage.

On the reverse side, the duller the students, the shorter the assignments—half-chapters, or a designated number of pages per week, or units of chapters prearranged in the textbook to keep pace with an assumed norm of capability on the part of the "average" student, with questions for discussion at the end of the chapters. The more textbooks that are used with the "average," that is, nonreading students, the more anthologies, the more course outlines, the more objective examinations, the more chance there is that if you are not a dull reader when you enter the university, the curriculum will make you that way.

When I use the word "dull," I do not mean that there is something irredeemable in the student, but only that his mind has not been sharpened by contact with other minds, among the students, the teachers, and the writers of books. He has not been taught to read in depth or to become involved in reading as a way of enlightenment and personal pleasure. Average students are exactly the ones who can profit most by learning to read for joy. That conception has slipped away from the educators. Most of the books students are asked to read in the mass of colleges are anti-intellectual in their effects. Students, bright and dull, are always reading for a deadline, to return books to the library, to prepare for the next class, to write a paper, to be ready for tests, to pass a course, and there is never enough time to do more than to read the amount of the author the assignment calls for.

When Theodore Roethke came into class he brought with him everything he was, his passions, his love of poetry, his tenderness, his awkwardness, his irrationality, his habits of scattered thought and scattered reading, his terrible jokes, his good ones, his clowning, sometimes his showing-off, and his deep and compelling wish that his students write, read, speak, and listen to poetry, speak it to each other and learn from it. No one in his class could mistake his meaning or intent no matter what they thought of his style. His assignments of reading were the outcome of what his meetings with the class suggested to him, what he thought would work for them, and they were of all kinds. His purpose in making assignments, as his purpose in teaching, was to tie his students to a love of poetry forever. Then there would be no need for assignments. They are only the means by which the teacher can help to give his students a beginning from which they will never turn back, and that is the ground on which the assignments should be chosen.

Roethke told one class at the beginning of the term what he meant to do with them and how he meant to teach them.

> To find out something about your life: that will be the purpose. It may be necessary to change some of your ways of acting and thinking in the course. The burden will lie on you a good deal more; but it also, I wish you to understand, will lie on me a good deal more. It is much easier for me to lecture than it is for me to store up your various reactions, attitudes, keep turning them over in my mind, letting my unconscious, my creative capacity evolve something, make a synthesis, come through with the right nudges, jeers, japes, kind or harsh words which will bring you into fuller being. Crudely put, it is like this: I am willing to give you a chunk of myself—my time, my patience, my talent—*if* you want it. . . . Faith. That's it. This course is an act of faith. In what? In the imagination of us all, in a creative capacity—that most sacred thing—that lies dormant, *never* dead, in everyone.[2]

What Roethke says in this is very close to the heart of what it means to teach and how an artist in the medium goes about his work. There is no talk here about theories of education, "ground to be covered," or assignments to be met, only about man teaching. I spent a week on an Eastern campus not long ago as a visiting professor and had a chance to see at first hand the opposite practices in operation, with students who, the admissions director was proud to say, were among the top 5 per cent of the students of the country. I found the freshmen and sophomores to be completely encased in the heaviest set of course requirements I have come across in a life of looking suspiciously at course requirements of every shape and size. As the week went by, on successive days I met with groups of freshmen, sophomores, juniors, and seniors nominated by the faculty as representative of the student body, and found that the liveliest ones were the freshmen and that the seniors had become more skilled in defensive argument, especially about the virtues of their institution and its academic record, about the number of students in the best graduate schools, and so on, but much less interesting intellectually than the beginners.

One young man asked me (he was a nominated sophomore) if I ever met, in my visits to colleges, any unofficial students. I replied that I could not tell unofficial students from any other kind and that I met whoever was around. The young man said that he knew where there were some students who seldom came out into the open, and harbored thoughts I would not otherwise come across.

At 1:00 A.M. the next morning I found myself discussing literature and writing with a group of seven students who had very strong views about education, their own and everyone else's. "We used to be able to write in high school, but now we can't. It's all dull prose; we have had all the English courses." They said they were locked up reading all the time, from a sense of duty and keeping up, with the length of the reading assignments having increased to match the level of their capability, with no time left for thinking about what they were reading. One of the men said, "What I need to do most right now is to read Paul Tillich. I read a little for last week's assignment and he is saying something to me that no one has ever said before. But I can't read him unless I stay up all night, and then I won't be ready for the classes tomorrow."

On the part of educators in that college and elsewhere there has been a refusal to come to terms with the reality of the student's experience as a reader. It is a refusal to take seriously the unconscious process which can only take place at its full when the objective phenomena of life are set aside for a while, in those moments of time when there is nothing at stake, nothing scheduled, when one's mind and heart and body have a chance to walk along on their own, when the fortuitous and the accidental are freely accepted, when the idiosyncratic can arise if it wishes. Now that we have open to us in mass circulation a full array of published literature in nearly every field of knowledge, the way is clear for teachers to make new curricula which range broadly into books and ideas capable of engaging the student in genuine reading and thinking, without regard to whether or not at this moment the literature is classified as great or the ideas are considered basic to the thinking of all mankind. Greatness in literature or philosophy is unlikely to be perceived by the young until they have first had the experience of a literary or intellectual kind which can make it possible for them to respond to ideas naturally and warmly. To become lost in the reading, to disappear into the writer's mind, and to come out on the other side enriched by the journey—this is what we should be trying to make possible for all students.

"I was a chemistry major, at first," says Jack Gelber, author of *The Connection* and other plays, "thinking I'd be a chemist or a chemical engineer. Then I wound up studying journalism, which dealt mainly with how to get a job in radio and television. Which I didn't want. Within two weeks after graduation, I got a lift in a friend's car to San Francisco. I had one hundred dollars saved from working summers as a sheet-metal worker and when that ran out I got a job as a ship fitter's helper."

Gelber's account of his education goes on to describe the people he met in San Francisco, his developing interest in free-hand reading and poetry, and learning by thinking, outside the California universities, walking the streets of New York, seeing dozens of films. Then he began writing his first play. After the success of *The Connection,* he was asked about his literary influences. "I haven't read too much, but at the University of Illinois I had a job in the library, where I came across a lot of things that interested me. *The Books of the Dead,* Egyptian and Tibetan, that give advice to people who die. Early Greek philosophy. I've been attracted to Turgenev, Gorki, Gogol. I never really read Proust, but I read Rilke and the German expressionists of the twenties. *Alexanderplatz, Berlin,* and *The Sleepwalkers* had a great effect on me. In the library, I first got interested in Buddhism. I've always had a great interest in religious states of being. That little baby in there knows everything right now that he's ever going to know, but some day it will be revealed to him. That's the way I was in the library. I was in a conducive state. I wanted to know." [3]

The crucial point in Gelber's description of his education is that this discursive reading was the most important intellectual experience in the whole of his education at the University of Illinois. Although it is not necessary to argue that the University of Illinois should entirely revise its curriculum in order that those who begin in chemistry should be prepared as dramatists, the least the university could have done was to have made it natural for Gelber to go to the library in a conducive state of mind without having to pay him to go there as an assistant. It is entirely possible that if Gelber had not had to work in the library and had not had the freedom of the stacks, he would never have learned to read. Or to write.

[III]

When you drop the word education and think entirely of teaching and learning, it then becomes necessary to look at teaching from the point of view of the student, to look at it from within his consciousness, just as a composer in writing a score has in his mind the sounds that will be produced and the way the sounds will be heard. This does not mean that he writes only for his listeners, but that the sounds are not in the score, they are in his listeners, including himself as listener.

The history of the arts has proceeded not by theories of art which have demanded that the artists work toward this or that end in this or that way. The artists have done what they had to do in order to make real what they wanted to say, and what theories they have had are the result of their work, within whatever conventions (theories) they have chosen. They are influenced less by theories than by other artists, by the forms of experience which have shaped their own view as to the nature of art. There is of course the context and content of their culture, and the images and reality of the society in which they work, and of other societies about whose art and reality they may or may not be informed. There are influences from a variety of sources, among them the intellectuals, the historians, the critics, and all the rest of the members of their culture.

The history of teaching and learning has moved in a parallel path, and the educational theories which have developed through history are the work of teachers who have discovered in their experience certain truths and ideas about their art which they have found the means to express, either by writing about them, teaching them to students, or by building institutions around them. Montessori, Pestalozzi, Dalton, A. J. Neill, Dewey, Bertrand Russell, Jane Addams, Horace Mann, and a host of others have done all of these. But the value of the educational ideas is tested as art is tested, by their persistence in the culture, by the practical question of whether or not they exist in the consciousness of those capable of responding to art and education, by the degree to which they stay alive as objects and ideas commanding a continuity of attention.

Persuasive ideas for the reform of education come from the minds of working teachers and working students whose experience with teaching and learning leads them to draw their own conclusions about what it is best to do. Students are constantly teaching each other, by what they do together, and can teach their teachers when they are given a chance to do so. Once educational theory is taken out of the hands of the managers and organizers and put in the hands of teachers and students, it becomes modified by their mutual influence. They are the practitioners of teaching and learning.

At the present time, it is as if the art critics, museum directors, and theater managers were in the position of telling the artists what to do by organizing institutions in which they all had compulsory training to produce works that would fit the museums and theaters. The only defense open to the artist would be to refuse to enter the institution, and therefore not show his work in the museum or the theater. In the case of the college student, he has the same kind of option, with the same kind of consequence.

A theory of education need not demolish all other theories in order to speak its own truth. It can only insist that it be tested in practice, that its results be measured by what happens to students. If the students either can't learn or will not learn what it demands, if, in the process of being educated, students are stunted in imagination or inhibited in the measure of their full growth, there is something wrong with the theory and its practices, not with the student. It is necessary to develop a theory of teaching and learning which works in practice to do the most that can be done in the development of the student, and its worth as a theory will be the extent to which it takes account of the reality of educational fact and gives better solutions to the problems all teachers and students must face than the theories and practices proposed by others.

One of the unhappy facts in the history of progressive education is that its advocates were lined up in a continual battle of assertion against people referred to as essentialists or traditionalists, who were usually caricatured as those who had never gone past Aristotle, who wanted to nail down the seats and the desks, line up the students for inspection, ram knowledge down their throats, and punish them with bad grades if they did not do as they were told.

On the other side, the traditionalists, and later the Hutchins-Rickover style of educational critics, sneered at the progressives as those who thought they had solved the problem by *not* nailing down the seats, by allowing children to do as they pleased, by substituting a sentimental, warm-hearted permissiveness for serious intellectual demands, basket-weaving for mathematics, citizenship for history, and a mush of a curriculum in place of the intellectual disciplines. It is still very difficult to get a serious discussion of progressive ideas in education going because of the overlay of ambiguity in the terms used to describe what the movement tried to do. The trouble was that neither side took the other seriously enough, neither tried to look at the kind of truth being told by the other.

The vocabulary of the progressives received abuse from its users, as it did from its detractors. Phrases about the whole child, individual differences, adaptation to the environment, reading readiness, the core curriculum, emotional factors in learning, learning by doing, the child-centered curriculum, not only became worn with use, but, in the hands of those who had learned about them in a school of education rather than in a fresh set of experiences with children, became devoid of their true meaning. The insight of Dewey became the banalities of the schools. When Dewey spoke of the relation of effort to interest, he meant just that. He meant that there was a direct and irrefutable relation between effort and interest, and that unless the child became truly involved in what he was doing he was unlikely to learn what the teacher assumed he could or should learn.

I talked with Dewey a good deal during the later years of his

life, and found him impatient with much that was done in his name
in the schools and much that was said about his philosophy of
education. He said that one of the primary ways in which he had
been misunderstood was in his concept of growth and experience.
What he meant by growth and what his critics meant by what he
said about it seemed never to be understood. The critics said that
he was confused, ambiguous, and hopelessly optimistic, and that
his idea of growth made no distinction between the growth of
weeds and the growth of flowers—it was sheer growth in whatever
direction the individual psyche cared to go. In fact, Dewey was
hard-headed, realistic, and profound, all at the same time. His
criterion for measuring growth was whether it led to further
growth, and the institutions and practices of education were to be
measured by the degree to which they freed the student to discover
truths, ideas, and experiences of his own. There could be no intellectual or personal growth until the individual learned to make his
own discoveries and injected himself into his own education.

What Dewey wanted was a system of education designed to set
things in motion, to make learning happen, to make it a transitive
verb, to make it of a kind which would lead to the next stage in
learning. There are many ways of doing that. Too often Dewey's
insight was lost by those who insulted the child by making learning
into a game of playing grown-ups. It is one thing to teach biology
to third graders by having them set up experiments in which they
can see with their own eyes and aid with their own hands the evo-
lution of the chicken from the egg, another to teach history by
eternally dressing up in the costumes of Puritans. When Dewey
said "learning by doing," he also meant just that. Doing mathematics. Doing history. Doing philosophy. Doing politics. That is,
acting in the way people act when they do mathematics, when they
write history, when they think philosophically, when they run for
office or elect representatives.

In any case, the issue is not Dewey, or his system of educational and social thought. The issue is, how can a theory of education be forged in the teeth of experience with live students in a
culture whose character and available knowledge changes from
year to year and which demands that changes in education keep
pace with changes in the society and in individual students? Dewey
was closely in touch with this question. So were others who were

anti-Dewey but who were very good teachers and often good educators. The test is in what happens to the students, and how well they are able to make use of the educational situations arranged for them, what kinds of knowledge and in what form are most appropriate for their intellectual and personal growth.

The progressives had a very great deal to say about individual differences among children. Rightly so. Without taking that into account, no theory can hope to be successful in dealing with the complexity of the total educational process in its cultural setting. They had less to say about individual differences among teachers. They took progressivism as zealously in its doctrinal form as their opponents took their own.

It is even doubtful that an effort should be made to re-establish progressive education as a theory, since its vocabulary works so much against it; even the word "progressive" has lost its meaning, and the name of John Dewey is overladen with false associations. Nor does a search for other words to describe a radical philosophy of education yield a ready substitute. I think of such a philosophy as both traditional and post-modern. It is traditional in holding that teaching involves moral action. It is post-modern in accommodating itself to the next stage of the movement in twentieth-century cultural history beyond what we have all become accustomed to calling modern—modern sensibility, modern architecture, modern dance, modern science, modern literature, modern education, modern life, without knowing exactly what is meant by modernity.

To be modern is to accept the reality of the new forms of art, culture, and styles of thought which broke with the traditions of the early twentieth century and made use of new ideas, techniques, and insights for the reorganization of experience and its expression in the culture and in new patterns of social organization. Having accepted that reality, a reality which has now become, in a sense, traditional, the ideas of post-modernity are still in the process of being formed and stated, for example in the experimental work of the mixed-media artists, in the links between technology and art, the intense subjectivism of the new literature, the theater of the absurd, confrontation politics, systems analysis, future-centered social planning, computerized industry, and so on.

At the same time, post-modernism in educational theory can

be identified as experimental, since it starts from certain hypotheses about how students may best learn, about the connection between education and social change, tests them in a variety of situations, and judges by their results. But post-modern education has too easily been identified with Summerhillism, Rousseauism, hippyism, and, in another sector, with innovations in methods of instruction involving electronic equipment, audio-visual aids, team teaching, rearrangement of schedules, reading techniques, ungraded classes. Until it is clear what is to be experimented with and to what end, what innovations are to be used for what purposes, experimental education remains a name for doing whatever seems to be a good idea to those who do it.

In any case, good education leading toward enlightenment and humane action has no need for other adjectives, and it is better to talk not about education as doctrine but about teaching and learning and what it entails. That puts the case in its active form and draws attention to the details of action which give any doctrine its validity and form.

[IV]

Those who support traditional education have things to say which are perfectly true. There *is* a body of knowledge which exists and which stands before each age as the heritage of its past. Ignorance of the heritage is just that, and those who know no history, while not necessarily doomed to repeat it, suffer the disadvantage of living outside the community of persons whose lives and ideas have set the conditions of the world environment we now occupy. This means not only the disadvantage of suffering a certain kind of ignorance and a possible arrogance, but a loss of the satisfactions and rewards of belonging to a bigger community of persons and ideas than the one which has happened to assemble itself on a narrow shelf in this part of the twentieth century. Modern youth has an anti-historical bias, induced in many ways by the influence of the mass media and various forms of contemporary self-absorption and introspection. Although this has advantages in the freshness with which it confronts old problems in new forms, and provides a freedom from the weight of historical precedent, it can be a genuine intellectual and personal deprivation.

In the ordinary life of the young, other persons with ideas, styles of life, wit, intelligence, and this or that kind of idiosyncratic behavior and character give stimulation to the young person's own consideration of himself, give him something to compare himself with, to learn from. So the study of the past gives to each generation a chance to see itself in a setting of various styles of life as they evolved from the variety of circumstances in which man acted upon the environment into which he came. To experience history in these terms is to establish one's own identity and the identity of one's era.

Where the traditionalists are wrong is in not making a distinction between experiencing history and learning about it. The theory of the educational tradition bases itself on the psychological mistake of thinking that being presented with historical accounts of past events is the same thing as gaining a sense of history, that a knowledge of what has been thought, said, and done is the same thing as knowing ideas by thinking them, that knowledge of the good leads to a concern for the good, either in action or in thought. It is only by acting upon knowledge, literally making it, or acting upon life, shaping it, learning from it, creating a life and a knowledge of one's own, that the individual can gain the values of education. That is why it is false to separate educational methods from educational content, and to assume, with the traditional educators, that the educational end has been reached when a body of accredited knowledge has been assembled in a curriculum and communicated to the student by the conventional devices.

The traditional theory is also sound in arguing for breadth of knowledge across a variety of its forms, so that the individual can see himself and his world from a broad perspective. The student must have a variety of usable knowledge, not a special collection of information and academic techniques. Otherwise he is not equipped to go on learning, since he does not know what else there is to be learned, what the world contains, what intellectual interests he might follow up. His aversion to certain kinds of knowledge, quite often in the physical sciences, may be simply ill-founded, due to lack of experience with them and with other fields of which he is ignorant.

But again, the mistake is to assume that breadth of knowledge is to be gained by formal exposure to a curriculum which intentionally groups its subject matter into broad areas involving a variety of fields, and once more presents it to the student in conventional ways. Then the problem is considered to be entirely a matter of organizing the subject matter, not of engaging the student in broadening his mind and opening up his interests. The three main ways in which the organization has taken place are: (1) To present surveys of Western and, in a few cases, non-Western civilization, surveys of literature, the social sciences, and the natural sciences; (2) to provide interdisciplinary courses, which sometimes draw upon three or four teachers in sequence in courses for a semester or a year; (3) to require that students take a certain number of courses in each of the four major fields, with the choice of the particular course in the hands of the student.

In the case of the survey, the unavoidable consequence is a rush through anthologies, texts, and brief references to events, ideas, and persons, giving a spurious breadth at the expense of serious involvement in depth. The interdisciplinary idea suffers from a similar handicap, in that knowledge is again subdivided, and most often the student learns, for example in the social sciences, something about what anthropology, sociology, economics, and political science have to teach, by reading and listening to representatives of the fields in question, or from one person who covers them all. The very purpose of ensuring this kind of breadth of knowledge defeats itself. Whereas the purpose should be to enable the student to find his way to an understanding of the society and the variety of conditions which shape human lives and which human lives have shaped, the effect is to put the student in possession of a knowledge of how the various disciplines of knowledge function and something about what is known by those who work in those disciplines.

The greater degree of freedom of choice in the third kind of program has more to recommend it, since it allows the student to work in a course and, sometimes, with a teacher of his choice, according to his interest. But once more, the organization of the subject matter and the method of instruction are not designed to broaden the student's mind and interests, but for the most part to provide the kind of introductory work appropriate for continuing into the succeeding courses of an academic sequence.

More than this, there is an over-all parochialism in the content of the curriculum and its approach to contemporary culture, a parochialism which in the long run is bound to defeat the purposes of a genuinely liberal education. Granted that a knowledge of one's own tradition is an essential ingredient in all humane learning, the bigger question remains unanswered. What is the nature of the tradition?

Is it the cluster of ideas, attitudes, and values which go to make up Western civilization, with its own philosophers, writers, scientists, and scholars, and its history of European culture? Or is it the tradition of mankind, man occupying the wider world of the planet, struggling with the circumstances of his local conditions and creating out of that struggle a variety of ways in which nature and man came to terms with each other and man came to terms with himself?

Obviously it is the latter, and to segregate the historic figures among the Western intellectuals and the governments and cultures of the West as if they represented the whole of mankind and as if their cultures represented the true models around which human progress has been made is to falsify the history of mankind.

In some of the curricula designed in each of the three patterns of requirement I have described, an effort has been made to go beyond the conventional Western civilization courses and the idea of the humanities as a private preserve of non-scientists and of superior minds in the historical West. This has been done either by including in the set of requirements for the general education courses a course in non-Western civilization, with a fast run through Africa or Asia or the Third World, or by offering among possible electives single courses in a country or countries of the East. The extent of these efforts can be measured by the fact that not more than 3 to 5 per cent of all teachers educated for service in the American public schools have taken courses in non-Western studies, and that not more than 8 to 10 per cent of undergraduates in all the colleges and universities of the United States have done work in a non-Western field by the time they graduate.

Even here the parochialism is still rampant in the very conception of a non-West. The world outside Europe and the American continent is not non-West, just as the world inside these geographical areas is not non-East. It is the world of man, with local histories in its various parts, some of them going back in time long before the West evolved its local culture and its passion for the use of science and technology in the conduct of its affairs.

There is no doubt that the approach to the discovery of truth through science and the work of the rational mind has a universal quality, just as the approach to the problems of agriculture in every sector of the world becomes part of a global body of knowledge and of practical information, from the stick plow to the mechanizing of the collective farm. But to teach American youth a set of cultural habits drawn from the history of the West, and, by the content of psychology, philosophy, economics, and literature, to assure him that the human mind is a Western phenomenon, working on Western principles, is to do both the student and the human mind a grave disservice.

[v]

A dramatic demonstration of the inadequacy of applying the present concept of a general culture of the West was given when in 1960–1961 the Peace Corps turned to the colleges and universities for educational programs which could prepare their volunteers for service in a culture other than their own. In a real sense, the method by which college students were being prepared to enter their own culture was put on trial by the need of the Peace Corps for curricula which could prepare the volunteers to enter another one. After the beginning months of experience with university and college planners who converted the usual system into programs for Peace Corps use, it became very clear, and especially to the volunteers and Peace Corps staff in the field, that most of what had gone on in the preparatory training was irrelevant to the service of the volunteers in a foreign country. They were not being prepared to enter a new culture but to learn what the academic profession had to say about it in the style of academics. The discontinuity between life and education, between culture and learning, was never more clearly revealed.

In the analyses made by the volunteers and the Peace Corps staff of the changes necessary to make an organic relation between preparation and service, it soon became clear that the educational goals of the colleges and universities and the kind of human skills and talents they were concerned to develop made it impossible for them to adapt to the true needs of the volunteers. In this fact is contained one of the most damaging indictments of the contemporary college. The literature of education has been immensely enriched by the internal memoranda of the Peace Corps staff as they began to work out their own ways of remedying the defects in the regular system [4] and by the cooperative programs eventually worked out with colleges willing to engage in serious experiment and reform. What has emerged, although it is too seldom conceived in these terms, is one of the most significant and far-reaching programs of reform available in the field of contemporary educational theory and practice. Not only did the Peace Corps and its Task Force on Education develop new concepts for the study of foreign cultures, but it developed a style of educational change of the utmost importance for the reform of the American college.

The essence of the style is in the continuing appraisal, by those who are using their education to carry out services to society, of the process by which they have been educated. The volunteers were taken seriously as educational critics and reformers from the start, and the insight and knowledge they gained through experience in the field was used directly in the reconstruction of methods and ideas in use abroad and in their previous preparation for service. There was no question as to whether they, as students, should be involved in decision-making about educational policy. They were in the decision-making process continually, since they were the persons who knew most about the reality of the problems with which the Peace Corps had to deal.

Since many of the volunteers on their return from service abroad entered the Peace Corps staff itself, what they had learned in their preparation and in their service abroad was put to work immediately in the self-generating process by which the Peace Corps made judgments about the success or failure of its mission. The volunteers did not have to wait until they had achieved academic rank before being listened to. They were basic elements in the planning and evaluation, with planning and evaluation conceived as two parts of the same process.

As a result, it became clear again what has always been true, that to separate practical and useful knowledge from liberal knowledge is in itself a major fallacy. For the Peace Corps the study of the history, sociology, literature, political science, or anthropology of a foreign culture had to be liberal in order to be useful. That is, it had to release the capacity of the student to understand the way in which this particular society looked at life and organized itself as one kind of response to its own history and circumstance, but it also had to make it possible for the student to put that understanding to work in adapting what he knew to the circumstances of his service. A generally educated person who can do nothing specific, or who knows something in general about cultures he has studied is of very little use to the society he intends to serve, whether the society is American or otherwise. It is the human element in the situation with which he must deal, not the generalized concepts of a body of knowledge.

This means a return to the idea of experience as the prime teacher, with organized bodies of knowledge considered as sources of material which can only be useful once the student has already learned how to gain from it what he needs to know in order better to understand how to cope with his culture. Roger Hilsman spoke of this recently in a comment on the inadequacy of State Department knowledge of the political system of the Thais. There is in existence a considerable body of knowledge about Thailand, but it was not until the State Department began receiving reports from an experienced observer who understood the family structure and the internal organism of Thai society as it was perceived by the people in it that any real understanding of the politics of Thailand could be gained for the enlightenment of policy-makers.

A further implication from the Peace Corps and VISTA experience follows from this, and moves in the direction of the need for practitioners of knowledge in the proper conduct of college education, for the teacher who has not only developed a body of knowledge in the field of his interest, but has had a depth of experience in its use within practical situations. In the case of the Peace Corps, a model of college education was created in which a whole variety of talented people, only a few of whom were academic professionals, and those few very carefully selected, were recruited for the preparatory programs. They were sometimes nationals from the host country, young people of experience in teaching or in agriculture, at other times foreign nationals from other countries with experience in the host country, or Americans outside the academic profession whose knowledge of the problems of social change and cultural diversity had been gained in the United States, or returned Peace Corps volunteers with special talents as teachers and scholars.

It also became clear that the entry into another culture had so many parallels with the entry into one of the subcultures of the United States that it was better to move the Peace Corps preparatory programs off the campuses into the Negro or Spanish-American or Indian communities in order that the students could explore the nature of alternate cultures by studying one in depth at first hand. The transference of knowledge from this kind of encounter, combined with direct knowledge of the foreign culture, made a transition from the United States to a foreign country much simpler to accomplish.

For American college education, there are many implications in this, including the obvious one that direct experience in an American subculture is one of the most important ways of learning to understand America as a whole. Going beyond that, the implication is that to study a culture in depth, through a combination of direct experience, one's own research, and teaching which deals with the meaning for human lives in the organized knowledge of the colleges, is a more direct route to becoming liberally educated than to be exposed to the curriculum of general education.

Aside from everything else, the Peace Corps experience with educational reform shows the open opportunity lying in the hands of the American college for broadening the cultural and social concepts of young Americans far beyond the limits of the Western and American curriculum now in existence. Young Americans who have returned from Peace Corps service abroad, of whom by 1970 there will be 50,000, now form one of the most potent forces we have in the United States for linking the educational system to the rest of the world and for disseminating throughout the American culture a knowledge and understanding of world problems, especially as these have to do with war and peace, education, and social change. Most of the volunteers have been seriously changed by their Peace Corps experience, in the direction of understanding themselves and the size and nature of American problems, and toward a commitment to human service which has deepened the commitment they took with them into the Peace Corps in the first place.

If every college campus dealt with its curriculum in the style of Peace Corps training programs and used the idea of foreign experience and experience in cultures other than the white American middle class, a whole new element would enter the quality of college education and the accomplishments of its graduates. The recruitment of returned volunteers to the faculty of the colleges and schools—and the reform of graduate programs to take advantage of the knowledge the volunteer brings back with him and to build his education around his talent and knowledge—is only one of any number of things which can be done once education begins to move in this direction. It is the educational concept more than the actual Peace Corps program which has in it the energy and ideas by which reforms can be generated.

12: Freedom and Learning

When the idea of education as entry into a culture is examined for its implications in radical reform, it carries education back to one of the original insights of the experimental college movement—that there *is* no complete body of knowledge common to all educated men which every student must possess in order to enter his culture and to live there as an educated person. There is a world culture, of which the American is a part, there is a world knowledge, of which the sciences, the arts, languages and literature, philosophy, the social sciences are all a part, and each man, unable to encompass the whole, must begin to understand it and to enter it by beginning with that part of it for which his talents and purposes fit him at the point of beginning.

The radical step of the experimental college movement was to declare that fact as a basis for planning a curriculum. It can be called a radical step only because it was taken in the 1920s in the context of a period in American educational history when education had moved away from the free curriculum of the latter part of the nineteenth century and back toward the idea of required studies, from which the curriculum of the nineteenth century had already broken. Long before the 1920s the philosophy of the elective system had been declared a radical principle, both by its major spokesman, Charles W. Eliot, who acted on the principle and put it to work at Harvard in 1865, and by a strong body of concerned democrats among nineteenth-century educators, who saw in the elective idea an instrument for the achievement of democratic education and the development of a democratic society. Not only did the elective principle break the grip of the traditional curriculum on the student and the faculty, it introduced a radical concept of the equality of worth within a variety of forms of knowledge, and shattered the hierarchy of classification of subjects into the pure kind, possessed by scholars in certain fields, and the practical kind possessed by those who wanted to put their knowledge to work. It combined forces in the 1860s with the land-grant concept of service to all citizens, and in the hands of university leaders at Cornell, at Michigan, at Wisconsin, and elsewhere, became a powerful instrument for advancing the idea that universities existed for the education of all citizens in whatever might be their dimension of need. By extending the range of possible subjects for study, and allowing students to choose among them, the universities placed themselves in direct contact with the public need, at the front edge of the growing society, and gave strength to the public view that higher education should be open to all those who wanted it and could profit by it.

What was introduced as a principle for organizing the curriculum had ramifications so broad in the development of the university's place in society that it radicalized the university. It brought the world into the campus—"real life" as Eliot put it—and took the campus into the world. Lincoln Steffens, in his enthusiastic description in 1909 of the Wisconsin idea as it operated at the University in Madison, said that this new kind of university had its center in the idea that it offered "to teach anybody—anything—anywhere." [1]

The idea is still as powerful as it was when it was first introduced. Its restoration in a reconstructed form in the American university of the 1970s would set in motion a train of consequences with an importance not only equal to those of the nineteenth-century developments, but going far beyond them into the re-establishment of the student at the center of the university community and in giving a broad range of answers to the most crucial problems the American system of higher education now faces.

The failure of the elective system and its replacement by the knowledge machine was not that it produced overspecialized students who entered courses of their choice and stayed there to the exclusion of all other kinds of study. Providing their teachers were competent, most students who became thoroughly involved in study within a given discipline had a better grasp of what serious intellectual effort on a broad front meant than those who have now been all around the general education curriculum. The elective system failed because the competition among the departments for offering courses according to the academic preoccupations and special interests of the faculty produced a proliferation of bad courses rather than an opportunity for good education. It failed also because the faculty advisers who were to work with students in planning a program of studies suitable to each did little more than sign cards on which unguided and unmotivated students had listed courses they felt would produce the greatest amount of academic credit with the least interference with their personal and social lives. Choices among courses became almost meaningless for students whose advisers gave no advice and whose teachers were giving courses, not teaching students.

The root cause of failure lay in the decline of teaching as an art and the lack of commitment by the faculty to the education of students. It was not the elective principle that was at fault, but the system of instruction. Since there was no unity of educational purpose within the academic community, there was no unity of knowledge in the curriculum. Since there was no sense of intellectual community within the student body and faculty, there was no community of interest between student and student or student and faculty member. The separation of the academic curriculum from the life of the student was already so complete that the mere mechanics of choice-making in the elective system could not be the main factor in the loss of purpose and unity in the student's education.

The faculty committees who installed the common curriculum and its variations in place of the elective principle and open choice never went beneath the surface to dig out the simple objective fact that if in the course of instruction the student is never called upon to engage himself deeply in his own education, or to make the kind of commitment to the ideal of humane learning it is the purpose of the college and university to create, then the question of who makes the choice of the subject matter, the faculty or the students, becomes almost irrelevant. In this situation, the deliberations and decisions of the faculty left the entire system intact while rearranging the compulsory arithmetic of its parts.

[II]

Spreading beneath the surface of the issue of a free elective system is the larger issue of freedom itself and its relation to life and education. Some of this has to do with who will be admitted to college, what they will study there, what they will do on the campus, and what part they are allowed to take in making decisions about policy. It is perfectly possible to conceive and to establish a college, as some students are doing in the ghettos, where anyone who wants to may come and study whatever he needs to know with persons who volunteer to teach it in the best way they can all work out together. Graduation from such an institution occurs when those who have been involved in it no longer need it or find better ways of finding out how to do what they want to do next.

In the work of the experimental colleges in their beginning, and the part which is most important to the reform of the present system, freedom as a concept was basic to a whole series of other concepts. The idea of freedom was applied to a philosophy of politics, social change, aesthetic experience, a psychology of learning, and methods of college organization. The curriculum was the whole college and the total body of experience available in it to the students and faculty—experience on the campus and in the society, private, internal, subjective experience, organized and unorganized knowledge, social experience, political experience, to be found in organizing the governance of the community and in taking an active concern for political issues and world affairs. There were varieties of knowing and doing, and the speculative faculties, intuition, imagination, empathy, creative intelligence, and social sensitivity, were honored along with the faculties of rational thought, the ordering of ideas, and the acquisition of a body of knowledge.

It is in this conception of freedom that most of the ideas to be transferred into the reform of the present system are to be found, not in the particular methods and techniques by which the experimental colleges operated. Those are in many ways, as their critics have said, a function of the size of the institutions and the character of the student body. But the total intention of the radical education movement, and the movement with which it is now joined in the work of student reformers and activists, can be transferred into any institutional or noninstitutional setting. Once the radical conception of freedom in its psychological, social, and political dimension has been taken as the starting point in a philosophy of reform, the methods of education and community organization for the college and university work themselves out in their own way.

The freedom from all requirements for specific courses is only one of the consequences of beginning with that conception. From the radical point of view, the free curriculum is not merely a device for making it easy for students to do what they want to do, or for making it possible to avoid "hard" subjects or the obligations of the intellectual disciplines. It is a new kind of discipline, the kind a musician observes in perfecting his art. All subjects are hard when badly taught, and the traditional "hardness" of mathematics and the physical sciences is more a result of insensitive teaching in science and the consequent cultural habit in students of assuming that they are "no good in mathematics" than it is of intrinsic difficulty in the subjects themselves. The educational radicals simply raise the question of whether the ability to reach a high level of competence in mathematics or physics, or in any other subject, or in all subjects, should be the criterion for intellectual and personal ability in general, just as the earlier radicals raised some of the same kind of questions about the study of Latin, Greek, and the formal eighteenth-century disciplines.

There is a common culture which contains a variety of forms of knowledge, no one of which is absolutely essential for entry into the culture. As soon as a distinction is made between knowledge and culture, a whole new area opens up for educational thinking and planning. The attention of the educator is then turned to the question of sensibility, of intellectual commitment, of the ability of the student to deal with ideas and to discover and pursue interests, or to handle problems of authority, intellectual and social, to act in his society. In other words, the educator must think about qualities of mind and of character, including the quality of cultural maturity and cultural proficiency, rather than of the single skill of acquiring someone else's body of knowledge.

In the radical view, therefore, freedom for the student is the natural and necessary condition for the accomplishment of a whole cluster of educational aims, of which gaining a specific body of knowledge is only one, and not the most difficult to achieve or, in one sense, the most important. The most important is entry into the culture, with readiness and ability to act in it in personal terms. The entry can be made by many different routes, any one of which can provide access—dance, theater, physics, literature, psychology. Once inside, the learner can move from his beginning into other areas as these are relevant to the organic body of knowledge and experience he is making his own.

Should there be need for further knowledge in any area which he has not entered in the four college years, the student has the rest of his life to enter it. If he needs to observe the formalities of admission to graduate school in a given field in which he has not concentrated, a full year of work in one field can usually deal with that. In the meantime he has had an education which he has created for himself, not only by his choice of areas and teachers with whom he has worked, but by the variety of experiences in the community of the college and in the world outside the college. It therefore has an inner meaning which is reflected in his total character.

The experience at Sarah Lawrence with an open curriculum refutes the argument that this degree of freedom leads either to an overspecialized education for those who know what they want to do before they come to college or a fragmented, dilettantish exploration by those who have no committed interests when they arrive. What appears on the surface of a transcript when a student graduates either from Sarah Lawrence or from any other institution does not reflect what the student has learned, nor do the subject-matter headings or course titles reveal much about what the student has done or what intellectual and personal qualities have been developing. In the experimental college, a transcript simply records what courses have been taken and whether or not the student has been able to do the work asked for by the teacher. It is not intended as a certificate of accomplishment. The only certification for that lies in what the student is able to do and what kind of person he is.

Most students when faced with an open curriculum make fairly conservative choices; that is, they already have in mind the idea of breadth and range of study, as do their advisers among the students and faculty members. Since the choice is theirs and they know they are committed by it, they are careful in what they commit themselves to. There needs to be room enough in the opening schedule of the college year and at other times to allow time for serious discussion of possible programs, and there need to be experienced persons enough, among the faculty and student body, to give advice where it is needed. The descriptions of courses and educational action projects have to be carefully written with the problem of student choice in mind, so that it is clear what the student will be expected to do and may expect to do when the course or project begins.

[III]

Another misconception of the way in which a free curriculum operates has to do with the goals toward which it seeks to move. Not only is it an effort to free the student into a situation where choices become a necessary part of his movement toward his own fulfillment, it is an effort to introduce the relevance of his choice to a goal which he must continually define. If the reason for taking a course in science is to prepare oneself to become a scientist or to become a medical practitioner or researcher, or simply to become better informed about the meaning of science, this is part of the choice, the choice is made in those terms. A student who wishes to enter government service, to become a poet, to become a *person,* which is altogether valid, along with other wishes, chooses the kind of intellectual experiences and the kind of knowledge suited to that end. Some of these choices are purely his own subjective judgment. Others are made necessary by the goal to which he is moving and the objective standards by which his knowledge and talent will be tested.

It is therefore perfectly practical to transfer the open curriculum to the larger institutions, where a variety of choices among departmental courses already exists and where many of the internal requirements within a given discipline are simply unnecessary. They have been put together by members of the academic profession with their eyes on the graduate school and the academic profession, and have been narrowly conceived within that framework. There is no certainty that setting down a regular curriculum through which all persons must go on their way to triumphs as academic sociologists, physicists, psychologists, or literary experts is the best means of accomplishing that end. There should be as many kinds of academic scholars with as many special interests as there are persons in the field. We are unlikely to have fertility of imagination and individually creative minds if it is assumed that all scholars in a field are alike and should be taught to stay that way.

The open curriculum also works in the direction of concentrating attention on the teaching. The choice of a program has to be one which makes educational sense to the student, who must see that it does not involve heavy reading assignments in all the courses, is not all in one style of teaching by the same kind of persons, and is genuinely related to what the student wants to do. In general terms, students in a free curriculum choose to work in about the same areas in which they would find themselves if they were subject to a required program. Nearly all of them will choose to do part of their work in literature, in the social sciences, in the humanities, in the creative arts, in the natural sciences, and some will think of the natural sciences and foreign languages as interests for those who enjoy the work for its own sake or who are entering a field later on in which they will be necessary.

If, as at Sarah Lawrence, the student works in three courses or areas in a given year (the courses are usually for the whole year), the student's choice of areas is made with the idea of breadth in mind. But since an entire third of a student's work is done for a full year in one field, the student with specific interests can start with them and go as far and as fast as his talents will take him, while at the same time working in two other fields which may or may not be related to the central one. Although it may look odd to the conventional educator to see a freshman transcript recording the fact that a student has spent a year studying physics, dance, and French literature, this is a perfectly natural and important thing for a student to do, if these are the areas of exploration or specialization in which the student is interested. The unity of knowledge of which the traditional educators speak so often is achieved in the only way it can truly be achieved—by the integration which the student makes within himself of the forms of experience and ideas which go to make up an organic whole.

The complete conception of freedom in this kind of education is the opposite of *laissez-faire,* assuming of course that letting people do things without hindrance is what *laissez-faire* means, and that that is bad for people. It is opposite because once the freedom is given, a transfer of responsibility and a considerable degree of authority has been made to the student, and what is done by psychological and social force exerted by the conventional system with its punitive devices is done in a completely different way by the internalized system of values developed by the student. In some cases, the internal control is already so great that one of the educational tasks is to break the grip of that control so that the student may become free of tightly held feelings of obligation in order to let his intellectual development range more freely. In other cases, it takes time for the transfer of external authority to an internally derived system of values to take place, and a greater degree of patience on the part of the teacher, combined with a gradual lessening rather than an abrupt release of the teacher's authority.

But in a community whose ethos is one of voluntary association and of self-realization, where students work with each other and personal influences act within the community with much more intensity, students learn readily from each other and learn quickly to help each other, since there is no competition between them for external rewards other than the satisfaction of being recognized by fellow students and teachers as an integral member of the community. The radical educational theory examines the pathology of obligation and compulsory learning as a whole, and is concerned not merely with the number and kind of courses, but with the quality of each person's experience in the total college environment.

Nor is the rejection of testing devices, grades, academic credits, and formal curricula a technical matter, another device for ensuring "freedom." It is a complete alteration in the idea of what education is for and, therefore, in how it is best organized. The testing and grading apparatus is rejected because it acts as a simpleminded control over everything the student learns, and is seriously inhibiting to the growth of the intellect, the imagination, and the native powers of the young.

Among the student activists and their liberal colleagues in the faculty there has grown up recently a literature of denunciation of testing and grading, in some instances accompanied by proposals and demands for their removal. Some cases of reforms have resulted in which one course out of the four or five a student takes is arranged with a distinction made only between passing and failing. But most of the students and many of the faculty are playing on the surface of the problem in concentrating on the marking and testing system.

Certainly the high comedy of the absurd in "grade-point averages" carried out to two and three decimal points is matched only by the high tragedy of the absurd practices of the military in their body-counts and kill ratios, and reflects the passion in America for a baseball-score approach to education, to culture, and to all forms of achievement, a passion which seems almost impossible to cool. But to shift from numerical to letter grades, or even to pass-fail arrangements, is only one small step toward sanity while leaving the norms of insanity intact.

[IV]

It is the control by the total system which must be analyzed, not the technical parts of it. The question to be asked and answered is, What effect does the testing system have on the intellectual and cultural life of the students and teachers?

Its first effect is to narrow the range of criteria for intellectual achievement to a thin sector of human ability—that of reporting back what has been retained in the memory—and, in removing the impetus to a higher form of learning, to substitute external rewards for the satisfaction of internal needs. The objective test is the worst offender, and can serve by its nature only to weed out those with incredibly bad memories and impossibly little information. But again, it is the character of the demand made by the tests, even when they are written examinations, which does the damage, not the implied assertion that there are standards which students must meet. It is perfectly possible to construct examinations which give the student a chance to show what he has learned and what he can do, and which can serve both as a source of satisfaction to the student in clarifying the nature of his own accomplishment and as an indication to the interested parties of what it is that he has accomplished.

If the purpose of education is to liberate the student's mind rather than to direct it toward a certain kind of thinking and learning, then the criteria of success are of an entirely different character. A student who is asked to provide a written report of a case study in the life of a three-year-old child has in this a useful and proper examination of what it is he has learned about children and himself. Or if he is asked to make a verbal report to a group of fellow students on an issue which he has investigated, this is a proper examination for him and for the others. The trouble lies in the artificiality of the conventional testing situation, in which the student is stripped of all the available aids to the demonstration of his ability—seated in a room with a hundred or hundreds of others, without books, notes, or the possibility of conversation and help from the most natural of sources, his fellow students— and asked either to check the right items in a list of word choices or to write on a broad or narrow question which has already been answered in the lectures and texts.

The natural tendency of a system of that kind is to produce the conditions for plagiarism in all its forms, from actual cheating by codes of communication, concealed notes, stealing tests in advance, or the other kind of plagiarism at one stage removed—taking from the lecturer what he has previously said in class and using it as an answer of one's own. The fact that the answer is the one the examiner wants does not remove it from the sphere of plagiarism. It is simply not the student's own answer.

The recent cheating scandal at the Air Force Academy, resulting in the dismissal of more than sixty cadets, is the natural outcome of a general approach to education across the country not confined to the military academies. The Air Force had simply taken the system to its extreme form, by having put the students into a tightly screwed vise which held every moment of their waking lives, having imposed an academic and technical curriculum of uncompromising severity, having demanded of its athletes that they not only fulfill the requirements of the academy but carry out their professional athletic training and performance at the same time. The rest of the institutions are less severe in the application of the doctrine, especially in the academic sector, but the results they get are only slightly less severe in the kind of learning it imposes.

If students were judged by means other than written tests and examinations, and were taught to judge each other and themselves by visible accomplishments, they would be free to make full use of their time in learning. I have known students in the experimental colleges who asked to be examined by the conventional tests, or by unconventional ones, in order that they would know whether or not they were able to meet the demands of the regular system, or to find out for themselves whether or not they were capable of remembering the specifics of what they had learned and could produce them on demand. In a system designed to give the student what is, after all, one of the most important of his possible possessions—the ability of self-appraisal and a clarity about his own ability—whatever test is made of what he can do must be made in the context of the learning, not external to it. His worth must be recognized by himself and measured against standards which he learns to set for himself with the help of his teachers and fellow students.

If the log-jam of the system were broken by pulling out the key log of course requirements and returning to the elective principle, the stream of change in most of these particulars would begin to flow again. It would be natural to follow out the implication in the principle of election that each teacher prepare and teach his own courses in his own way, and the invention of new ways of appraising student achievement would then be made in the context of the work the student and teacher did together. If at present a single teacher, in search of remedies for defects in the system, acts unilaterally to remove grades and tests completely, either by an act of defiance in giving A's to the whole class, or leaving assignments and attendance at class as a matter for the student's personal decision, he is likely to find himself in an impossible situation. Since the rest of the student's program continues to make the same academic demands, and the administrative officers, including the registrar, are duty-bound to make their demands, the rebellious teacher is faced with the fact that he is not only in trouble with the system, but that a fairly large proportion of his students, being unaccustomed to the removal of conventional requirements, do not come to class, do not carry out assignments, and classify him as a soft-headed fool or a romantic revolutionary with whom it would be either useless or dangerous to study.

It is the whole system of instruction which is in need of change, not merely the testing part of it. Teaching and testing are so closely intertwined that the particular kind of appraisal the teacher makes of the progress of his students is a major factor in the effects of his teaching. If his appraisal is designed to make it possible for the students to learn how to appraise themselves, then he teaches in such a way that the responsibility for learning is shifted to the students, and the test of their intellectual and personal qualities lies in the demonstration they make of the intellect in action.

13: Education by Influence

The student's education in college begins with the experience and knowledge he brings with him to the culture of the college. He has already entered one part of the general culture through his high school years and his membership in the mass culture as it is represented in his native community. The task of the college is then to take him, not simply out of the mass culture and into a narrower one, but into a wider dimension of experience with a larger variety of ideas and a wider range of cultural and personal values.

I turn to Ortega for a definition of what this involves and how it creates a new and more complicated set of educational obligations than the simpler ones of the conventional curriculum.

> The usage of the expression "general culture" shows an underlying notion that the student ought to be given some ornamental knowledge, which in some way is to educate his moral character or his intellect. . . . But the fact is that if we go back to the medieval epoch in which the university was created, we see clearly that the relic before us is the humble remains of what then constituted higher education, proper and entire.
>
> The medieval university does no research. It is very little concerned with professions. All is "*general culture*"—theology, philosophy, "arts."
>
> But what is called "general culture" today was something very different for the Middle Ages. It was not an ornament for the mind or a training of the character. It was, on the contrary, the system of ideas, concerning the world and humanity, which

the man of that time possessed. It was, consequently, the repertory of convictions which became the effective guide of his
existence.

Life is a chaos, a tangled and confused jungle in which man
is lost. But his mind reacts against the sensation of bewilderment: he labors to find "roads," "ways" through the woods,
in the form of clear, firm ideas concerning the universe, positive
convictions about the nature of things. The ensemble, or system,
of these ideas is culture in the true sense of the term; it is
precisely the opposite of external ornament. . . . A man belongs
to a generation; he is one substance with it. And each generation takes its place not in some chance location, but directly
and squarely upon the preceding one. This comes to mean
that man lives, perforce, at *the level of his time,* and more
particularly, at *the level of the ideas of his time.*[1]

In this conception of culture, it is the repertory of convictions
as a guide to existence and the capacity to live at and above the
level of his time that is the mutual concern of the teacher and the
student. How such convictions and capacities can be reached then
becomes the central question in making the curriculum, and the
curriculum becomes the whole community and the culture it creates by the free association of its members.

Those who enter the community with no bewilderment and no
strong impulse to find a way through the chaos need to begin a
journey in some particular way by taking first steps, inward toward
themselves and outward toward the world. Confronted with the
necessity of a choice among journeys, they may make a choice
which involves no deep commitment to continue in a path, or one
which has no fundamental basis in their own psychic need. But
that too will be a start. For many it will be the first time that such
a choice has had to be made in connection with their own education, and it is then the obligation of the college to find ways in
which the seriousness of choosing can become part of the student's
psychic development. Without the confrontation with choice, there
is little opportunity for the student to learn to know himself and
what it is he wants from his education and his life. If within the
context of his education his choices are eliminated in what he will
choose to study, how he will learn to study it, and how he will
choose to live, he is unlikely to find either motivation for what he
does or a full intellectual character of his own.

One of the most obvious characteristics of those who come to college from the American high school is the extent to which the entrant is conditioned by the external stimuli and cultural phenomena of the society in which he has been living. The style of life in the high school and the community reinforce each other and condition him to see the world as the sum total of its external conditions. For many college entrants it is literally true that they have no very definite self-image, never having looked within nor examined with any pleasure or profit the internal life which has been proceeding on its way without having been called into consciousness. The entrants have not extracted meaning from their own experience, in spite of the fact that without having done so they have almost nothing to bring to the encounter with new experience, whether in college or in life. Since it is out of experience that the self is made and a psychic identity is formed, it should be clear to the educator that whatever plans he makes for inducting the young into the culture and giving him a chance to find ways in which he can live in it and act upon it should be based on the idea of raising the level of quality and intensity in his experience and what it contains, rather than on plans for continuing the banality of his previous style of life and way of learning.

[II]

It is for this reason that the radical view, and the one taken by student activists, is that personal action, intellectual and cultural, must precede and become wholly a part of any serious learning to be done in college. We are therefore back again with the concept of freedom and its necessity as a condition for learning. This has come to be described by its critics as permissiveness rather than freedom, and a host of hostile witnesses has risen to testify that this is the fatal flaw in the culture of a modern America which has lost control of its children. In view of the emotional overlay which rests on the word, and in view of the better quality of sound and inner meaning invoked by the word "freedom," I would prefer to put "permissiveness" and "permissive" out of the vocabulary for a while to let them simmer down, while reviving the concept of freedom and free persons to refer to the atmosphere and character of the kind of educational situation I have in mind.

But before doing so, it might be useful to examine again what is meant by permissive and permissiveness. In the public mind in recent years the terms have come to be associated more with Benjamin Spock than with the original sources from which modern attitudes toward education and child-rearing have come. This has been especially true since Spock turned his attention to the politics of peace and began rendering immense service to his country in the leadership he has given to the opposition movement to the Vietnam war.

The critics of the peace movement often link "permissiveness" with radicalism, and find an easy connection between Spock babies and the student protest movement. They are right to do so, even though their terms of reference are misleading. There *is* a direct connection between the politics of peace and modern ideas of education. Both go to the roots of the idea of liberal democracy and nonauthoritarian, nonviolent approaches to human relationships of all kinds. The country is greatly in debt to the generation of parents who, with or without the Spock books, have brought up their children in an atmosphere of warmth and affection and a feeling for the worth of others. If only a larger proportion of the population had been affected by the inherent liberalism of the modern educational movement rather than by old wives' educational tales and obsolete political rules of thumb, we might never have had the twin catastrophes of war in Asia and civil disorder in the United States.

As far as education itself is concerned, the radical view turns in many ways on the kind of radical empiricism supported by William James and his concept of the stream of consciousness, and in many other ways on the kind of thinking about psychic behavior which stems from Freud and the psychoanalytic movement. From both sources and their allied intellectual tendencies comes the evidence that the intellect and the emotions are so closely intermingled in their function in a life that, to put it baldly, we think what we feel and we feel what we think. One of the problems for the person who wants to think clearly and feel honestly is to strip away his own defenses against what he does not want to think and to open himself up to ideas, feelings, and experience which can act upon him in their full reality. It is not possible to do this in an atmosphere of distrust, or in an atmosphere of authoritarian control, since the psyche has its own defenses against intrusion or invasion of the self, defenses which are no less crippling or damaging to the psyche because they have not yet risen to the level of consciousness.

The psychiatric model therefore provides the most compelling notion of all in suggesting a relation between parent and child, teacher and student, man and man, and the influence for the good they can have on each other's lives. R. D. Laing, whose thinking in these matters and whose way of writing about them is of the most profound character, has described the model in its most attractive form in defining psychotherapy as "an obstinate attempt of two people to recover the wholeness of being human through the relation between them." [2] When this is transposed into a philosophy of education and a philosophy of society it demands gentleness, affection, openness, freedom, concern, honesty, and a willingness to permit others to act as they are without invoking sanctions against them; that is, it permits people to be themselves.

That is what permissiveness truly means. It does not mean that everything is permitted. It means that one man permits another to be himself in his full particularity, and that the rules of society are to be drawn up on the evidence they can give that what the rules call for will enhance the life of the free individual.

In the matter of authority, at one end stand the police of a police state, ready to beat the citizen into submission to the state's conception of law and order as defined by the abstract will of the state. At the other end stands the teacher, ready to help create a situation in which his fellow man may act in freedom, secure in the faith that in an atmosphere of trust, acts will turn themselves away from destructiveness, aggression, and hostility toward cooperation, mutual respect, and affection. In between stands the conventional educational system, sometimes moving toward the police, at other times toward the teacher as a healer, but in general unaware of the psychological or political meaning of its own actions.

We are back then to the double problem of creating a free environment in which the student may act as the member of a cooperating community and an agent of his own growth. The intellectual content of the curriculum is an open question, since the variety of contributions to it are as many in number as there are students and teachers who act in it and on it. The role of the teacher is also an open question, since this will be determined by his own place in the community of learning and the kind of talent and knowledge he brings as his own offering to its members. But both questions can be answered fairly easily when it is agreed that the essence of the free intellectual environment is that actions in it should be voluntary, and that the testing of the worth of learning and teaching together comes for the teacher and the student in the experience they share and the modifications they make in the course of their work.

The teacher as a finite person has in his possession the personal content of his own private curriculum. This he offers to those who can make use of it. The student as another finite particular person has a similar but presumably more limited possession of knowledge and experience which he offers as his contribution to the community and to the teacher. If he asks to join forces with a teacher by "taking his course," he is making a tacit and, in this system of ideas, an explicit agreement to invest himself in learning what the teacher has to teach. Otherwise there would have been no point in his having accepted the teacher's willingness to teach him.

But the singular fact is that he is being treated as a man, not a boy, as an equal in the community of learning, not an object of instruction. Then something else happens. When the idea of a learning community replaces the idea of a knowledge machine, each member of the community begins to affect what the other members learn, and out of the spirit of voluntarism on which the community rests comes the cooperation of students in teaching each other. No matter how large the university or what vast numbers of students are collected together, the formation of internal communities around mutual interests is as natural on the campus as it is in the society. The difference is that on the campus the experience of working and acting together for ideal ends—in this case, the mutual education of the members of the community— can create a high form of human enterprise and can transform a group of anonymous persons isolated within their separate selves into the fullness of shared lives.

[III]

I would now like to put what Ortega has to say about the culture as the curriculum into a context supplied by R. D. Laing in a passage from his work which extends the idea of teaching as a

healing art. In this passage, Laing is describing what amounts to
a method for imparting Ortega's content. In the sentences preceding, Laing has been speaking of the difficulty of "achieving a
human understanding of man in human terms," and of the way
in which ideas are created. "Theory is the articulated vision of
experience," he says.

> If we are stripped of experience, we are stripped of our deeds,
> and if our deeds are, so to speak, taken out of our hands like
> toys from the hands of children, we are bereft of our humanity.
> We cannot be deceived. Men can and do destroy the humanity
> of other men, and the condition of this possibility is that we are
> inter-dependent. We are not self-contained monads producing
> no effects on each other except our reflections. We are both
> acted upon, changed for good or ill, by other men, and we are
> agents who act upon others to affect them in different ways.
> Each of us is the other to the others. . . .
>
> It is quite certain that unless we can regulate our behavior
> much more satisfactorily than at present, then we are going to
> exterminate ourselves. But as we experience the world, so we
> act, and this principle holds even when action conceals rather
> than discloses our experience.
>
> We are not able even to *think* adequately about the behavior
> that is at the annihilating edge. But what we think is less than
> we know, what we know is less than what we love, what we
> love is so much less than what there is. And to that precise
> extent we are so much less than what we are.[3]

Most of the thinking about behavior in education is not about
this approach to experience, or even about this approach to education. As in the case of the response of the officials of government,
the politicians and the law enforcers, when there is violence or
trouble in the society and behavior at the annihilating edge, the
concern then becomes to put down the violence by counter-
violence and repression, not to think deeply about the behavior
itself and its causes. The leaders of a liberal democracy should
be thinking about the best means of enhancing the quality of life
of the citizens as the prime duty of their public position. So should
the educational leaders. Were they to observe this duty in action,
they would have developed plans and social institutions on behalf
of human welfare which went to the root causes of positive and
negative behavior, without the necessity of sudden action in re-

sponse to outbreaks of the aggrieved against situations which, it is obvious to all, are literally intolerable.

What is required by the principles of liberal democracy is an educating society, one which in the normal course of its daily life gives its citizens the kind of social institutions, especially in the citizens' schools and colleges, through which they learn continually to live in a cooperative community. The structure of institutional influence should be moving constantly in that direction. To meet force with force is to move toward fascism. To think in terms of a structure of order to be sustained by force is to create a society in which eventually half the population of the most talented of all the citizens will be in prisons and the other half in mental hospitals.

In the case of the university, the kind of thinking necessary for developing an educating community calls for the creation of a self-regenerating, self-correcting governance, the purpose of which is to use all the available resources in the society and on the campus for the education of the members of the community. This is very hard to do if the conception of the internal order of the university is that of a center to which commuters come, some of them faculty members, others students, for as little time as possible, in order to transact their business.

The radical proposal in education is to shift completely the conception of teaching as a process of instruction into the idea of learning and teaching as the influence of persons on each other. What Laing, James, and others as sensitive as they to the psychic process have to say about experience is proven daily in educational institutions. The institutions strip the student of his experience, take his deeds out of his hands and into their own, and, in doing so, fail to use the deep resources that lie within the student for learning and growing, once the process can be started by intensifying his experience through his actions.

Begin with the act, move from acts to thoughts, considering always the quality of experience, and the new system of education evolves from there. Assume that everything educates, that some things educate more than others. Springtime educates, for example. So do oceans, cities, poems, plays, books, sounds, situations, sights, people, sorrows, catastrophes, joys, and, in the last analysis, raw experience. The direction of learning is from emotion to thought to expression, in words, symbols, or symbolic action of some kind, not the reverse, although symbolic action and the use of symbols, lecturing, listening, reading, and so on, may start up a psychic experience if that is the purpose in teaching, and the teacher knows how to do it and knows what acts and symbols to choose. Intellectual action, the act of the intellect, is the imposition of oneself on the materials of learning; it is to enter consciously an experience of thought, to create for oneself an act of comprehension.

Since the use of language has to do with the formation of concepts and the development of intellectual power, the act of talking, writing, and thinking is all one act—the use of personal energy to express what is latent and hidden. The interest among student groups in sensitivity training sessions, some of which, in their amateur but nevertheless useful form, turn out to be sessions of appalling personal frankness carried on for interminable periods, is in effect an effort to free the psyche for open thinking of all kinds, to make a start in a new way toward an intellectual and emotional life of one's own, uninhibited either by internal or external obstacles to honesty and authenticity.

It follows, for the beginning of a college education, that until that process of opening up and commitment to learning has been started, there is little use in trying to teach subject matter by itself, since it will always remain external to the self around which the education should be built. That is why, in the experiments with children in Head Start programs, in various versions of the street academy, in new efforts to reach the drop-outs and the ineducables, sensitive teachers begin by giving the child or young adult the fullest opportunity to use the materials of his own experience in writing or saying whatever it is he knows. The teacher in these programs *must* start with the experience of the child, since there is nothing else to start with except the child in his stark reality. If the child had been able to cope with the subject matter of the disciplines, and he wanted to cope with it, he would not be a drop-out, he would not be reading at third-grade level at the age of twelve, he would not be incapable at the age of four of knowing his own name or identifying his beginning self.

What is true of the child is true of the adolescent, the young adult, the older adult. The process goes on from birth to death, and the enlargement of experience can be continuous once the process has begun. The college is the place where, if it has not yet begun, the opening up to experience can be started, and the entry into oneself and the culture can then be made under the best possible circumstances, since this is the last officially arranged, open period of life, and the college is exactly the place for that kind of enterprise.

[IV]

The fact is that the latent power of teaching—teaching considered as the influence of one person on another—lies in the student body and not exclusively or necessarily in the teacher. At the present time, that latent power is untapped. In a new kind of college it would be, since this would be a college for students in which all the students became teachers of themselves, each other, and of the community of the campus, including the teachers. At present, individual teachers affect individual students, some many, some few, and the teacher's influence extends beyond himself and his students once the student has carried away something of his own from what the teacher has given him. The teacher at his best is one who sets many things in motion in the lives of his students, and one of the best of these is to give to the student the capacity to go on learning and to influence others by what he has learned. To that extent, he too has become a teacher whether or not he intended to be.

In the smaller colleges the presence of even a few strongly influential and powerful teachers can set the tone and implicit values of the whole community. In the experimental colleges, where the radical democracy of the governance and the freedom of the curriculum combine to render the community almost completely open to the influence of individual teachers, it is possible to deflect the aims of the institution into negative attitudes and a cynicism about the aims themselves by the presence of only a very few teachers of a cynical disposition and a sophisticated teaching talent.

The same thing is true of the presence of negative students whose disposition is intellectually sullen and socially destructive. A sufficient number of these in a small community can turn it into a place where the difficult ones are working out and acting out their own problems at the expense of the rest and of the mental and social health of the whole community. It is as if in every community there is a basic minimum of positive emotional energy which must be released into the stream of life if the organism is to retain its integrity and its educating energy. That energy is supplied by the students *and* the teachers, but in the long run by the students, who in their very youth have a resilience and a power of adaptation which can overcome all but the most impossible curricular circumstance.

If I wanted to remake a college quickly into a lively center for intellectual and personal development, I would send out for a national cross section of juniors and seniors from the student movement, add a group of selected graduate students, bring them into the campus on scholarships and fellowships where needed, and invite them to develop teaching and learning programs for themselves and for the rest of the student body with the help of faculty members and students who were interested, leaving the rest of the college and its faculty to go along in its own way. Within a very short time, the ideas generated by the influx of new students and the programs they developed together would have the same effect on the quality of educational performance as the recruitment of a cross section of the country's best athletes on a college's intercollegiate athletic program.

Many colleges whose interest in athletic achievement is in excess of an equivalent interest in the intellectual growth of their students have the imagination to understand how the athletic achievement occurs. Aside from assembling a competent teaching staff of coaches and their assistants (graduates of former classes, or, as they are called, teams), whose responsibility it is to instruct the new athletes in such a way that each person may develop his talent to the full in his own specialty, the most important task for the college is to assemble a group of students whose athletic talents are of a variety of kinds which supplement each other and combine to create new energies and a rising level of creative ability. The degree to which these students accept their responsibility for learning and for teaching each other is displayed in a group examination, which also gives opportunity for individual displays of ability, every Saturday afternoon in the fall semester and one or two evenings a week in the winter.

Colleges with interests of this kind spend their scholarship funds and arouse community support for additions to the teaching and learning budget to recruit student athletes who will add their abilities to the development of higher levels of achievement in the field of athletic learning. The student athletes are highly motivated because of the opportunity the college thus provides for ideal learning situations for the beginning of a career in graduate school, that is to say, a career with the professional athletic organizations for which the students are prepared while in college. The students are not only learning by doing, they are practising their profession in a realistic way as a central part of their general education. Each year a chosen national group of them test their education in the field against the veteran professionals in football and tennis.

It seems to me short-sighted not to apply this imaginative approach to the development of cultural, social, and intellectual achievement in the colleges by recruiting young poets, writers, painters, dancers, philosophers, teachers, race-relations activists, educational reformers, political experts, mathematicians, peace advocates, and social critics, while making sure that the coaches in in these fields on the teaching staff are persons whose own experience is of a practical kind and who can serve as realistic models of what the best talent in their specialty is like. In the field of sports, the great teacher is measured not by his publication record or his reputation for research among professional colleagues, but by how well his students have absorbed his teaching and put it to work in performance.

There is no reason why public performance in the presence of the community, supported by community funds, should not be a regular part of the college teaching program in the social sciences and the humanities—for example, in community action having to do with race relations, or with the intellectual poverty of the public schools, or the dearth of aesthetic experience for children and adults. The streets, that great arena for the arts and social change, can serve as the setting for this kind of student performance, as can church basements, store fronts, student apartments, playgrounds, or buildings constructed by the colleges themselves in the middle of that part of the community where the educational and social needs are at their height. When education, teaching, and learning are conceived in these terms, the morale of the students, their teachers, and, if programs are successful, the community, is raised to the level at which thought and action are fused into their true meaning in education.

For the radical college, just as for the radical political organization, the structure and ethos of participatory democracy makes the question of emotional tone a crucial one for the success of this style of education. For the educator, it also involves a deliberate effort to bring together a student body and a faculty which will create its own environment, and to ensure that the environment they make together will act as a creative force for the individuals in it. That is one reason why it is so foolish for the colleges to rely so heavily on test scores and scholastic aptitudes for admission. A student body composed of achievement-oriented, high-scoring, professional students has its own inner dynamic which can drive the college in any number of undesirable directions, including straight into the waiting arms of the graduate schools.

It is also a reason why it is so foolish not to make the creative arts a central area of the undergraduate curriculum, since their absence in equal status to other fields not only deprives the students of the supreme advantage of being educated through the arts, but it deprives the college community of the spirit of the arts and the life-giving influence of those who love them and practise them. A student whose raw scholastic ability is limited at the outset is likely to have virtues of other kinds which are crucial not only to his own development but to the development of the community and of individuals in it. As William Arrowsmith has said about the university faculty, "What is wanted is a repertory of convincing, visible, and powerful life styles," not a row of academic professionals in classrooms. This is equally true of the student body, although the repertory must be extended both for teachers and students beyond visibility and the power to convince, into styles of gentleness, affection, intuition, social concern, and any number of others in a situation which encourages each to develop his own style in relation to all others.

In the case of the big universities, the individual influence of teachers and students is absorbed into an anonymous community, unless, of course, a critical mass is reached in the number of teachers or students who are serious about the quality and degree of influence their work entails, and have a clear idea about the kind of influence they wish the university to exert.

[v]

By a devious route we thus come back to the question of the influence of the college and university on the character of its students. It is a question which agitated all the colleges and universities in America after the Civil War, especially those which had been founded by the religious associations with the training of a certain kind of character precisely in mind. The center of the debate as far as the nineteenth-century universities were concerned lay in whether or not a scholar was to be chosen for a teaching appointment on the basis of his character, his religious point of view, his social, personal, and intellectual attitudes, or on the basis of his scholarly achievements.

That debate subsided after it had been won by the scholars, as it had to be, until revived in an outrageous form in the 1950s when the same kind of question was raised, inside and outside the universities, about Communists, radicals, and potential subversives. But in the meantime, winning the debate meant not only deciding that scholars must have the freedom to be themselves, but deciding that there was no particular point of view about either education, moral values, social responsibility, or cultural aims which should exert an influence on the character of the students. As I have already pointed out, that kind of thing was handed over to the personnel workers, where it either died or suffered from serious malnutrition.

On the other hand, without benefit of philosophy, an implicit set of aims, apart from their rhetorical statement at public meetings, had been built into the university, where they are now attended to by the humanities section of the curriculum, by courses in the ideas and values of Western civilization, and by the student personnel services. The fact that neither institutional device has serious influence on the behavior and attitude of students is no longer a question the curriculum-makers have cared to deal with. In recent years, the shift away from the paternalism explicit in the university administration of college rules has not improved the situation as far as influencing the character of students is concerned. The move from paternalism is a formal recognition that the regulations seem counterproductive in influencing student behavior, and that in view of this the university should give up any pretense or intention of dealing with the social and personal attitudes of students.

In the case of a college like Amherst, with its religious tradition, and its short spasm of freedom for students under President Julius H. Seelye in the years following 1877, the older pattern of influence was designed on the religious model, all the way from compulsory chapel to required courses in religion. At contemporary Amherst, chapel attendance has been replaced by student assemblies, God has a corner in the chaplain's office and in a small number of courses in religion. But the tradition of duty, responsibility, and a tough-minded, jealous Deity was transformed into the All-required Curriculum, which took over the duties and appearance of its Predecessor and demanded the penance of the religious man.

Removing God and substituting either the academic curriculum or a dean's office is no answer. You have also removed the sense of a community of interest. The failure of the nineteenth-century colleges to influence and control the moral values of their students, who had the good sense to revolt against the ponderous way in which the attempt at control was made, was due to the authoritarian pedagogy and the unsophisticated assumption by the educators that human conduct could be guaranteed by formal education. The society was working against both the assumption and the educators.

When the faculty members of the American colleges and universities in the 1940s and 1950s began considering the question of what to do with the colleges, they had gone only a few steps beyond the nineteenth-century debate. The Harvard Committee spoke of the "rational guidance of all human activity" as an end to be sought by the new courses to be introduced. The others since then have given up even that kind of rationale and have turned to the concept of law and order. They have tended to agree with Robert Hutchins that concern for student character is child care and custodial work. Train the intellect and the rest will follow.

In moving in that direction, the university has not answered the major question of the degree and kind of influence it is responsible for exerting in the life of the student. It has simply given up and abdicated the field. The students are the ones who are bringing it back. They bring in the moral questions with them in two ways: by their personal acts and the way they live, and by the challenges they make to an educational system which ignores the moral and social values with which the student activists are concerned. There is a very serious question here to which the colleges and universities must make answer.

Granted that the intrusion of college authorities into the personal life of students, or efforts to control their behavior in ways going beyond a simple need for community order, is a genuine intrusion and that more enlightened policies must be developed. But the general notion that the university, aside from its efforts to push the students through the academic curriculum, should have no concern for their personal values leaves all value questions in the lap of the gods and of society.

The older style of colleges, in their assumptions about building character, did nothing about the creative arts, for example, since the conception of good character in their minds did not include sensitivity to aesthetic experience or its objects. But is this not a proper concern of the modern colleges, just as it must be their concern to develop a sensitivity to intellectual experience itself, to social justice, to political and cultural issues, to the self and to others? Students need to learn what it is like to think clearly and honestly because of the sheer joy in doing it. They need to learn how it feels to act beautifully, to create something, to give part of themselves away, to know what it feels like to be entranced by the work of artists and to experience the delight of using the senses to the widest range of their possibilities. These are personal values which go to make up the character of the liberally educated person; and where, if not in the colleges, are these values to be honored, celebrated, and imparted?

Where else can the chance be given to the young to break free from the self-conceptions and emotional habits which exist in them? If they have never learned to look at who they are and how they came to be that way, or what they might be instead, why do the colleges not help them? If the earlier colleges failed to impose a character on their students, this was not because an antidote was not needed to the anti-intellectual and material values the students brought with them from their society. It was because the gap be-

tween the interests of the faculty and those of the student was too
wide to be bridged by the primitive means of an academic curriculum. As Lawrence Veysey has put it, "Except in a small minority
of instances, nothing the professor said or did could change the
student's mind, for his mind was shaped far more powerfully by his
parents and his peers." [4]

Although the shaping is now a function less of his parents' influence and more of his peers and the mass media, the problem is still
the same in a world which makes it easier to adapt than to change.
The colleges exist to enable the student to find a way to a character
of his own, by the kind of study and experience with his fellow
students and his teachers which can explore his inner resources.
If the humanities curriculum is to do what humane learning is
intended to do, it would turn the students to look within themselves,
as far down and around as they can see. The links between one
kind of knowledge and another then become visible; the myths of
man in anthropology are linked to the insights of psychology,
literature, and politics, and the connection between an internal
world rich in imagery and an outer world described by social
scientists can be seen in ideas through which both can be understood.

If the earlier colleges failed because they took up the wrong
mission in the wrong way, the present colleges need not. The need
of students is for exploration, for trying out roles, for feeling that
they are in a life that is real, where ideas and personal commitments matter. That is what the college can give them.

[VI]

In the experimental colleges, questions of personal growth and the
effect of the college on individual lives have been matters of central concern, as have been questions of how best to involve the
students in their own education. Research studies and informed
observation have shown that there is little positive effect on the
personal values of students in attendance at conventional colleges,
and that the standard criteria of college success in high grades and
academic achievement have almost no correlation with success in
later life. Yet we are told that although the experimental colleges
have actually been able to touch the lives of their students in ways

which are highly significant both for them and for the society, this kind of education cannot be transposed into the big universities because there are too few teachers, too many students, and the system does not allow it.

In the face of this, many radical critics have simply written off the big universities, and have proposed that the best way for the student to pursue his own intellectual and personal development is either to drop out entirely or to secede and found new voluntary communities near the universities or in other places where there is access to books and to people. But if we write off the big universities and all the other educational institutions which are now imitating them, we also write off the mass of students, leaving them on their own, while suggesting secession for those whose own intellectual development has gone far enough to make them fully conscious of the absurdity of the regular system.

The free university movement has carried out the implications of Paul Goodman's deep-going analysis of the failure of the university and has adopted the idea of secession which stems from it. As it has been operating on or near more than a hundred college and university campuses, the free university in its various forms has injected new ideas for change into the regular university programs. Aside from the work with its own students, it has given other students the courage and initiative to experiment with student-run programs of all kinds.

But the free university is essentially conservative in its educational philosophy, and tends to turn in on itself without the possibility of linking its ideas to anything more than its own internal movement. In this sense, Goodman's idea for change is also conservative, taking the medieval *studium generale* as its model and calling for a version of the apprentice system in which "veterans," who have not only a body of scholarship but a fund of experience to draw on, serve as the teachers. That is certainly a great deal better than what we have now, but it does not go far enough. The students have their own veterans, and they know where the other veterans are without having to isolate them in a separate enclave.

The secessionist enclave suffers from the inherent weakness of the philosophy of anarchism on which it rests, which by its own doctrine cannot build a program capable of dealing directly with systems of power and turning them to ideal uses. The strategy of anarchism lies in deliberately working outside whatever system is in effect, and from there, by demonstration, criticism, and action to influence the course of what happens inside the system. In another sense it involves living inside the system without accepting it, something which can be done and has been done by the new student movement, and shows very great promise of creating the changes the system needs, not by continual confrontation but by continual demonstration of new styles.

But the free university, as an offshoot of the regular university, stays with the tradition of the academy, meeting classes, holding lectures and discussions, and differing from conventional curricula only in its subject matter and the choice of its teachers. In some instances its freedom to develop is inhibited by the ideological base on which the instruction rests, and as in the case of all education with an ideological base, whether the conventional kind of the American high school and college curricula or one more sharply defined in philosophical terms, at a given point it becomes involved with an authoritarian conception of learning in which certain truths are handed out to those willing to receive them.

When the free university is on the campus itself and organized by the students there, it takes such an amount of time and energy in the administrative problems connected with it and in the counter-work which the students are doing that in many cases after a lively beginning it fades out without a new infusion of leadership. On the other hand, if it stays resolutely outside the system, recruiting its own staff from outside and inside, it has little direct effect on what could be done to make its ideas a permanent part of the university program. In the preservation of its adversary stance, it keeps throwing itself on its own resources without getting new ones.

The tragedy in many cases is that the students who form the free college, the free university, or whatever the internal counter-curriculum may be called, are trying to find their way toward a greater intensity of educational experience and a higher form of learning, but are not quite able to get there by themselves. They have the impulse, know something about what it is they want and how students on other campuses have achieved it, but find it very hard to put what they want into a form that will work. One of the difficulties for the student reformers is that there are not enough others who want to make the effort to go beyond what is ordinarily given to them, and those who are ready to make the effort have not had enough experience in organizing education to keep the momentum with which they began and to use it to spread the interest throughout the whole student body.

They find themselves the object not of hostility so much as an amused tolerance on the part of the faculty, and apathy on the part of most students. The faculty will point to the ineptitude or naiveté of the students to show that the faculty was right all along: students do not know enough to be brought into educational planning, their interest is skin deep and will disappear in a month or two. Or the faculty seizes upon the fact that the rest of the student body does not respond to the idea of student-centered education as a clinching argument against it, and complains that when meetings are called by the faculty to which students are invited to come to discuss educational issues with them, only a few students turn up, usually the same ones who have already been either protesting or planning new projects.

All of this simply proves how very badly the present system is working, and how crucial it is that the kind of efforts students are beginning to make should have the full support of the faculty. Why should it be necessary for the students to be left with the sole responsibility for improving their own education? If faculty members do manage to see that the campus is wild with apathy, should this not indicate that the debilitating virus is in the educational plan and in themselves, and that that is the source from which the students get the disease? Apathy toward ideas and toward one's own education *is* a disease and should be treated that way. It is a mental health hazard, a dangerous psychological and social condition which can damage a student for life and infect other people around him. It is infuriating to have the existence of apathy used as the reason why there is no point in rearranging the educational program to give the students more freedom and responsibility, when the absence of freedom and responsibility is what has been producing the apathy.

Since so few of the faculty members have the time or the inclination to help to organize free universities, student communes, or secessionist enclaves, the gap in leadership is usually filled by students with experience in this kind of organization. Some of them from the National Student Association, others from Students for a Democratic Society, or civil rights groups who organize educational programs around special issues, travel from one campus to another to hold meetings with interested students and to show the other students how to get an experimental college or reform movement started.

This can help to give courage to those who are neglected or frustrated on their own campuses as well as practical help when it is needed, in supplying study guides, suggestions for action programs, bibliography, the names of interested graduate students, undergraduates, faculty members, and others to come to speak and organize support for new educational programs. The Radical Education Project at the University of Michigan has been very useful in the Midwestern universities in all these ways, and has stirred the apathetic and aided the activists.

Students on other campuses have invited intellectuals and scholars to come as their guest professors in residence for a week, a semester, or a year, without a specific teaching assignment in advance, but with the understanding that the visitor will collaborate with the students in any ways which can advance their educational projects. I spent a week at the University of Colorado in Boulder in the fall of 1968 as visiting students' professor as part of a year-long project in educational reform organized by the Commission on Academic Affairs of the Colorado student government. It was a fascinating week in which nearly every issue presently agitating the country's campuses came up in one way or another—from interference in the university's internal affairs by the Regents to the question of whether or not SDS should be banned from the campus —with mass meetings of students, conferences with student organizations, meetings with philosophy and education classes, faculty members, administrators, and community leaders. Student initiatives can and will continue to draw upon the pool of intellectuals available to them outside the campuses, to be supported financially with the use of student funds.

Another kind of initiative has begun among students who have taken over boarding houses and have turned them into student communes where those who live together—some students, others not—are writing, reading, talking, working on community projects and sharing a set of interests in the arts and social change. They teach others whatever it is they know, and in some cases work on problems of university reform by action programs on the campus and study and planning back home at the commune. Others who live in the communes are teaching or counselling children in the ghettos and writing about their experience; some are doing nothing but reading and talking. In the process, the communes are working out new forms of education which could very easily be applied to the general residential policies of the university, with students choosing their own rooms in university housing in such a way that they can form the enclaves of mutually congenial persons without having to take over houses elsewhere. A variation of this would be for the colleges to buy or lease houses in nearby cities where students could live and work in community programs for a semester at a time, with a curriculum made up of whatever studies and projects they wished to carry out. The Rochdale experiment, in which a group of Canadian students have done just this, outside the university, could be extended more broadly into general reform policy by the colleges and universities themselves.

I would also like to see an extension of the idea of student travel and collaboration from campus to campus so that wherever there are energetic and experienced students who can help the others to make some moves, their influence can inject some life into the dormant situations. I would also like to see some help by the faculty and administration within the state college systems to the students who are most vigorous in their ideas for free university programs, so that some collaboration could take place among the colleges through their students.

One way of doing this would be to invite students from one campus where there is a free college, or student enclave-college which is working well, to come to another campus for a week or two to help organize the same kind of program there, with exchange visits by groups of students among all the state campuses, paying special attention to those where there is some lively educational action, and using the students from those centers as student teachers to the others. There is no reason why a college could not supply a small bus for a group of students and invited faculty to spend two to three weeks travelling through the state, stopping at various colleges for open meetings, educational reform sessions, recruitment of volunteers for new projects, to act as a stimulus and organizing force to circulate new educational ideas among the students.

An even simpler version of this kind of help to the students would be to arrange for a member of the faculty in the social sciences or the humanities, one who had a serious commitment to educational reform, to take a class of volunteers in a course of his own on a month's field trip throughout the state to examine the educational system at first hand and to start some relations between the students at one institution and those at another. It has been my experience that not only are the students in each state unaware of themselves as potential educators, but they are unaware of what is going on at other campuses, even those within the same city. One of the greatest needs is to open up the conversations and introduce the new ideas from campus to campus as they are developing there. In this the administrators and the faculty members can give help, if not by taking initiatives of their own, at least by making it easier for the students to take theirs.

The positive value in the idea of the free university movement spreads in dozens of directions and is not confined to any of the forms in which it has so far been demonstrated. Starting with the central idea that students can and should conduct their own education, it moves to the elective principle, the idea of a community of persons voluntarily associated with each other, and implies the concept of education as a teaching-learning community, in which students who have a concern to know seek out the people who in their judgment can teach them. The more projects of this experimental kind the students can start, the more chance there will be of loosening up the regulations and rigidities of the required curricula. Counter-forces to the system are set in motion, ideas begin circulating which do not have to go through the channels of the committee system, but simply begin to work on their own wherever there are a few people who want to learn together, on or off the campus.

The strategy of change suggested here is for students—and the faculty members whose help they seek because they know it will be given and is the kind they want—not to try to reform the entire institution at one stroke. If there are no serious issues around which public debate and controversy is turning (this is the usual case) there is no point in trying to heat up some issues until they blaze. Unless they are real issues, perceived as such by the students, they won't ignite. Instead, the strategy must be to invent the programs and start the projects which are most important to those who are interested, and then press for the acceptance of the programs as a regular part of the college curriculum. This strategy has a great advantage over the frontal-assault style, which will only work if the situation is of a certain kind in which the legitimacy of student grievance is matched by the insensitivity of the administration and faculty. The educational advantage lies in the fact that by starting something of their own the students can immediately begin to enjoy the fruits of their educational ideas and efforts in the experience of the project itself. Otherwise they are likely to spend all their time fighting a battle for an entire new curriculum, a battle which, even if won, will not show its effects in the improvement of education, theirs or anyone else's, until the peace treaties are signed following protracted negotiations and occasional new outbreaks of hostilities.

On the other side, the advantage is that the demonstration of good, valuable, interesting, important work in education which absorbs young people in a set of interests of their own is a powerful way of answering the question as to how reform should proceed. It addresses the question to the specifics. If not this kind of reform, then what kind? If not this kind of course or project, then what other kind? If academic credit is not to be given for serious and important intellectual work, then what *can* it be given for? The reform of the curriculum proceeds then not by committee discussion of what they are doing at Harvard or Columbia, but by whether a given project is a practical and workable thing to take on. If enough interesting new projects were introduced, the entire institution would then be changed without having to go through the boring process of trying to change education on paper by discussion of paper problems.

The strategy of change which calls for work both outside and inside the system simultaneously is supported by the experience of the Educational Development Center in Watertown, Massachusetts, which evolved from the original work of Jerrold Zacharias in the reformation of the science curriculum of the schools. The support of the center by foundations and government grants gave it the opportunity to work, independent of the regular system, yet closely related to it, by inviting direct cooperation from teachers and schools in experimenting with new curricula. In the case of the Peace Corps, for example, one of the most interesting and productive models for a three-month training program for Nigeria was developed under contract to the Educational Development Center under the direction of Roger Landrum, a returned Peace Corps volunteer with experience both in the field and in the training staff of the Peace Corps.

Landrum recruited Nigerian teachers and returned volunteers and other teachers with appropriate experience, located the program in the middle of the Boston Negro ghetto of Roxbury, carried on community studies with student field work by the volunteers who lived with families in the area, arranged for practice teaching in local schools, and used the resources of community leaders and university staff whenever their talents were relevant to the program. A variation of this approach is now under way under Landrum's direction in the New York City ghetto areas for preparing teachers for the urban public schools, with a private organization entitled Teachers Inc. which recruits its own staff and acquires its own legitimacy and financial support from foundations and by direct iinks to the New York City school system and the Bank Street College of Education.

This kind of program, through outside contracting agencies, could very well be applied in the educational reform movement of the colleges. A university might, in this case, contract with an imaginative educator outside its present faculty to organize a student college either on its campus or off it, giving the contractor an appropriate budget and 500 student volunteers for his experiment. One of the greatest values in this approach lies in its revival of the general idea on which the liberal arts colleges operated during the period following the Civil War, the idea that if you didn't like the kind of college you were attending or in which you were teaching, or you thought there was a better kind to be made, you set off to start another one. That attitude has begun to revive, although until now it has suffered from the fact that only a few of the new institutions have taken the radical step of founding colleges for students and building a curriculum designed to involve them in its beginning and future development. Rather than breaking with past models, most of the new colleges, and particularly the community colleges and state colleges which have grown up inside the state systems of education, have concentrated on the design of the subject-matter curriculum and on methods of instruction rather than on a reconstructed conception of what the college can do in relation to the new society and the new generation of students.

14: The President as an Educator

Suppose education were defined as a social force, and the subject-matter of the curriculum and everything about it, from the natural sciences to poetry to the way students talk to each other and what they do with their lives, were considered as the means through which the total intellectual, moral, and social strength of the culture can be mobilized to enhance the quality of the national life. Suppose it were assumed that education defined in this way is the single most important asset possessed by a democracy for establishing the unity and character of the national purpose.

There is no conflict here between the interests of the individual and the full development of the society. Through individual development the ends of the society are achieved, and the individual has become part of a massive cooperating community rather than a competitor for purely personal gain. Nor is there a conflict between the radicals and the total establishment, since the radicals are then seen as those who make their contribution by raising the crucial questions in their most extreme form, keeping the educational system in touch with issues and forces within the society which it must take into account if it is to remain relevant to the problems of a society in a state of revolutionary change.

The place of the university in the society is thereby redefined. It becomes the nerve center of the society, sensitive to the persons, ideas, and values making up the total human community and its universe of discourse, a place where the opportunity exists for taking the kind of action which can help the creative forces in the society to coalesce. Rather than waiting to serve society's needs when the society demands it, the conception calls for reaching out to the society to anticipate its needs and to link together the means for meeting them, with the college and the university as the center of the linkage.

The radicals in recent education have been in the same position as the political radicals, for some of the same reasons. They have been able to make devastating criticisms of the system, but are less successful when confronted with the practical business of changing it. Part of the lack of success lies in the very intensity with which the attacks have been made on the university system as a whole, rather than the systematic development of radical changes in the particular parts of it which need change the most— the curriculum, the teaching methods, the community life, the admissions and testing programs, the relations between the races, the administration of the university community.

The system can be changed, from the inside as well as the outside, and as the educational changes grow in number and in depth, the society will change, as it already has in the past five years no matter who has been in charge of it. The real question is whether it will change fast enough to deal with its problems.

In the meantime, the society has been changing education from the outside faster than it is being changed by anything education is doing inside its own system. While I admire sporadic efforts, new counter-groups, good education in one college, protest movements against bad education and other injustices, I do not see why we have to settle for so little, or why we have to remain at the level of radical criticism with occasional bursts of overt action, the formation of enclaves, and guerilla raids from prepared positions. This is not serious enough, thoughtful enough, nor radical enough. At a certain point it becomes self-indulgent, and begins to take up the posture that everyone in the universities should immediately drop everything he is doing and do what the radicals tell him to. Change is not only necessary, but possible, on a sweeping scale. Even if it were not, that is what we should be talking about and that is what we should be trying to bring about. Part of the change has already begun. The question is how to enlarge its dimension, deepen its force, and increase its pace.

One of the first ways to make the next beginning is to get rid of the notion that educational administrators are always the enemy, and that, simply because they provide the sitting targets for demonstrators and critics, they are the agents of reaction and the tools of the establishment. In *The Community of Scholars* Paul Goodman laid down the proposition that "the president [of the university] has a remarkable freedom to determine policy whether educational, architectural, or financial . . ." and that among his time-serving administrators "he is the master in his own house. He is freed from headaches in his dealing with legislators, the press, parents. He can control the student organizations and newspapers. . . ." [1]

This comes as a delightful surprise to college and university presidents, in both public and private institutions, who spend most of their time dealing with legislators, potential donors, pressure groups, trustees, government agencies, and all the various constituencies Clark Kerr has described, while exercising very little authority in educational policy. That policy is the jealously guarded territory of the faculty, which has its own entrepreneurs and fund-raisers to promote its own educational policies through forming institutes, curricula, research centers, and, in the sciences and technologies, profit-making companies. In fact, so heavy a responsibility does the university president carry for serving his institution in its economic and political affairs that it is only very rarely that an appointment to the presidency is made of anyone with a deep interest in educational policy or a talent for sustained thinking about educational issues. That is the way most of the faculty want it, and, in view of the size of the political and economic problems of the university, only a person with the skills of a serious administrator who functions as if he were mayor of a town or the governor of a small state could handle the problems.

The students are the ones who want administrators to deal with education and to take educational action, and most of the administrators in office show a willingness to encourage educational change if good plans can be made and a way found to get around the collective faculty. The presidents who have been most spectacularly unsuccessful in dealing with changes favorable to students and their education are no longer in office, and stand as examples of what can happen if change is resisted or is badly managed. Chancellors like Samuel Gould of the State University of New York, for example, and his colleagues Harris Wofford, president of the State University in Old Westbury, New York, and Martin Meyerson, president at Buffalo, are men who understand as well as the radicals the meaning of educational and social change and are capable of bringing it about. For the rest, what is needed are new plans which are creative and will work well on behalf of the students. Armed with programs of serious merit, the students will often find that their greatest allies are the administrators who know how to get things done and are interested in setting new programs in motion.

[II]

At the present time, the role the university president is forced to play by his place in the university's corporate structure prevents him from acting as an educator with direct links either to the faculty or to the students in what he does from day to day. The custom of the universities is to appoint a vice-president for academic affairs and a vice-president for student affairs, along with the other vice-presidents for finance, buildings and grounds, athletics, public relations, making it apparent in the chart of organization that academic affairs are simply another section of the organization along with the buildings and the students.

In the case of state university systems, which can include fifty or more institutions of different kinds, each with its own president, the president of the state university not only does not have working relations with a faculty or student body, he does not have the basic privilege of having his own campus. Whatever he can do to develop educational policies must be done by collaboration with the existing political leaders, from the governor to the appropriations committee of the state legislature, with existing officers of the board of trustees or regents and with the chancellors and presidents of the colleges and universities under his jurisdiction.

One of the difficulties, both for him and for the other presidents, is that while on the face of it the state university president is in charge of the others—they report to him, work out their budgets and allocations and general policies under his guidance and direction—if he becomes too interested in what is going on in one of the universities in his state, he is intruding in the affairs and responsibilities of its president. On the other hand, if one of his presidents gets into difficulties with the students, the faculty, the public, or the state legislators, whether he is right or wrong in a given case, the state university president is responsible for what he does but usually has had no direct knowledge of or responsibility for what the issue involves and what the president has done.

In relation to student affairs, the state university president must be a man of particular sensitivities who can help to give direction to the solution of student problems by the strength of his intellectual position and the powers of his persuasion. These he must use in dealing with the power structure in which he functions and with the principles in which he believes as these are relevant to the issues, yet all the while, by reason of his position, remaining out of touch with the reality of student life and the inner university community. He must be a most unusual man to be able to deal with all of this in a way which gives leadership to his colleagues among the institutions under his jurisdiction and to education at large, since he needs not only the resources of a scholar-educator but the toughness of a politician and the skills of a first-rate executive.

There is also a great difference between the role of the president of Harvard and the president of a state college, between the president's role in a small or medium-sized college of liberal arts and in the Massachusetts Institute of Technology. In the case of the liberal arts colleges and the famous private universities, the president does have the opportunity of direct association with his faculty and students, and usually that opportunity is reflected in the kind of person chosen for the post and the kind of concern he displays in his public actions and public statements about the social and educational issues confronting his institution.

The basic difference in the choice of presidents lies in whether they are considered to be representatives of the community of scholars who have had a part in choosing one of their own members to act in the capacity of an administrator of university affairs, or whether they are persons appointed by boards of trustees to carry out responsibilities delegated by the board under its grant of powers from the charter of the institution. Students who are now of the opinion that they should share in making the decisions about basic university policy are often of the corollary opinion that they should share in the process of choosing a president. When they express this view, they are implicitly asserting a proposition similar to that of the faculty—that the president should represent the community of students and faculty, not the community of business, industry, finance, government, the military, and the existing social order.

There is something else implied, something which has not been explicitly stated but which lies at the heart of much of the present student discontent. It is the fact that the true role of the president of the university and his trustees must be, in the long run, not to control progress but to advance it, not to rule but to initiate, not to block students but to hold them accountable, and to look for the creative, the useful, the imaginative, and the possibilities of joint effort among all concerned. Merely to say that the president must be a representative of the faculty does not solve that problem, if in fact the collective faculty is an unwieldy body of ambivalent opinions making its slow way toward the dissolution of long-held preconceptions, and is out of touch with the complex constituencies which have grown up around the university as an institution.

The students are right in raising the question as to who the president represents. Until now he has seldom represented the students, nor the invisible constituency of the poor and the uneducated, nor, in most cases, even the faculty, if one thinks of the faculty as the source of informed intellectual and cultural policy. There are ways in which the students' ideas about the duties and responsibilities of the presidential and administrative offices and about the persons who might best carry them out can be put to use, both in the selection and in the care and treatment of presidents. In the past, the appointment and duties of the president have been the prerogative of the trustees, modified in some instances by consultation, informal or formal, with the faculty.

In recent years, the influence of the faculty has increased without an equal precision in the description of the particular duties the president is expected to undertake on its behalf. A joint committee of trustees, faculty, and students to determine the general criteria by which the qualities of a president should be judged, and to suggest particular persons who seem, in the judgment of each sector of the joint committee, to be most likely to meet these criteria, would give substance to what is now a vague and unsatisfactory conception of the presidential office. The final responsibility for choosing the president could be left, if necessary, with the trustees as a governing body, but on the way to their decision they need to be made much more aware than they can be at present of what they are asking for and what they are likely to get.

It may just be that the situation of the university and college president, aside from the manner of his appointment to the office, has now become impossible. If he has the virtues necessary to be elected mayor of the town which has now formed itself out of the materials of higher education but is still referred to as a university, he is unlikely at the same time to possess the virtues of the scholar who can genuinely represent the intellectual community. If he has both the professional and political skills to administer the town of students, faculty, staff, alumni, trustees, and members of the public, and he possesses the qualities of a serious intellectual, he is not only rare but is so completely immersed in sets of problems which interlock with the social, economic, political, and intellectual disorders of the present moment that he has no time to be a person. His intellectual and social capital are soon exhausted by the intensity with which they must constantly be used.

In the case of the smaller liberal arts colleges, the president is so close to the interface of every one of his constituencies that his emotional strength and his physical energies must be at least the equivalent of a finely trained astronaut combined with the temperament of a saint and a complete philosophy of nonviolence. It seems to me that unless the president is relieved of the primary responsibility for raising the funds to support his institution, and unless some better ways are found of financing higher education than by government subsidies for services the government wants and the personal contributions of private citizens and private foundations, we will very soon be in a position in which those best suited for the presidency will refuse to accept the office. In my judgment, the best solution would be to arrange a division in the responsibilities of the president similar to the pattern at the Massachusetts Institute of Technology, where the chairman of the board deals with major financial and administrative problems, leaving the president free to work as an educator, in touch with the going concerns of his students and faculty.

It may also be time to consider the fact that chancellors and presidents should accept appointments for designated and limited periods of time, perhaps five to eight years, with the understanding that during that time the administrative officers will map out a plan for the use of their energies in specific and calculable ways, with emphasis on the educational and social policies of the institution, rather than on the improvement of its economic position. That should be the responsibility of the board of trustees.

Or, to put it differently, if, over a period of three to five years, the duties of the president's office are to be concentrated on the solution to economic problems, then a person who enjoys that kind of work and who understands the way it can be done without damaging the morale and purposes of the institution as a whole should be appointed to the post. Having accomplished his mission, at least to the degree that this is possible in the present situation of the colleges and universities in the economic system, the president can then move to another post in the field of public service which can use to the full the talents and experience of one who has been in university work.

In my own case, the appointment to the presidency of Sarah Lawrence College came as the result of discussions with key persons in the faculty who served on a committee of faculty members and trustees to find a president who would be a representative of the faculty. I would not have been interested in any other kind of presidency, nor would the college and its trustees, since the nature of Sarah Lawrence as an experimental college was such that the president, the faculty, the students, and the trustees were associated together in a cooperative community devoted to teaching and learning.

On the other hand, it seems to me in retrospect that the period of fourteen years of my administration was too long a time for the most effective use of what talents I possessed as an educator and an educational administrator. The testimony of my colleagues among the presidents coincides with my own—that one tends to become more and more deeply involved in every sector of the college life the longer one remains in office, while at the same time, the more deeply involved one becomes, the less effective may be the long-run results of that involvement. It is not merely that the routines and duties become over-familiar, and that over the years one finds that there are only a certain number of ways of doing what has to be done, but that the duties and routines grow in number and size while one's intellectual and personal resources find too little opportunity for replenishment.

What is needed is a new start, by someone who enters the situation from a fresh beginning and who is different from his predecessor in style and in the interests he holds and is capable of evoking in others. The time has gone when the assumption can or should be made that the appointment of a president should continue until his automatic retirement at a prescribed age, or until a point has been reached at which either he or his constituents decide that everybody has had enough. This is especially true now that universities are appointing younger men to the presidential office. Unless more sensible arrangements are made, the president is likely to go on until he is physically, emotionally, and intellectually exhausted, and finds that he cannot face the renewal of the eternal problems without a parallel renewal within his own resources. The case of Nicholas Murray Butler, who kept outliving the members of various selection committees to find his successor at Columbia University, is the most extreme of comparable instances.

[III]

All this is of special significance when we go back to the theme that the mass of students in the American system of higher education are being educated and will be educated in the state universities, the state colleges, the large private universities, and the community colleges. What is done there by the presidents and administrators is in many ways of greater importance than what is done by the collective faculty body, since the procedures and speed of change if left to the present collectives are proving, and will prove, to be inadequate to the needs of a whole new sector of American society.

In view of this, it seems to me that some alteration in the structure of the college and university is absolutely essential if the chancellors and presidents of the future are to give the quality of educational leadership the country must have for its own social health. Rather than establishing administrative posts for vice-presidents of academic affairs and for student affairs, would it not be more in keeping with the true role of the educator for the president to be given as his central responsibility the work in education with the students and the faculty, and the administrative posts in fund-raising, management, buildings and grounds to be considered to be supporting roles for the president as educator? In the reconstructed university, there would be no reason why, during a full semester, the president or chancellor should not devote all his time to working on issues of educational policy with the students and faculty, re-serving other parts of the year and substantially less time in his total schedule for the business side of the institution. When the crises arise, that is what happens in any case, although the con-text in which it happens is often fatally disarranged by the fact that this is the president's first entry into full-time work as an educator.

I have known university presidents whose first meeting with their students to talk seriously about education came when they found their offices overrun with a large and unusual collection of unin-vited and agitated students with a selected list of educational de-mands which had not previously occurred either to the students or to their president. Students, like everyone else, want to see the man in charge when they want their business attended to. Although there are others with legitimate demands on the president's atten-tion, it is up to the president to establish his own priorities and to make certain that the students are at the top of the list.

The same philosophy could be applied in a different way by allo-cating generous stretches of the president's time during each week of the college year to educational issues and involvement with the intellectual community, all the way from organizing all-university conferences of students and teachers to consider basic policy ques-tions, to studying the problems brought to university attention by the students, whether through protests, demonstrations, sit-ins, or through more conventional agenda items.

The tendency of the president in the present situation is to spend what educational time he has available in going to conferences on education where presidents, generals, executives, and administra-tors tell each other what the university problems are in plenary sessions and in the corridors. This has the effect of creating some feeling of solidarity and educational rectitude inside the educational establishment, and kind of educational self-righteousness among the administrators as members of their own class in what now amounts to a class war. But it does little to solve the serious issues which are agitating the minds and emotions of the internal communities of which the presidents are, at least by tradition, ostensibly the leaders.

One of the useful effects of confrontation between the students, the faculty, and the administrators in the heightened atmosphere of encounter which is now so frequent a phenomenon of the campuses is that the president himself gains a great deal of education in the very issues about which he needs most to be informed. Ultimately, when the showdown comes, if it does, the president is responsible for its outcome. Unless he is part of the community as an educator involved in the process of events, at that point he finds himself with acres of responsibility but only inches of authority, either intellectual or political, since he has given it all away to others or has never had it in the first place. It is not possible for the president to perform as a mediator, an arbitrator, or an educational force unless he has taken the educational initiative and holds a set of principles with which he is publicly identified.

There is also a mystique which has grown up within the radical movement that there is something intrinsically evil about any form of self-government that has organization in it, and that participatory democracy is the same as direct democracy, with everyone in everything all the time. The idea of radical democracy and its concept of participation is at the heart of what is most important in the restoration of social health to an over-organized and oppressive educational system; and the students who have formed their own groups have invented their own ways to reach decisions without the conventions of bureaucratic practice. But after a while it becomes clear that somebody has to run the mimeographing machine, answer the mail, get out the notices, act on his own without conferring with the entire membership from hour to hour, and, in a word, exercise some degree of freedom after having accepted so much responsibility. This is the eternal problem in the exercise of democracy. But it cannot be solved simply by defining the person who does the work of organizing as a power-hungry bureaucrat or a tool of some other establishment.

There is a wealth of testimony in the experimental colleges to the fact that eternal self-government becomes tiresome once a new program has been set in motion unless it is mitigated by some delegation of responsibility for action. The time spent in arguments over details which do not matter creates a gradual attrition in enthusiasm for the venture itself. I still remember vividly my own enthusiasm for participatory democracy which led me in my first year as a young president at Sarah Lawrence to bring to the Student Council the question of whether Commencement should take place on a Thursday or a Friday. Three weeks and four 2-hour meetings later the Student Council was a mass of writhing antagonisms, which could only be resolved by my deciding in favor of Friday because I thought that day would be more convenient for more people.

It is also true that some teachers and some students are not very good at getting things done, and that some with a passion for democracy and self-government become either hard-nosed and autocratic when elected to office or soft-headed and inefficient when asked to do something useful. In the pathology of self-government among liberal and radical intellectuals, the most frequent symptom of breakdown is the refusal of the community to allow anyone, elected or appointed in no matter how democratic a way, to make any decisions or to act, and to turn on its own elected representatives the moment they have been elected. They have suddenly become "administrators." The Black Mountain experiment was a case in point. The experiment ceased, among other reasons, because it produced a kind of self-government in which anarchy could only be modified by total consensus, and policy-making involved more *ad hominem* argument than enlightened judgment.

Some of this total suspicion of all power is carried into the student reform movement, and in many cases makes it impossible for the reformer to accept any relationship but that of adversary with the educators with whom he must deal. A paradox then appears in the fact that the reformer is continually looking for ways of mounting more power for his side rather than thinking of ways in which the existing situation can best be changed. As in the case of foreign policy questions, there are other ways of accomplishing good ends than by the application of force. There is the power of example, of persuasion, of appeal to ideal possibilities. A strategy for the reform of the educational system must think in big terms and must not rest content with the limiting tactics of immediate solutions to immediate problems. It must look deeper within the system for the trends and forces which are either actually or potentially moving in the direction of creative change.

15: A National System

It is the argument of this book that the most promising trends and forces for desirable social change are to be found in the student movement, and that the connection between that movement and other creative movements in the society can be made through the organized efforts of individuals and groups of teachers, students, and administrators in the colleges and universities. It is the further argument, which I would like to develop more specifically in what follows, that in order to find ways in which these forces for change can mutually support each other and coalesce in a new form, the colleges and universities must consider themselves to be teaching institutions whose intellectual and cultural influence in the society is made possible and actual by what the students do with their lives.

Among the forces of change now at work in the society there are four which interlock with the American system of higher education. The first is the one released by the mass of government programs since 1965, ranging from the community-education section of the Civil Rights Act to the various forms of VISTA, Head Start, Job Opportunity centers, the Peace Corps, the National Teacher Corps, provisions of the Elementary and Secondary School Act, and the programs supported by the Educational Professions Act of 1967. The thrust of all of them in concert has been to make the educational system more responsive to the reality of contemporary social need, and to give thousands of young people and others a chance for engagement in tasks of social service whose importance to the national welfare the participants can recognize. As far as the young people in the programs are concerned, this has meant an induction into the culture by a direct route which has given them an experience in education and social change unavailable in the regular educational system, and has turned their intellectual and personal interests in a new direction. They have been called upon for educational and social action as responsible young adults, not as students trapped in a college curriculum.

I will be told by my radical educational colleagues that this is all busywork on behalf of the system, patchwork to repair the worst parts of it, ways of trying to keep a dead body alive. To which I reply that it isn't. It is the beginning of a social movement which has already made changes and which will make many more as soon as the radicals and liberals, among others in the colleges, put their minds on larger matters than complaints against defects, and turn toward a more accurate and positive analysis of where the power in the system actually is, and what elements in it are on the side of creative change and democratic reform. Another way of putting this is to say that before the Eighty-eighth and Eighty-ninth Congress and its social legislation, and before there was an Office of Economic Opportunity or an agency for Housing and Urban Development, there were few opportunities for the younger generation to use their talents in places in the society where their personal efforts could help to bring about change. Now there are thousands of such opportunities and thousands of young people have taken them, with more to come.

The second force is of course the student movement itself, which is directly linked to the first force by the interests and actions of students. But what we do not have as yet is a recognition by educators that the schools and colleges can serve as instruments of coalition between the two forces. If the colleges were to consider themselves to be teaching institutions where students learned to teach by teaching each other with the help and cooperation of the faculty, and the students were given responsibility for working in the community in programs linked to their own curricula in the social sciences and humanities, they could invent a completely new style of education in which the work of students on the campus would connect directly with the work of students in the society.

This would not only enrich the college curriculum by the new insights and actual research knowledge brought to it by the students, but would create a new source of talent for the teaching profession itself, among those students whose lives and interests had been caught up in a new sense of what education can be when it is used to liberate human lives. The absurdity of many of the present requirements and educational practices would dissolve in the confrontation with students whose experience in teaching and social service had starkly revealed the inadequacy and irrelevance of much that is now done in the colleges.

The third force is again obvious, and forms a basis of comment throughout most of what has been said in these pages—the social revolution within the black community. What we have seen as of now is only a beginning of what we are going to see in the months and years ahead. Something has been said in the newspapers and journals about the effect of the return of black veterans from the war in Vietnam and the double problem of absorbing them into the work force and into the educational system. Men who have had money and a place of their own, many of them for the first time, having proven themselves in the society of the military, are going to strengthen the social force of the black movement, and will speak and act with the legitimacy of those who have already served their country in one of its most highly regarded roles.

What are the colleges prepared to do for them and with them? To continue the kind of curricula and admissions programs now in effect is to reject their legitimacy and their accredited talent, just as it has been rejected in the black youth who have not been to the war.

At a conference called by the U.S. Office of Education in the summer of 1968, representatives of 150 colleges and universities were asked by the government to develop ways of attracting and educating the thousands of veterans with backgrounds of poverty and racial slums who are returning to the society and whose academic records would ordinarily keep them out of college. We had the same situation following World War II, although not as directly connected to the Negro community, and we solved it by revising admissions standards and college programs in ways which benefited both the veterans and the programs. But almost as soon as things returned to normal, that is, when the regular flow of young high school graduates replaced the veterans, the upward climb of scholastic aptitude tests began once again, with a curriculum to match.

What a gold mine of talent for teaching exists, not only among those from the war, but throughout the entire black community, where there are thousands of young men and women who need the kind of education the Defense Department, VISTA, and the U.S. Office of Education are urging they be given and which the colleges have until now not thought to provide. Here again, the link with the second and first force can be made by the colleges, by making a regular part of the curriculum the kind of tutoring and mutual education which it is the function of the college to give. Whatever else happens, we can count on the force of the black community to shake loose the educational preconceptions of those who have thought of the college as a place for the academic talent of those who have the preparation to use it. It is a lesson for educators that it should have been necessary for the government to take the initiative in preparing the ground for a new form of education in the progressive tradition.

The fourth force is the world student movement in educational change and the new world community of youth which is forming itself on the basis of a common set of interests and alliances. There are upwards of 100,000 students and 12,000 teachers and scholars from foreign countries now in the United States and thousands more who are eager to come if there were provisions which made that possible. But until now we have not made use of the talents they already bring to the colleges for joining together what they know with what we need to know. They have been integrated into an American campus life in which the main concern of the educators has been to assimilate the foreigners and to have them understand American culture as it is found on the campuses. Yet among the foreign visitors is another gold mine of teaching talent for presenting the reality of cultures foreign to our own.

Once the concept of a college for students is accepted, it becomes natural for students from foreign countries to join in the mutual education process by taking a leading part in seminars, tutoring, group research, and discussion, to share their experience of a life and an education unlike that of our own students. It also becomes natural to recruit students from abroad, some of whom have been active in the student movements of their own countries, to join with American students in working at the problems of world education and the reform of the universities. We have a rich and unprecedented opportunity to use our resources to help in the formation of a network of world youth, linked together not in Soviet style, by the political organizations of the countries in which they live, but in an international style in which American campuses can act as international educational centers for the consideration of the whole range of problems having to do with world affairs and world peace.

An experimental summer project to test out that idea was begun in 1963 under the sponsorship of a group of Quakers in Long Island who wished to found a college in which a true internationalism and a world point of view would be ensured by the character of the curriculum and the world diversity of the student body. With the present writer serving as director, and the collaboration of twenty-two United Nations countries representing Eastern and Western Europe, Africa, North America, South America, and Asia, a World College was designed with a completely international faculty, student body, and curriculum for a summer program of work and study.

The curriculum grew from the initial assignment to all students and faculty members of an autobiographical account of their own education and a statement of what in the judgment of each were the essential problems of world society which should be studied, and to which college curricula should respond. They were also asked for a statement of the status of these problems within their own society and the contribution which each could make to possible solutions. The written material from the student body and faculty was mimeographed and distributed to all college members and served as the basis for choosing issues and problems to be considered by the whole college in panel discussions led by the faculty and students interchangeably. The material also served as the basis for grouping students and faculty into research teams, for the development of a library of materials ranging from United Nations documents to the literature of Soviet and Latin American writers, for field trips to the United Nations and national embassies, and for individual student research projects, with the faculty and other students serving as supervisors and tutors. Foreign scholars were invited for special sessions as the curriculum demanded, and papers written by students and faculty members served as the main basis for seminar discussion.

Since few of the standard texts in history, politics, social science, and the arts were written from a completely international point of view, the main source materials came from original documents, including the newly written and signed test-ban treaty of 1963 for the control of nuclear weapons, disarmament papers from the Geneva eighteen-nation disarmament group, the recently published UNESCO *World History,* and the literature of the countries represented in the college. As the curriculum and the college developed, ideological conflicts which in the beginning produced tensions and disruptions gave way to joint research projects on everything from the world student movement to the role of international trade in easing ideological tensions. The curriculum was formed by the cooperative use of the knowledge and experience of the Communist students, the socialists, the liberal democrats, and the right-wing activists to deal with questions of political and social structure both in national and international terms.

Although the pilot project did not last long enough to establish either a full-fledged college or a full curriculum, the idea of a world college was explored in depth and in action, and proved not only workable but immensely valuable. The concept is easily transposable into models which will work, in the United States and abroad, particularly in this country with its large foreign-student population and its access to other students and teachers through the variety of international organizations established here. The original group of Quakers who sponsored the 1963 experiment have gone on to establish the Friends World Institute, which has now become the Friends World College, with a charter from the State of New York and a student body which will gradually be internationalized by the addition of representatives of other countries to the present student body of Americans. The plan now in action calls for four regional centers to which students move from one year to the next, in Mexico, in Scandinavia, in India, and, when it can be arranged, in the Soviet Union; programs of study and community involvement are worked out with local authorities for the students during their period of residence.

If the necessary funds were appropriated by Congress for the Center for Educational Cooperation designated by the International

Education Act of 1966 as its main instrument, a great deal of this kind of education would become more readily available in this country and elsewhere. In the meantime, the present resources of government and university funds and educational talent are sufficient to make many more such experiments possible.[1] If the resources of the private foundations were used for the plans and activities of the students themselves, some of the most effective ways of introducing world issues into the American student community and for sharing the implicit sense of community which now exists within the world student movement could be set in motion.

Among the ironies which riddle the history of the Columbia University uprising of 1968 is the additional irony that the one source of action and planning for bringing the international student movement in touch with itself was the Columbia Strike Coordinating Committee. Early in June of 1968, following the events on the Columbia campus, the committee sent invitations to representatives of the European student activist groups to attend an International Assembly of Student Movements to be held for a week in New York City. The students who organized the assembly did so entirely by their own efforts. They simply wrote to the appropriate students in Europe, invited them to come, and raised ten thousand dollars for the expenses while calling on the help of the universities in New York City to supply the meeting places and to organize the audiences. Their intentions in doing so are stated in explicit terms:

> The necessity for holding such an assembly is primarily educational. In general it has been impossible to gain any real understanding of the different movements throughout the world, and the recent actions they have engaged in, by reading the press. . . . We feel that many of the movements are similar to ours—yet this is impossible to gauge correctly without first-hand knowledge; and all concerned citizens are faced with a situation in which the entire capitalist world has been upset by movements led or originated by students about whom they know practically nothing.
>
> No one can leave the task of understanding why these movements erupted when they did, or the ways in which they acted, to those same academics and political scientists who have consistently misrepresented and deplored the action students have taken—actions they often-times have known nothing about. Such men have not shown even a disinterested sympathy towards

the actions taken last spring. Unless the students, and other
concerned persons, take upon themselves the burden of discovering the nature of their allied movements and what has
taken place within them, the same distortions will be allowed
to continue, distortions against which people without their own
sources of knowledge have no defense.[2]

Although it is possible that one of the subsidiary purposes in
having called the assembly may have been an effort by the Columbia Strike Committee to gain support and understanding for its
own work in this country, the Columbia students have rendered the
kind of service the universities are responsible for giving to concerned citizens, to the international student community, to the
cause of international understanding, and to the understanding
by Americans of what has been happening in other countries. By
their project they have acted in an area of initiative in which the
United States government is unlikely to operate, and where university leadership has been most reluctant to assume a role. With
the help of students, here is a way in which that reluctance can be
overcome.

[II]

What possibilities are there for linking these national and international movements together by what is done in the colleges and universities?

It seems to me that the possibilities are very great indeed, and
that within movements already in existence and new ones now
being formed, some of the educational reforms are beginning to
find their own ways of intrusion into the future. In the first place,
there is a growing community of interest between the government
agencies and the American student body based on a common concern for the American social revolution. The students and the
government come to that concern from different points of view,
but at a central point their interests coincide. The problem for the
government is to face and correct inequities in the social system
and its possible disruption by those who are blocked from its benefits. To do so, the government must find among the available
resources of the population the kind of persons whose intelligence
and social concern can give the initiative and leadership for carry-

ing out its programs, and can help to create the indigenous leadership by which long-run solutions may be reached. While it cannot take direct responsibility for breaking the grip of the present bureaucracies in the social institutions of the local and state governments, the national government can start new currents flowing by which the power of the bureaucracies can be shifted into the hands of the community and its members. In this, the students are their allies who, by voluntarily engaging themselves in social action, in the government programs and in their own, have already had an effect on the educational system and on the society.

The city of San Francisco provides an example. The Federal government, the state, and the city are all interested in solving the local problems of social change, for a variety of reasons, political, economic, and practical. The educational institutions of the city are involved in those problems at the front edge, although the public schools have not yet been at that edge long enough or persistently enough to find solutions.

On the other hand, the students at San Francisco State College over the past four years have developed their own ways of tackling the problems and furnish an example of what could be done on a national scale to achieve the reform of the American college and university both in its social outlook and in its educational programs. I have chosen the example of San Francisco State College to illustrate the possibilities for educational change through student action, because the college represents in a well-developed form tendencies and movements in the country as a whole, and because, as a state college, it represents the sector of the national system of higher education in which the expansion of student population has been greatest. There are many other institutions, including the University of Michigan, Wayne State University, the University of Minnesota, Antioch College, Earlham College, and dozens more, where in various ways the idea of student education has been developed in the past and is being encouraged in the present.[3]

The instrument of educational change developed by the San Francisco State students lies in their Experimental College, an internal college organized by the students through their own student government and with the use of its funds. Courses are taught by students to other students, often with the help of the faculty; in 1968 the Experimental College included 1,200 students of a total of more than 18,000 enrolled in the regular college. The range of courses offered by the students runs from the study of the avant-garde in the arts since the 1920s to issues of community change, race relations, education, foreign policy, war and peace, economic inequality, and the place of black culture and the arts in contemporary America.

The student experiment, although initiated, sponsored, and supported by the Associated Students of San Francisco State College, has had the cooperation of the faculty and administration, and, since its beginning, has made arrangements through which student-initiated courses when taught or supervised by members of the faculty receive academic credit toward the college degree.

The result has been that the curriculum of the whole institution has been enriched, not only by the new courses included in the degree-granting section but in the intellectual ferment produced by the students among themselves in their own college. A style of curriculum reform which has broad national and international significance was brought into being, a style which uses the resources of the students, the college community, and the community at large to develop changes in educational content and method which go far beyond the grant of the right of students to serve on college committees. The students have recognized themselves as educators and have been recognized as such by their college.

Out of the student Experimental College in 1966 grew the Community Services Institute, originally called the Work/Study Program, which was made up of a combination of student groups, the Community Involvement Program, the Tutorial Program (for teaching children in the slums), and the Black Students Union. Sharon Gold, one of the students in it, reports:

> The intent of the program was to provide a vehicle through which students, faculty, and administrators at San Francisco State, and residents of the various communities of San Francisco, could work together to begin to solve the problems of an urban and suburban society undergoing rapid social change; and to provide a means by which students at San Francisco State could receive academic credit for the community work in which they were involved. Since its inception in the spring of 1967, over 500 students have worked in community projects in 9 districts of San Francisco. Approximately 120 faculty

members and many administrators from the college have been involved in the program. . . .

In May of 1968, the Community Services Institute, together with the Black Studies Institute and the Special Admissions Program, became part of the newly created Division of Innovative Programs at San Francisco State College. The establishment of this division indicates the college's support for the development of alternative forms of education which meet the needs of students committed to changing the attitudes and institutions of contemporary American society.[4]

In cooperation with faculty members and administrators, the students of the institute have now worked out a bachelor of arts program in community work to be installed in the regular college curriculum

The educational objectives of the institute are described by Miss Gold as:

1. To assess students' needs for an educational experience relevant to the work they are doing in the communities;
2. To meet the college's responsibility to provide the resources necessary to community groups in the process of making social change, so that these groups can make informed decisions concerning the directions of their change;
3. To extend educational opportunities to individuals in the community who ordinarily would not be able to take advantage of the college;
4. To eliminate the cultural and social barriers which exist between members of the college community and members of the communities outside the colleges.

. . . [the Institute] is an attempt to re-educate and train college students so that they may participate intelligently and work effectively to end racism in their own communities.[5]

In this example it is not only clear that the United States government both in the language and intent of its social welfare legislation shares the goals of the Community Service Institute with the San Francisco State students, but that the students have built a model for the use of educators in developing the kind of educated persons so desperately needed for making the government programs work. There is no other future source of talent for carrying out the work of the human services in all the complexity of their demands than in the high school and college students who have had the kind of education Miss Gold, her fellow students, and their college are providing. Through the extension of the present government support for students through loans, scholarships, and fellowships, through the extension of the work of VISTA as proposed by Senator Gaylord Nelson in linking its volunteers to a two-year program of teacher preparation, through the use of existing U.S. Office of Education funds under the Education Professions Act, through links made with Job Opportunity Centers, the National Teacher Corps, Head Start projects, and the Department of Housing and Urban Development, and in countless other ways, support can be given to students in carrying out projects of their own. There is no other base in the society for mounting programs of this kind than in the colleges and universities.

What is required for making use of this base as a staging-ground for national educational and social action is a coalition of the students with the administrators and faculty. Plans can then be made by the students, with whatever help they receive from the faculty, and presented, with the backing of the colleges, to the sources of national funds in the foundations and the government. A further coalition can be made between the government officers who are working with the government programs, the administrators, and the students, in which a representative committee of students, faculty members, and administrators on each campus could work directly with the agencies of government to help increase the speed and range of the work being done.

At the present time, when students have ideas for reform, or if they organize to create their own kind of education, they do so against the opposition of the regular system and the regular convention that students in college are there to be educated and that policy-making is none of their business. They seldom have access to funds with which to operate, either from their college or from outside sources. There is a mere handful of foundations which will even consider making grants to students for their own use. At the present time, only the Office of Economic Opportunity, certain sections of the U.S. Office of Education, and the Peace Corps have a serious understanding of the way in which the student movement can handle educational and social projects of its own. In this interim stage, before the country comes to the realization of the quality and degree of talent which lies in the student movement, the intervention of university administrators in support of student projects would not only increase the speed of necessary change, but would involve a wider section of the American student body in the teaching side of the educational system.

In some ways, this is the most important factor in the work of the students at San Francisco State. They have hit upon the most effective and creative way in which the colleges can act to reform their curricula and at the same time to stay in touch with the true needs of their society. What they have done is essentially what the experimental colleges were founded to do—to experiment with education which is built around the talents and needs of the students—and they have proven what the experimental colleges were unable to prove, that this is an education which is not only of crucial importance to students, but will work in the large-scale institutions of the country. When a continuing responsibility for educational change is put in the hands of the students and faculty together, with students given the opportunity to take an equal share of initiative and policy-making in inventing their own programs of study and action, the curriculum is then in a continual process of development, changed and corrected through the experience of teachers and students.

To trace the development at San Francisco State from the Work/Study Program of 1966 in the student Experimental College to the Community Service Institute, from there to the Division of Innovative Programs of the College, and then to the bachelor of arts degree in community work is to trace the natural history of how educational ideas can best be developed in the American college. The students started it, worked it out with faculty help; the college took it on from there. It would have been possible at the beginning for the faculty and administration of the college, at San Francisco State or any other, to have established both the Division of Innovative Programs and the new bachelor of arts degree by faculty and administrative action in the conventional way and to have then allowed qualified students to enter.

To construct new projects of this kind is certainly the responsibility of the colleges, and one which only a few have accepted. But that way of doing it would have deprived the college of the creative thinking of the students and the rich detail of information and insight which they brought to their task, while depriving the students of the opportunity to become educators in their own right, to educate themselves as they explored the problems of education. It would also have deprived the black students, not only those in the Black Students Union, of their role in bringing something of their own to San Francisco State, and learning, through their part in the Community Services Institute, how the connection could be made between the college and their own community.

These students proved something else which badly needed proving. Just as they proved that the ideas of student-centered education were workable in a large institution, they also proved that students who were not part of a highly selected élite, especially chosen for academic proficiency, had talents for learning and teaching which went far beyond the expectation and knowledge of educators about the quality of the mass student body. I have been told time after time by my colleagues that the Sarah Lawrence style of education would not work either in a large institution or with a relatively unselected student body. While not wishing to deny the particular merits of Sarah Lawrence students or of the institution itself, I have persistently argued that such a view is nonsense and that it is in the large institution with an unselected student body that this style of education is of such crucial importance, *because* so many students in these institutions are unmotivated and will remain that way unless a new philosophy of education can arrange a different situation for their learning.

An example of what can happen when educational philosophy is supplanted by political confrontation is provided by the events at San Francisco State College in the fall of 1968 when the college was forced to close in order to avoid complete disruption of the educational program and the possibility of violence and destruction on the campus. Rather than allowing the regular process of student and faculty government to settle the question of the dismissal or retention of a graduate student who had been teaching classes for disadvantaged students and who had been accused of urging black students to bring guns to the campus, the board of trustees of the state colleges of California and its chancellor ordered Dr. Robert Smith, then president of the College, to dismiss the alleged offender.

After urging the chancellor not to intervene and to allow the college to settle its own affairs with the dignity of a true educational community, Dr. Smith obeyed the order. He then found himself with a group of militant students from the Black Students Union, who called a strike against the college and presented a set of demands having to do with the retention of the dismissed teacher and with establishing a Black Studies Department with the addition of twenty-one more faculty members, the admission of a larger number of black students and Third World students, and student control of the formation of educational policy in faculty appointments and the content of the black curriculum. The striking students backed up their demands with forays into the classrooms and laboratories, the destruction of educational equipment, and threats of more violence to come.

The result was that the faculty, the students, and the administration of one of the most creative colleges in the country were split into dissenting factions, some sympathetic to the demands of the black students, others opposed to both the tactics and the demands of the disruptives, nearly all of them united against the action of the state board and its chancellor in interfering in the internal affairs of the college. There is no doubt that if the administration, faculty, and students had been left to settle their affairs by the application of the principles of educational philosophy consistent with their practices in the past, a fair solution to the problems of curriculum and of faculty appointments would have been found without submission either to the blackmail of the militants or to the orders of the state. If the issue is joined as a political confrontation, no such solution is possible. Instead, there is increased turmoil and trouble for everyone.

[III]

When serious consideration is given to the actual accomplishments of students in developing new educational programs and in accepting responsibility for administering student affairs and educational policy, it becomes natural to assume that they should be represented in the membership of boards of trustees, of administrative and faculty committees, and in all the sectors of educational policy in the governance of the college and the university. Any board of trustees would benefit from having the advice, opinion, and educational insight of two or three students of the quality of the leaders of the National Student Association, the Radical Education Project at the University of Michigan, the Experimental College at Dartmouth, the Antioch Community Government, or the Students for a Reconstructed University at Columbia.

Although boards of trustees might not agree with everything the students said at the board meetings, they would learn a great deal that they would not otherwise know, and university policy would be a great deal wiser and more comprehensive in dealing with the issues before the board. Before such student membership becomes possible, boards of trustees, governing officers, and faculty members are going to have to reconstruct their notions of what students and their leaders are capable of doing when they are given responsibility, and what intellectual equality means when it is not based on age level and social or cultural status.

In the meantime there are some approximations to full student status which are feasible and even probable within the present university, and which would simply extend present tendencies. If the idea of making coalitions between the college and outside movements toward common social ends were taken seriously, the board of trustees and the governing officers of the colleges and universities would find some workable ways in which student groups with ideas for reform could meet with those responsible for university policy, in situations in which the student ideas would receive a hearing in the same spirit as any other ideas from trustee, administrative, or faculty sources. They would also find ways of conferring directly with the black community, with educators and executives from the government, and with foreign students and scholars, so that whatever joint plans could be made would be the result of the best kind of thinking all of them could do together.

As it now stands, members of boards very seldom meet faculty members, students, community leaders, or foreign educators. Their agendas are usually burdened with financial decisions. The subject of education itself seldom comes up, and when it does, it comes in relation either to a crisis in the status of faculty members or students about whom a decision must be made. Yet discussion of the educational program is the most interesting part of being a trustee, and there is no reason why trustee membership should not entail the enjoyment of educational advantages. There are approximately 35,000 members of boards of trustees, regents, and other governing bodies in the United States; among their ranks are some of the country's most capable executives, citizens, and public representatives, drawn from a narrow circle of the corporate and business structure.

The conception they usually hold of their role in education is one consistent with their background as employers of manpower. They usually think of themselves as members of a corporation empowered to hire and fire presidents, faculty members, and staff, and to make rules about students and faculty members—what they are allowed to do and what they are allowed to say. Yet as trustees and regents they seldom have enough experience or knowledge in dealing with educational issues to become qualified to engage in the very matters in which they pre-empt the authority of educators, teachers, and students.

I have mentioned the interference of the board of trustees of the state colleges of California in the affairs of San Francisco State College, and the subsequent effect of the interference on the stability of the college. The interference of Governor Reagan and the regents of the University of California in ordering the president, the chancellor, and the faculty of the University in Berkeley to cancel nine lectures by Eldridge Cleaver in a course officially approved through the regular faculty and student procedures is another example of recent actions of a political kind taken by boards of control. To this might be added the continual interference by the board of regents in the internal affairs of the University of Colorado in Boulder, Colorado, ranging from the issuance of sets of rules for student and faculty behavior without consultation with student or with faculty representatives, to the banning of SDS from the Boulder campus.

Although the analyses conducted by radical critics of the university governing bodies are quite accurate in identifying the interlocking connection of most boards with the most conservative economic and social forces in the society, there is no certainty that this will remain true in the future as the colleges and universities evolve past their present role in the society. In those states where regents and trustees are elected by the state, students, faculty members, and citizens concerned with education can mount election campaigns of the kind which have been successful in the election of new and better school boards in local communities. In some cases, where student organizations and their members are sufficiently interested in politics to be able to create an organizational force, they could not only seek out and support candidates among citizens with an interest in educational change, but could put up student or faculty candidates of their own, with speeches, meetings, rallies, and a political campaign organized by students and faculty members on the state campuses.

If a coalition of citizens, public school teachers, faculty members, labor unions, including the liberal agricultural unions, were formed, with the students taking the initiatives and acting as the members of their own staff of speech-writers, organizers, research teams, and speakers, a new conception of educational trusteeship and its possibilities would be introduced into politics. Even when unsuccessful in electing a candidate, either to the state legislature or to the boards of higher education, the election campaign could accomplish a great deal more than is presently being accomplished in making educational issues and the role of students in them a significant part of public discussion. It would also produce a greater awareness of responsibility toward a wider electorate, including students, on the part of the politicians and the members of university and state educational bodies.

In the case of private universities and colleges, and in states where members of the governing bodies in higher education are appointed rather than elected, a similar student-faculty-citizens coalition could become active in putting forward its own candidates and in following closely the work of the governing bodies and their members. In several public schools, for example, groups of students have formed what might be called shadow boards of education, to which the student body elects its own representatives to serve as student counterparts of the governing bodies. The students gather information and materials about budgets, policies, programs, and other items of the board agenda, and hold parallel meetings or, in some cases, joint meetings with the board of education. They then develop policies of their own which they put forward as recommendations for action by the regular board.

A comparable shadow board of trustees could be formed by university students in those instances where there is little access by students to the decision-making bodies, with a parallel agenda, discussions with individual board members, including the board chairman, with requests for joint meetings on matters of policy.

This approach has the advantage of concentrating student attention on the issues as seen from the point of view of the policy-makers themselves. A body of student researchers and reformers can then be developed whose knowledge of university affairs is much more informed than is usually the case when the criticism of board policy is based either on generalities or on a program of action to gain the right of students to board membership and a role in board decisions.

From the point of view of the trustees themselves, whether they are the ones condemned for their social and economic connections by the radicals, or whether they are simply citizens whose interest in education is serious enough to merit spending their time and energy on university affairs, there is little communication between the trustees of one institution and those of another. The result is that often when policy questions of national and international consequence are raised in the setting of one university, the trustees have no preparation for considering the questions in their larger dimension. Since it is unlikely that the present corporate structure of the university will change in a direction which would remove ultimate power of decision from these governing bodies, the efforts in reform should be directed straight at the policies themselves. This would be crucial for the education of the governing bodies and of the individuals in them whose interest in education and in students is serious but whose direct contact with students, community groups, and other universities is limited by the present structure and attitudes.

There are other ways of unifying the structure, attitudes, and policies of governing boards than by outright condemnation, by political action, or by actual membership of students and faculty members in the boards themselves. A degree of privacy in the conduct of trustee business is necessary to its operation, just as it is necessary to the relation between faculty members and their students, the editors of newspapers with their reporters, and persons with persons. Members of policy-making groups of all kinds have the problem of needing to be free at meetings to make any number of indiscreet or hypothetical suggestions or comments in the discussion of policy questions if the eventual policy decisions are to be sound and enlightened. At the same time, unless there is a generous degree of public access to the governing bodies of colleges and universities by the interested parties among students, faculty, and community members, the policies suffer not from privacy but from isolation.

The trustee membership at Sarah Lawrence College benefited a very great deal by the presence of representatives from the faculty, from the parent body, from the alumnae, from the community, from the field of education, the arts, sciences, and letters. Although the board did not at the time of my presidency include students, students were often present with trustee members who visited classes, came to the campus for educational meetings, and joined in the life of the institution as interested members of the college. The discussion at meetings of the trustees gained a great deal, not only by a membership which included a cross section of educators and citizens from many areas of the culture, but from an agenda in which educational questions were raised and discussed with the full collaboration of the faculty and the students through reports, visits to the board, and symposia at the college.

The issue is therefore not entirely in the official representation of students and faculty in board membership, desirable as this may be, but in the way in which the education of trustees is carried on in the issues of educational and social policy which confront them continually. Aside from reforms in the present membership to include a wider section of representation, would it not be possible and useful, for example, for a delegation of one or two trustees, administrators, faculty members, and students from a college or university to spend two or three days or a weekend visiting one of the institutions where new programs of student reform are going on and to bring back reports to the appropriate groups about the work there? Or to arrange three- or four-day institutes with several colleges represented by equivalent delegations in order to discuss reform and the links to the national movements in education and social change?

The idea could be extended to summer study-travel projects in which a delegation of this kind could go abroad to confer with educators, students, and political leaders in Western and Eastern European countries, or in Latin America, Africa, or Asia. There is already in existence a network of relationships in the international community through the programs of the International Secretariat for Volunteer Service, the Peace Corps, UNESCO, and the International Educational and Cultural Exchange programs of the

U.S. State Department, and dozens of voluntary organizations like the American Friends Service Committee and the Experiment in International Living, through whom an itinerary could be arranged. Since we are in the middle of a world system of education, with the United States as one part of it, it is time that the reality of that system be brought closer to the people who are deciding the future of American colleges and universities.

[IV]

In many simpler ways, ideas of this kind can be put to work by students, teachers, and administrators across the United States. I would like to extend the San Francisco State example to its next stage, in illustration of what is meant by the possibilities of a coalition of forces for change which links together the social welfare programs of the government, the students, the black community, and the world generation of youth. In 1967, Karen Duncan, one of the students active in the student Experimental College in San Francisco, was invited by the National Student Association to extend the range of a community-action program for the improvement of race relations which had been developed by a former Oberlin student of the association staff. Miss Duncan was asked to see what could be done to enlist the support of a national cross section of colleges and universities to put into effect a community-action curriculum, that is, a curriculum of college studies based on student work in race relations in the community. The idea, independently suggested to the National Student Association by students from several parts of the country, is an extension of the San Francisco student community-service curriculum. Students from San Francisco State had already spread the word through the national student movement about their work in student education by preparing papers, research evaluation, and descriptions of what they had been doing, and by attending student conferences to discuss their ideas and program with others.

With a small grant from a private foundation, Miss Duncan, a junior at her college, spent six months in 1968 travelling to campuses explaining the community-action idea and conferring with college officials and students about the possibility of installing programs through which the community-action projects, some of them already under way, could be included in regular college curricula. Four universities—Central State University in Wilberforce, Ohio, the City University in New York, Brandeis University in Waltham, Massachusetts, and Ohio University in Athens, Ohio—have now begun experimenting in their own terms with the idea, fourteen others have either introduced field programs or are planning to, seventy-three more have expressed an interest or have already put the concept into effect and are prepared to exchange information and ideas with the others. One hundred and twenty additional institutions are presently being surveyed for their ideas on educational programs of this kind, since they are known to be involved in one way or another with similar projects. Miss Duncan now proposes an expansion both of the number of institutions who are actively engaged in this kind of education and in the distribution of information about what is going on to a much wider variety of institutions across the country.

As Miss Duncan puts it, in a statement about the need for expansion and the direction the movement should take, "It is clear that in addition to working with those who are oppressed, we must begin to work with those who are oppressing. That means working not only with individuals, but also with institutions, school systems, businesses and churches that either covertly encourage racism or become a party to it, encouraging it by not actively working against it. . . ."

The accomplishments, first of the students at San Francisco State in whose Experimental College Miss Duncan was educated, then in the direct and single-handed way in which Miss Duncan set to work to give substance to her educational ideas on a national scale, then in the initiative of the National Student Association students in appointing Miss Duncan and her predecessor to the post of travelling educator, point to a simple fact. If one student, working with a single student organization can stir up so much initiative in educational reform in a single year, the possibilities for reform through the cooperation of present students, here and abroad, in the black and white community, using the financial resources and connections of the government, the private foundations, the educational organizations, and the colleges, are incalculable, once the colleges themselves turn their students loose with the ideas they have created among themselves.

Consider, as another example, the work of the Southern Student Organizing Committee, organized in Nashville, Tennessee, in April of 1964 by a group of students from Vanderbilt University, George Peabody College for Teachers, and Scarritt College at a conference attended by forty-five student leaders and representatives from fifteen predominantly white campuses in ten Southern states. Having admired and been influenced by the union of black Southern students with Northern whites in the years following the first student sit-ins in 1959 and 1960, and the founding of the Student Nonviolent Coordinating Committee, the white Southern students declared at the conference, "We, as young Southerners here pledge to take *our* stand now together here to work for a new order, a new South, a place which embodies our ideals for all the world to emulate, not ridicule. We find our destiny as individuals in the South in our hopes and our work together as brothers."

The students not only made good on their pledge, but by the college year 1967–1968 had organized a program of action with a staff of fourteen students, eight chapters of the organization in the South, and twenty-five affiliated groups, had held conferences involving white and black students in community action in collaboration with the labor unions, and placed eight student organizers in as many Southern states to extend educational services and social action. All this was done in accordance with a constitution whose preamble states that the Southern Student Organizing Committee is "an association of young, concerned Southerners dedicated to social change." "We wish," says the preamble, "to join with other individuals and groups in building a democratic society predicated on peace and racial equality; a society in which every person is guaranteed physical well-being and the opportunity to develop to the fullest extent his native abilities." [6]

A review of the committee's literature and reports shows a range of activity which includes not only projects of political and social action, but educational materials written on the basis of research studies by students, a magazine which reports university and community life in the South, student speakers at one hundred and fifteen campuses, seventy pamphlets made available to students and community groups, and eleven films in continuous circulation. The achievement of that small group of students back in 1964 has already grown in size and influence and has become a serious new force in Southern education, with no institutional help from the colleges and universities in which the students have been enrolled.

Or consider the work of the Student Press Association, founded in 1963 by a group of student editors who found that there was no available source of accurate news about student affairs in the national press, and that at that time there was no way in which the student newspapers of the country could communicate with each other. The student dispatches now available from the association include student reporting from Vietnam, editorials, descriptions of student action and educational events on university campuses, coverage of national politics from the student point of view, and a continuous series of intelligent and well-written dispatches from the campuses, used by 400 of the major news magazines and newspapers as a means of keeping in touch with the student movement.

The total of indigenous student projects of this kind which are beginning to assume national and international importance has never been collected, but is well over 250 if the smaller organizations are included, like *Vocations for Social Change,* a one-man effort by a student recently graduated who now has a staff of six other ex-students and provides a clearinghouse for advice and information to students and others interested in using their talents for the human services. All of these organizations are related in some way to the colleges and universities, either by having been organized by enrolled students or by students who have dropped out of college to give all their time to education of the kind they believe in, or by graduates who intend returning at some future date better to prepare themselves to carry on their work within the university community and its surrounding environment.

16: Social Change and Student Action

To put the matter broadly, there is already in existence the basis for a movement of student national service going far beyond the existing arrangements provided by the selective-service system, the poverty program, and the social-welfare projects sponsored by private organizations and the national and state governments. The two most potent sources of emotional and social energy for change within the society since 1965 have been the anti-war movement and the movement for racial justice. The issues raised within them include all the moral and social questions at once, and they are central movements which will grow in strength within this generation and the generations which follow, expanding their scope and the strength of student attitudes into a movement against all wars and all racial injustice.

There is a real question as to whether a democratic society can adopt a foreign policy in the future which assumes the use of the conscripted military service of its young men to fight declared or undeclared wars. It is a question which will not only haunt the policy-makers and political leaders of the present and future, but will determine a significant part of American foreign policy. Having been educated to despise the rationalizations made by their government in explanation of the Vietnam war, this generation is educating its successors in the moral and social issues implicit in the use of war as an instrument of all foreign policy. If the government continues to conceive service to the United States entirely in military terms, as it has by its refusal to allow forms of alternative services to qualify its youth for exemption from conscription, it will not only drive deeper the alienation of the young from their government and from their elders, but it will lose the greatest opportunity this country has ever had to build upon its greatest strength, the voluntary efforts of concerned citizens and the talents of its democratic youth.

Here is the conventional list of problems, growing in size and intensity by the day:

> Millions of American children in cruel need of an adequate education.
>
> Twenty-two million American families living at or below the poverty level; four million families near or at the starvation level.
>
> Millions of American children and adults without adequate medical or health care.
>
> Millions more who have never seen a live play, heard a symphony orchestra, seen a dance company, responded to poetry, painting, sculpture, opera.
>
> Two-thirds of the world living below the level of an adequate standard of living, illiterate, uncared for, without the resources to care for themselves.
>
> Continual depletion of national and international resources in clean air, water, minerals, and the beauty of the natural world.
>
> Continual tensions between societies and groups within societies over issues of race, political control, and ideology.
>
> Threats of annihilation, genocide, human cruelty, rising antagonisms capable of producing an American civil war and a civil war on a world scale.

Here is a short list of resources available for dealing with the problems:

> Millions of American and foreign students ready and willing to use their talents in the service of mankind.
>
> Hundreds of colleges and universities whose stated purpose is to aid mankind in all the dimensions of his need.
>
> Billions of dollars now used by the American government and the governments of the world for armaments.
>
> Millions of concerned citizens in the United States and abroad ready to do what they can for making a better society.

Technological devices of incredible versatility for removing the obstacles to human growth and development.

A body of knowledge in science and the arts rich in insight for the solution of human problems.

An international community of scientists, scholars, teachers, and youth capable of using their brains and energies for human betterment.

The most powerful country in the world, with a democratic form of government capable of bending its efforts, if it had the collective will, to the solution of its own problems and giving aid to the solution of the difficulties besetting others.

Yet at this point in time, the United States has not found the ways to match the problems with the resources, at a time when the youth have already volunteered their talents and have already shown by what they have done that they have a capacity for altering the shape of the future. A presidential commission in 1965 estimated that there were a minimum of 5,300,000 jobs in social service to be filled by persons with a minimum of educational preparation and experience if the country organized itself to assure its social health.[1] Very few of these jobs will be either established or filled unless a comprehensive plan of national service is made and adopted to use the resources of youth and the educational system to build a better society.

There are in the United States Senate and in the House of Representatives men and women who understand the potency of the social movement represented by American youth and have taken steps to create the legislative ground for its extension. I have mentioned earlier the work of Senator Gaylord Nelson and the proposed amendment to the Higher Education Act for student service in the Teacher Corps as volunteers, teachers' aides, assistants, and to bring together the schools, the universities, and the community in joint projects. Senator Fred Harris has proposed a Youth Participation Act to "provide opportunities for American youth to serve in policy-making positions and to participate in National, State and local programs of social and economic benefit to the country." [2]

> ... it is the purpose of this Act to create a new program, planned and administered largely by young people themselves, which will help to direct the resources of youth to the solution of critical needs of the country, and encourage fuller partici-

pation of youth in the American public life, by offering young
people opportunities to participate in the planning, administration and evaluation of programs which benefit our society and
economy, and by establishing National and State forums for
the discussion and resolution of problems facing youth.

Here are some of the elements of a broad-scale and potentially
radical program of reform in education, and it is time the colleges
and universities joined forces with those in Congress who are at
work on such reform, by volunteering the services of their institutions to aid in the accomplishment of the legislative aims, and by
becoming politically active in support of the legislation itself.

In my experience with the educators involved in preparing teachers in the colleges and universities, I have discovered that few of
them are either knowledgeable or active in relation to the educational planning now carried on by the congressional and executive
branches of the government. This is not only a lack of knowledge
by educators of the educational planning itself, but a lack of information about existing programs in which they could collaborate,
and a lack of connection on these questions with the Senators and
congressmen of their own states and districts. In most cases in the
development of new programs for youth, the initiatives are coming
from the government, without the help of the educators. Yet the
colleges and departments of education and the faculty members in
the arts and sciences departments of the country have between them
the responsibility for educating the entire teaching staff for the
country's public schools. Their lack of initiative in these matters
amounts to an intellectual and educational scandal.

The colleges and universities are at the center of possibility for
these and other educational changes, and in any number of ways
are at the center of power which can make the possibilities actual.
If we accept the argument, as it is clear we must, that the colleges
and universities are the manpower center for the entire American
society, with the power to persuade and to educate the public and
the government, and to decide what kind of manpower and what
kind of help they propose to give to both, then the case is made for
using this central position to enable the student population to fulfill
its own ambition to improve and remake the country.

A plan for national service can begin on the campuses, not only
with proposals for educational change in the service the young can

presently give in conjunction with their college studies, but by the development of comprehensive plans and policies to be urged upon the government for alternatives in service to military conscription. Only one more step need be taken beyond the present situation— to form a national service corps for youth, with scholarships, fellowships, and stipends to match, containing in one concept the Peace Corps, the National Teacher Corps, VISTA, Job Opportunity Centers, Head Start, and all the others, with more besides— in which youth can serve not war but peace, not social status but social need. The autonomy of the present programs could be preserved, while the administration of the human-services curricula and projects could be arranged by the colleges, with direct grants to qualified candidates in the same style as the GI Bill following World War II.

Although it does not appear on the surface, the volunteer movement linked to national service is an extension of the idea of land-grant education, defined not only as the idea of bringing to the citizens the education they need, but doing so by Federal subsidy which leaves the educational programs in the hands of the colleges, universities, and the students. It is also linked to the elective principle by the fact that the subsidy would be provided, as was the case with the veterans of World War II, directly to the students, who might then choose the institutions and the programs which they wish to enter. Because their education would then be linked to a form of community service, there would be a generous degree of latitude in the form their education would take. Part of what has been proposed by the Carnegie Commission on Higher Education in their 1968 report, "Quality and Equality," can be converted to this concept. The report recommends a civilian GI Bill, with direct grants to students and a cost-of-education allowance to the colleges of their choice. A modification of the idea could provide for direct grants to students for work in the human services linked to college studies in the humanities, social sciences, and education.

I can remember the development of this approach at a time when some of us were working with Adlai Stevenson and the Eleanor Roosevelt Memorial Foundation on plans to carry on Mrs. Roosevelt's life work in human rights and education following her death. Over and over again the students with whom we conferred asked that whatever foundation funds were available should go directly to the persons involved, to support projects of their devising, rather than to the educational institutions, where they would be absorbed into the usual budgets and programs and never reach the students. There is no other way to create indigenous leadership than to nourish it at its source, with the institutional arrangements responding to the ideas of the potential leaders among the students rather than fitting the students into prearranged patterns.

There are very great possibilities here for the support of important reforms in colleges which are either predominantly or completely Negro in their constituencies. The Jencks-Riesman account of the Negro colleges in *The Academic Revolution* describes fully the actual situation of these colleges and their place in the national system. But it does little to suggest how the educational level can be raised and how the cultural and social integration of the Negro colleges into the American community at large can be arranged. A small part of the problem is being touched upon by the increase in numbers of Negro students accepted into the predominantly white institutions, with appropriate admissions and curricular changes which should have been made a hundred years ago.

But the black institutions exist and enroll nearly two-thirds of the black students of this country, and one of the effects of the shift in policy of the white institutions is to deprive them of some of their best students. As the movement toward autonomy within the black community continues to increase in strength under the impact of the new generation of black youth, it will no longer be possible for the administration and faculty of the Negro colleges to continue an educational philosophy of vocationalism, control of students, and submission to the policies dictated by the white society. The resistance to that philosophy is already apparent in the black student protests at Grambling University, at Howard University, and elsewhere. The insensitivity of Howard University to the real needs of the black community was indicated by the plans made for the second hundred years of that institution to become "a first-class university," which meant doing all the usual things about test scores, admissions standards, and curriculum, and developing an integrated student body by an influx of white students, who obviously would replace black students more in need of education and deprived of an opportunity to find it elsewhere.

Just as in the case of the white poor whose schools and colleges are inferior in quality, the black poor and the Southern blacks in general do not have the means, either intellectual or financial, to raise the level of their own institutions. But the black student movement has its own goal—to establish the identity and equality of the black people by their own efforts in their own ways. Just as the student teachers who worked in the Mississippi freedom schools found new and effective ways of raising the educational level and intellectual interests of the children and high school students assembled in the schools, the black students are capable of forming their own leadership and working for the transformation of the Negro colleges.

They will do so, not in the interest of integrating them with the white community or with a white student body, but in the interest of developing an equality of acceptance within white society by whatever means are most effective. By the exercise of their present talents, whatever may be the accredited academic level, they can supply the missing elements in the cultural structure of the black community once they have been given the support they need to set about their work.

Although at the present time the black student movement is moving away from collaboration with white students on either social or educational issues, for reasons related to the whole question of developing indigenous leadership, the virtue of the elective principle and student education will lead them to seek allies and intellectual companions wherever they can find them once their present enclaves have formed themselves and they set about their plans for the next phase of action.

They are in a situation similar to the white students who wish to choose their own curricula and their own teachers. Once this becomes possible for the black students, the choice of teachers and associates will not be confined to blacks. Provided the choices are made by those who already have their own identity, the freedom of choice then becomes real. The interchange of students, white and black, will in the long run be determined by the degree of equality established between them in the educational community as well as in the society as a whole. In the interim, more Black Student Unions will be formed and will collaborate with other

blacks and whites as such collaboration advances the interests of
the black community.

[II]

The difference between the American and the European educational systems lies in the fact that this kind of educational and social
development through students is more possible in the United
States than in Europe. The influence of students there has to be a
frontal attack on a fortress, not an amalgamation of student efforts
to organize programs around ideas, with the help of other students,
teachers, and administrators. A centralized, government-controlled,
European system of institutions gives very little room for flexibility
even among those in the system who want to be flexible. The
example of the Free University of Berlin, which began with the
idea of something closer to the American style of relation between
teachers and students than the German tradition allows, shows
what can happen when an educational philosophy is grafted on a
culture which cannot sustain it. As faculty members were added to
the group with which the Free University began, the idea of democratic fusion of student and faculty responsibility shifted back to
the reality of faculty control, which then formed a target for the
student protests of 1967 and 1968. The students had gone on with
their own conception of the students' role in their university; the
faculty had reverted to an official and conventional university
position.

This is what will happen in most situations where the system is
centralized both internally within each institution and externally
within a whole society. If there is one dominant philosophy which
is either imposed upon or accepted gladly by the faculty, and that
philosophy gives the power of curriculum-making and student
control to the faculty, there is very little chance, aside from a frontal
assault, that the curriculum and educational policy will change of
its own accord. Even in the experimental colleges of America, failure by students to use the existing rights and responsibilities for
student policy-making results in the loss of influence by the students.
New faculty members who join the college seldom have the same
degree of interest in the experimental side of education which inspired the founders and the earlier teachers, and bring conventional

educational attitudes with them from their graduate schools and other teaching posts. In the radical democracy of the experimental colleges, the influence of every newcomer is constitutionally as great as any of the older settlers, since there is no faculty hierarchy, and a small group of persons with only a few more added from year to year can, unless checked by an active use of student power as granted by the college constitution, turn the college into a faculty-centered institution whose original spirit of adventure is gone.

This argues for the *necessity* of a grant of authority and genuine decision-making power to the students, not merely the desirability of such power. The founding of the San Francisco State student Experimental College and the serious improvement in the quality of learning and teaching by the students and the faculty which resulted could not have happened without the sympathetic interest of a sufficient number of the faculty members and administrators in helping in the beginning. When the faculty senate at San Francisco State voted to allow courses developed by students and supervised or taught by faculty members to receive regular credit toward the bachelor of arts degree, it strengthened the basis on which the student college could continue to grow. A hostile faculty, or the absence of key persons who worked directly with the students to support their ideas, would have led to the abortive sort of educational experiment to be found on many other campuses.

The addition of students to the decision-making apparatus also gives greater strength to the work of the college president and faculty members by giving the administration a larger constituency of support for educational reform, not only by the increase in representation of all elements in the college community, but through including, by way of the parents of students, a new body of representation in the electorate. To extend the San Francisco State example once more, this time into the state politics of California, it should be remembered that a strong force in support of adequate budgets for the continuance and expansion of the state colleges has come from citizens of that state who are very much concerned about educational opportunities for their children.

At a time when the issue of the budget for higher education in California is one which has divided the state between conservative and liberal views, with inadequate funds for the state colleges a general fact of life, a central board of trustees administers the policies for all eighteen colleges. As Rudolph H. Weingartner of the San Francisco State philosophy faculty puts it:

> The function of this board with its bureaucracy is other than might be expected. It has never faced the State in behalf of the colleges; it has never understood the goals of the colleges and interpreted them to the public and to the politicians who make the laws and appropriate the monies; it has done little fighting for the needs of the State Colleges as genuine institutions of higher learning. If one sees through occasional flurries of rhetoric, the central governing body of the State College System has unfailingly served as a one-way funnel through which the untutored desires of politicians are forwarded and implemented.[3]

If this is the case, and the indications are that it is, then the long-run solution can only be provided by the involvement of parents, students, and other interested citizens in the political work necessary to correct the situation. One of the greatest sources of direct knowledge and understanding of the work of the state colleges lies in their students, and it is no longer enough to consider *pro forma* representation on the colleges' internal bodies as having exhausted the possibilities for informed and intelligent political action for the improvement of college education.

I am therefore arguing for the acceptance of students into full citizenship within the American political system, and into full equality in educational planning on their campuses, in order to preserve the health of the political system and of the college curriculum, to give to both the freshness and immediacy of relevance to the life of the culture. This is not so much a question of student rights or political representation of the student sector of the university community, but of an enlightened educational philosophy which takes account of the reality of the educational process. Once the idea is accepted that the leadership of future intellectual and educational movements is in the hands of freshmen who become sophomores, who then become juniors, seniors, then graduate students, it becomes clear that the more that can be done to give responsibility for teaching and learning to the students at the very beginning, in high school as well as in college, the better will become their talent in education and cultural affairs as they move up through the system and into their culture. As they move through the system they carry their ideas along with them, gain the experience of organizing them into programs, teaching them to others, both inside and outside the college, learning from the teaching, and creating a new reservoir of talent for a new kind of college and university teacher, which is what many of them will then become, a teacher whose commitment to a life of learning includes a natural commitment to teaching what he knows.

[III]

There is at present a teaching shortage in the public schools alone estimated at 170,000, and one which is increasing annually as the need for educated persons in the whole area of social welfare and community action draws upon the general resources of the teaching profession with its allied branches. The supply of college and university administrators to match the demand for first-rate educators is already dangerously low. Upwards of three hundred new appointments must be made each year in the college and university sector, aside from the administrators needed for the community colleges, which are expanding at the rate of a new one each week and have a projected need over the next five years for 1,000 to 1,500 presidents and deans. In the matter of college and university teachers, even to keep up with the expansion of the student body and to retain a national ratio of sixteen students to each faculty member will require 150,000 new appointments for each million students, at a time when approximately 15,000 Ph.D. graduates are available each year for the teaching profession. Unless we turn our colleges and universities into a major instrument for developing teaching talent of all kinds, by making the internal life of the colleges one in which it is as natural to learn to teach as it is to learn to learn, there is no other place in the society to which we can turn to satisfy what is presently its most desperate need.

I am also arguing for the extension of student decision-making in education, and for student projects in innovation, research, and educational change, for the sake of the faculty. Otherwise the faculty will remain out of touch with the qualities of leadership the students possess and blind to the needs of a changing society about which the faculty members need to know at first hand if the curriculum is to reflect the best thinking available in the university community as a whole.

The most important single reform proposed by the Muscatine Committee at the University of California in Berkeley was the creation of the Board for Educational Development, which has the authority to include in the regular university curriculum any student or faculty-initiated educational program which in the judgment of the board has serious educational merit. When there is a way, as in this case, in which ideas developed by students outside the regular curriculum can be put into effect on their merits rather than on the ability to work their way through the faculty committee system, the spirit of initiative is nourished at the source. The spirit of voluntary association with its own internal energy then begins to operate in bringing about change in one sector of university life and in influencing change in other sectors.

The process of growth thus becomes natural and organic to the intellectual and cultural life of the institution. Whatever the tensions or disagreements which develop between faculty, administration, and students, or between one group of students and another, will be over substantive educational issues; controversy and discussion will not be about who has the political power and authority to decide, but about the issues. The result will be a clearer understanding on the part of the students about the real issues, not an enforced opportunity to retreat into the pleasure of being able to denounce the organized finkery of the entire establishment.

A good example of what can be accomplished by a status of full equality between faculty and students is the report I have already mentioned of the student-faculty Commission on University Governance at the University of California in Berkeley. There were five students and five faculty members on the commission. Here the effort was not only to analyze the effect of the university structure on the life of students and to find ways in which the structure could be improved, but to find how to create a new environment

> ... which values the student as an individual and demonstrates this respect by soliciting his participation in significant policy-making for the community, which thrives on the discomforting intellectual challenges that encourage the search for answers to

questions previously unasked. . . . Our goal is the creation of a
community in which students educate themselves and attain
intellectual autonomy, not an institution which gives an education (including a certificate of completion and a transcript
which may only be viewed under glass in the presence of a
clerk) to all those who put together a jigsaw puzzle of course
units, breadth requirements, grade points and an examination
in American History and Institutions. . . . Students should share
the responsibility for developing innovations in the curriculum,
for evaluating the success of the entire program, and, indeed,
for devising the indices most appropriate for measuring and
assessing a student's individual growth. Learning should not be
regarded as an isolated classroom experience, but rather as a
sustained, continuous public experience. Hopefully, so communal a venture would blur the lines of authority between
dependent students and dominant professors. Intellectual exploration would become a common experience of developing
understanding and would include sharing the pain and the
triumph of intellectual creativity, instead of concealing that
process and displaying to the student only the finely distilled
result.[4]

There is evidence to show that the improvement in tone and
philosophy, and the realism of the commission's proposals over
most committeee reports on education, is already a tribute to the
equality of membership in the student side of the commission
itself. The report makes the major point that if a university is
organized into sectors of students, faculty, and administration, with
powers of governance arranged according to each sector, and roles
assigned in advance which delegate most of the least important
questions to the students, not only does student government become meaningless, but the various sectors are immediately put in
antagonistic relation to each other.

Many of the detailed recommendations of the report apply to
the University in Berkeley rather than to universities as a whole,
since they deal with problems in the local institution. There are
two points, however, that have broad educational significance: the
first, a recommendation for reconstructing the governance of the
university to involve students directly in it; the second, for the first
two years of undergraduate education to give the students the
opportunity to assemble together in informal "colleges." These

would contain approximately 250 freshmen and 250 sophomores, with 40 half-time teaching assistants and ten faculty members, three of whom would be full-time, the others half-time, with each college deciding on its own staff, the members of which would be drawn from the regular departments.

The curriculum would be organized around topics or a set of disciplines, with the choice of electing a "college" left to the student according to his interests. There could be one such college in mathematics, physics, and philosophy, for example, or one in economics, psychology, and statistics. Among topic-centered colleges could be one in The Developing Nations (economics, political science, sociology, and anthropology), Language and Culture (linguistics, philosophy, and English), Myth and Ritual (anthropology, classics, comparative literature, Near Eastern languages). One professor would act as the head of each college; there would be a minimum of lectures, with independent study, tutorials, and other arrangements at the discretion of the students and faculty.

What is proposed here is a fairly conservative program, suited to the possibilities of reform in the situation at Berkeley, and emphasizing the traditional academic disciplines and approaches. But the core of the idea lies in the revival of one part of the elective principle, and in the way in which mass education can be decentralized by the voluntary association of students together in an area of their choice, and by the voluntary association of the faculty (no one need be appointed to the internal "college" unless he wanted to be) in a teaching program congenial to faculty interests and careers.

The idea of the internal college has been applied in a different form in many institutions, for example at Michigan State University, where a group of faculty members planned Justin Morrill College as an organization of approximately 1,200 students inside the larger university structure but with links to it through the faculty and the opportunity for students to take courses outside the college in other sections of the university. Justin Morrill is planned as a college with an international point of view, involving field work in the United States and foreign countries, and experiments in student teaching. At the University of Michigan in Ann Arbor, in addition to the appointment of an ombudsman to act on behalf of the students, an internal college has been formed in which the students choose their own texts, work out sectors of the curriculum, grade each other's papers, and are in a situation of full cooperation with their teachers in developing the college.

Until now, among ideas for internal colleges or for the colleges as a whole, one of the most important sectors of education has been entirely omitted—the area of the creative arts. Educational thinking has not yet reached the stage of acknowledging the capacity of the arts to educate, or the possibilities of the use of theater, dance, music, painting, design, sculpture, film as instruments of liberal education essential to the undergraduate curriculum. It is assumed that persons with talents in these fields should develop them in special courses in the departments and professional schools, and the function of education in the creative arts is to prepare professionals for their work in the culture. The Harvard Report on General Education, to use that document once more as a touchstone, specifically eliminated the "applied arts" from the field of general education on the grounds that they were vocational subjects and that the proper function of the college curriculum was to teach about the arts, but not to practice them.

This is one of the deepest fallacies in the whole of contemporary education. The arts, all of them, should be available to the beginning college student in exactly the same terms as any other form of knowledge, from physics to literature, and should be a central part of the curriculum for the entire four years. The place of the arts in education should be one which seizes upon their extraordinary power to educate, to liberate, and to inform. That is the reason why they should be in the curriculum, not because the country needs more professionals.

At a time when so many of this generation are genuinely interested in the arts, the colleges should be doing everything in their power both to encourage the development of education in the arts in the high school by adapting college admissions requirements to those who have practiced them, and by providing the opportunity to dance, to act, to paint, to write plays, and to gain a body of knowledge and experience in these fields which can raise the level of aesthetic awareness throughout the whole campus. Out of this will come the new talent for creative work and professional training, the new audiences for whatever is done, and the sensibility which the educated man must have if he is to be worthy of the name.

17: The Idea of
Internal Colleges

I would like to urge the idea of internal student colleges as a primary means of reorganizing the big university, and combine that with the idea of collaboration and equality in teaching and learning between the students and the faculty. At one stroke, the college can then become what it should always have been—a community of persons joined together by common intellectual and cultural interests. Many things, including the prevalence of joy, become possible, and a whole series of implications begin to unfold.

In the first place, it is clear that in the foreseeable future, even if the present system were to remain intact, there are not enough faculty members available or likely to become available to teach the students in ways more personal in style than the ways of the lecture system and all its parts. Nor is it likely that there will be an immediate rush of the academic faculty to the kind of over-all reforms demanded by the radical critics. Whatever is done to move the system from where it is now into new educational forms will have to be done in a way which deals with the present students, *now,* and which takes account of the present structure of the faculty departments.

This was the original insight of the Meiklejohn idea for his Experimental College at the University of Wisconsin in the 1920s and 1930s. Meiklejohn saw that it was possible by radical re-arrangements in the curriculum and style of teaching to create new colleges inside the existing system, and to recruit a volunteer teach-

294

ing faculty from the regular university departments. That meant that the faculty members could keep their place in the hierarchy of the system, no violence would be done to the university budget, and the faculty of the college could teach what they wanted to teach in the way they wanted to teach it.

The Meiklejohn idea, although it worked with great success over a limited period of time in Wisconsin, cannot be transposed, curriculum and all, into the contemporary student body. Meiklejohn's philosophy called upon the Experimental College students to accept a prearranged curriculum designed by Meiklejohn and taught by his faculty, with one year spent on studies in Greek society and culture in the age of Pericles followed by comparative studies of modern America. The pattern of instruction lay in one lecture a week to the whole college, with the rest of the work done in discussion groups led by the faculty, tutorials, and independent study.

It worked because Meiklejohn was a certain kind of genius, as a teacher, educator, and intellectual. His intellectual interests were so intense, his mind so richly stocked with ideas, his style as a teacher so provocative and stimulating, that everyone around him felt the impact of his character. He enjoyed controversy and argument, he loved having enemies and friends, and, as Robert Frost once said, he enjoyed his failures the way most people enjoy their successes. Although there was a high degree of personal relationship between Meiklejohn and his students and the students and the faculty, and although the college was connected to the wider world by summer research assignments to the students for studies of their own communities, the Experimental College remained as an intellectual enclave inside the university, with the students as apprentices to Meiklejohn and the faculty.

The problem of reviving the Meiklejohn idea as he conceived it, complete with a ready-made curriculum, no matter of what quality, lies in the radical change in sensibility within this generation of students. Those who followed Joseph Tussman's experiment in reviving a version of the Meiklejohn college at Berkeley in 1965 observed that the 1920s style was one which now had to struggle against the contemporary student sensibility. To achieve success in making it work in 1965 required a revision in educational philosophy much more drastic than either Alexander Meiklejohn or Joseph Tussman contemplated.

What is missing in it is the conception of a students' college, and student involvement in curriculum-making. Unless that is added to the idea of the internal college, the proposals for reform do not reach the center of the need. A great many new educators who support the idea of cluster colleges, with groups of students formed within the larger university framework into colleges of five hundred or so, liken it to the Oxford-Cambridge college system, with its tutorial program, general examination system, general areas of study in the humanities and the sciences, absence of lectures, and long stretches of vacation time. But too often they fail to recognize the archaic character of the British program, with its implicit paternalism, élitism and its nineteenth-century conception of the curriculum itself. The reason the British college worked so well in the past and is appealing to visiting Americans, both students and scholars, is that it is not as heavily organized as the American system, and that the student body has already been inducted into a cultural tradition before it arrives at the university.

The combination of high selectivity through difficult examinations for the individual British colleges, an intellectually and politically sophisticated student body, and a tradition of student respect for educational authority have made it possible for the British to work with students in their own way. Student responsibility toward the tutor and the college can be taken for granted. In the case of the main body of American students who have not learned either how to learn or how to develop an intellectual life of their own, neither the British college idea nor the curriculum in it is a satisfactory model for decentralizing the American university. The British universities in the last twenty years have begun to confront for the first time the meaning of diversity in cultural, economic, and social status in the British student body. They now face the necessity of a radical alteration in the paternalism which could be taken for granted in the years when the universities served the interests of a narrow sector of their society. The conception of useful knowledge which is at the same time liberal and the conception of the role of the university as a democratizing institution have now become necessary components in a new educational philosophy for use in Great Britain.

The need in the United States is essentially the same. It will not be met by a move toward the earlier British model, but by a return to the radical American tradition of the land-grant college, with its elective principle, "useful knowledge," and the emancipation of the students from the control of the curriculum. There is no single way in which that move must be made. The opportunities for movement vary from campus to campus, depending on size, present structure, the student body, disposition of university resources, and present mood of the faculty and administration. What can be done at Yale is not the same as what could be done at Michigan State, or Antioch as against New York University, Temple as against the University of Chicago, Berkeley as against Harvard. There are educational problems common to all, but a world of variety in how they can best be handled in the various stages of development of each institution toward its own destiny.

However, in the general structure of higher education, in that part of it which is growing in importance from day to day, that is, in the state institutions and the large urban universities, there are some common problems which will yield to solutions, which, if not identical, are capable of being generalized.

[II]

In the first place, it is necessary to look for the things which can be done immediately to improve teaching within the present system, while the rest of the reforms are going through official channels. This calls for reinstating the teacher as a scholar who offers a course which is truly his own, for which he is willing to be held accountable in the eyes of his students and his colleagues, for whose methods and content he is willing to take responsibility and with which he is willing to experiment. At present, too few teachers take advantage of the fact that even in the existing system, in the last analysis each faculty member is teaching his own students. If he chose to do so, he and others of like mind who cared to volunteer could create their own internal colleges inside their own classes.

My impulse in talking with my colleagues who are teaching in the colleges and universities is to urge them to stop the theoretical discussion of reform and the complaints about how hard it is to change the university, and, without asking anyone's permission, to begin whatever reforms they think would be a good idea. Go as far as you can until stopped by insurmountable obstacles or implacable colleagues and deans. In nearly every case, a teacher who is determined and imaginative can go a fairly good distance, usually as far as he wants to. He will encounter serious opposition more often when he makes proposals involving other people's teaching, under the guise of all-university curricular reform or a comprehensive educational philosophy. In his own case, if he is willing to put himself on test, with or without a few others in the test, he may raise eyebrows but he will not raise a storm.

This approach is especially important now that new demands are being made on the time and energy of faculty members in taking responsibility for students and educational change. There is a finite amount of time available for that kind of work. No matter how concerned, energetic, and devoted a faculty member may be in turning aside from his interests in research, scholarship, and his own intellectual development to work with students and colleagues on educational reform, the committee system with its endless meetings and discussions devours a man faster than tigers. There is a point at which a teacher must stop short and say to himself and his students, I am a teacher with a life of my own, you are a student with a life of your own, and although we share a number of interests and should spend a generous amount of time together in fulfilling them, there is an inviolate part of myself and my life which is neither yours nor the university's. It is my own, and I will not allow it to be completely absorbed by committees or by responses to protests. I will use my energies in the act of teaching and learning, not always at one stage removed from them both in discussions about the politics and organization of the university curriculum as a whole.

If even a minority of the faculty members begin their work in reform by a combination of action with their own students and collaboration with congenial colleagues, the curriculum is changed by that amount, and the process of university reform has begun. The existence of new forms then begins to generate other forms. Justin Morrill College at Michigan State University was organized and started within one year by a few faculty members who wanted to start it, made their plans together, then made the necessary arrangements with the other faculty members and administrators.

Theirs was not a theoretical discussion of what changes were desirable, but a program which a group of scholar-teachers were committed to trying out.

In a similar way, with initiatives of this kind, the big issue of student involvement in policy-making is solved at the point where it really matters—that is, in the actual work of the courses. A faculty member or group of faculty members simply bring together a group of their own students and their friends to talk about what kind of course, courses, or projects they could work out together which would be interesting and useful, and in which the students can share the teaching and planning. The students are then already in the policy-making because they want to be and are invited to be, and the idea of this way of sharing the responsibility for educational planning spreads to their general attitude to education and the rest of their learning.

Even if the students have this kind of experience in only one course or in one section of the curriculum, it gives them a base in the institution on which they can stand and from which they can make their expeditions into the rest of the terrain. The most important factor is to have students involved in the educational policy-making at the point where their lives intersect with the going process of the intellectual life of the campus, and not always with the abstract forms of government by student representation. Once such direct involvements begin, they spread outwards to the conception of government and policy as a whole, and form the basis for possible action in the larger sense of reorganizing the campus community and the entire curriculum. In the meantime, something can be done in one place in their lives to start it all moving. The general movement will be in the direction of giving the students more choice in creating their own education, and the elective principle is on the way.

[III]

There are also some general propositions useful to the aim of loosening up academic requirements, some general rules for what to do until the elective principle comes. Suppose, in an ideal sense, the whole institution of the modern university were conceived as a learning-teaching center, a true educating community, and suppose the students on a university-wide scale were invited to choose the areas of their study and, wherever possible, to choose the teachers and the other students with whom they would work. That conception can be held in mind as a goal by students and by those teachers who believe in it, whether or not the existing situation allows the practices that go with the ideal.

Among the existing rules and academic requirements, many of which are simply bookkeeping measures, there are a fair number of exceptions having to do with the requirements as they apply to special cases. It should be entirely possible to develop an educational program out of the exceptions, or, putting it more positively, for a group of students and faculty members to develop an interesting year or two years which could be put forward as their own way of meeting the requirements. They could be given the only kind of permission which really counts in the big university, to apply academic credit for the work that is done toward a university degree for the students, and to the teaching schedule of the faculty. A faculty member respected by his colleagues who cared to take the leadership could gather around himself a group of students and faculty members who agreed to stay together for a year, add others to the group, and build a curriculum jointly with the students. Or they could build one based on student models which the faculty could modify. What would then emerge would be a one-year college or a two- to four-year college which met the requirements but did so in a free and imaginative way.

Suppose the teacher in such a college, or, if there were no "college," within his own course simply asked to have the amount of credit for his course doubled from three to six. This would immediately double the amount of time the student could spend with him, and the amount the teacher could count toward his teaching schedule. It would involve no additional appointments to the teaching staff, no increase in the budget, nothing but the consolidation of the teaching and learning under far better conditions. It would also mean the reduction of the number of courses the student was obliged to take from five to four, or from four to three, while still enrolled as a full-time student. One of the greatest obstacles to good education is the overcrowding of the student's schedule each semester with too many courses and not enough time for any of them, with its corollary defect, the lack of concentration by the faculty with one group of students long enough to do any serious work with them.

There is room for a completely new sector of educational experiment inside the present system if a way could be found to alter the regular student schedules to allow for a different rhythm and different duties during the ten to fifteen weeks of each term. The quarter terms, or the two or three semesters, should be thought of as blocks of time, to be used in a whole variety of ways and durations. There is no need to keep the automatic scheduling of four to five courses taught in three fifty-minute sessions a week with a fifty-minute discussion added to each course. There is no reason students should be enrolled in five courses at a time. That is only the result of having chained the program to the units of credit and the subject-matter requirements. Educationally, it is madness.

The students' weeks are now filled with an average of fifteen periods of listening to lectures and five hours of discussion with graduate assistants, and whatever reading or laboratory work is done during the rest of the time. That is literally the extent of the students' education. In the case of the commuting students, who in most cases in the urban universities and state colleges make up from 60 to 70 per cent of the total student body, there is not even the informal conversation and discussion of the residential campus. Under the present system, the commuting students naturally make an effort to arrange their schedules so that their classes fall in succession on given days, so that they can be dealt with as quickly as possible before the student goes home or off to work.

When the matter is put baldly, in terms of how the students are *asked* by the system to spend their time and how they actually spend it, the one-dimensional quality of the definition of education itself is revealed in all its weaknesses. For the student it is like listening to an orchestra playing a repertory always with the same volume of sound, like Muzak, the same instrumentation, the same gestures by the conductor, the same style of music played by musicians who are tired of it. We know from personal experience in a country filled to the brim with after-dinner speakers, meetings with speeches, politics with public-address systems, churches with sermons, that what is taken away from listening to a speaker is enormously less than what the speaker thinks it is and what is desirable for educational purposes. We have enough educational research at hand to prove a hundred times over that concentrated effort on the part of the learner for consecutive periods of time is not only a more natural way to learn, but that more is learned in the equivalent period. Life is not divided into unnatural fragments of temporal units; it flows from one moment into the next, and it is only in institutions that life is converted into artificiality.

[IV]

One immediate change which could be made, aside from bringing students together with teachers of their own choice, would be to change the schedule to make two- to three-hour blocks of time available within a given course, with the course defined as a project for organizing a variety of experience for the students who are in it. If there must be lectures, let them be short, not more than twenty minutes to half an hour, in a session running for an hour and a half, in which, for a large class, there would be questions from the floor, a half hour of discussion by the students in small groups, followed by further questions, perhaps to a symposium of students with the teacher as chairman. The students can prepare themselves in previous weeks for their appearance in such a symposium through research, reading, and discussion.

Another change which could be made even before throwing out the apparatus of credit would be to reduce the number of courses taken at one time, with the student's schedule divided into half-days, allowing time for field research, community work, evening sessions, and greater depth of concentration. This could be linked with the idea of three or four faculty members collaborating in a sequence of studies which allowed full-time concentration by the student over a period of three to four weeks within a given field, followed by an equivalent length of time in another field; or what might be called a series of institutes could be organized throughout the year, in the style of the three- and four-week summer institutes which concentrate on a given set of studies in a single area.

This would bring the commuting students together with everyone else for the sustained periods of work which they rarely have either the invitation or the opportunity to undertake, but which they badly need. There are many new ways in which the outside life of the commuting student could be connected with his life on the campus by simply rearranging his schedule and by locating him in a student-organized seminar from the freshman year on. There he would find a place in the university which was his own. He would find himself with that group of companions in learning which every student needs in order to take his place within the larger community.

Suppose the teacher, equipped with his luxurious six-credit teaching time in an internal college or in his own course, worked with a loosely held syllabus, a general guide to what he intended to do, with open spaces in which 200 students working with him in the social sciences and/or humanities would be able to move. Suppose the students were asked to work in groups to form the design of their studies, to decide on research they proposed to carry out, and to make assignments among themselves of the persons who would take responsibility for this or that task. These could include writing a short research paper to be used, for example, as an annotated bibliography by the other students, or for information about a special problem. Others could take assignments for making arrangements with community groups for the study of community issues, for leading seminar discussions, for giving an occasional lecture. Suppose that most of the writing the students did was written for use by the other students, read by them and discussed by them, with a record of the discussion kept by one of the students and mimeographed, as would be the other papers, for distribution to the rest.[1]

In completely practical terms, this would reconstruct the teaching system in a way which is perfectly natural for the students, who, in their work as student activists are already teaching each other in this style, and in many institutions have already prepared their own courses, study guides, annotated bibliographies, counter-curricula, and work-study programs. Instead of going against the students, as in theory and practice the present system requires, this would build from student strength and inclination, with the ethos of participatory democracy accepted as the center of the educational conception. The students would be choosing their own student leaders, having chosen their own teacher. The external struc-

ture of the "course" or "action" is set in broad outline by the knowledge and professional skill of the teacher; the inner structure is
the work of the students in building a body of knowledge and an
intellectual and cultural framework for themselves. Each student
would have his own place to stand and, as among athletes and
musicians, would have his own place in the esteem of the others
by reason of the commitment and talent he demonstrated in his
performance as a student in the company of others.

In a reconstructed teaching system of this kind, many things
would begin to happen, two in particular. The pernicious and
pervasive goal of competitive academic achievement and grade-
getting would be dealt a fatal blow, and the student would be recognized as the person he revealed himself to be in the eyes of his
teacher and his colleagues among the students. The talented student
would be honored in the tribute he received from the others by
their invitation to him to take on assigned tasks, not by being sin-
gled out for awards in connection with the Dean's List. The faculty
member chosen by the students would be at the center of an internal community composed of the members of his course. He would
be a teacher in the usual sense—one who knows more and is better
able than non-teachers to teach what he knows and to teach how
to do what he can do. But he would also be an educator, that is,
one who applies what he has learned in teaching to the problem
of creating situations in which others can learn what they need
to know.

The decentralization so crucial to the reduction of anonymity
and apathy within the big university could then proceed by natural
causes, not by administrative rulings and committee reports talked
to death by the entire university. With the restoration of only this
part of the elective principle, even those in the university who are
repelled by the idea of student freedom and involvement in policy-
making would still have their own chance to teach in their own way.
For some students, the regular system and its teachers might be
more appealing, since it is an easier one, with fewer expectations
and demands. But even here, as in the past, the precision of reference in the folk-wisdom of the student body about the quality of
teaching and of the persons who teach would act as a deterrent to
downright bad teaching and as an encouragement to good teaching.

[v]

Most of the attention among student reformers toward the evaluation of teaching and teachers has until now been concentrated on formal, all-university ways of organizing student committees or student-government projects. Most often, the students send around questionnaires whose results are to be used either in the guidance of students toward good teaching or by the administrative officers of the college in considering appointments and judging the qualifications of the faculty. There are many sensitive questions here, difficult for students to answer. Among them is the prerogative of the community of scholars to choose its own membership, and the defensiveness many faculty members feel toward the idea of having students given the power to influence judgments about the position of faculty members in the university when the students do not have the knowledge and experience in scholarship to qualify them to make such judgments. The specter of the Latin American university is summoned up by the critics, as are fears that if students had the power of appointment they would turn the faculty into sycophants or political manipulators.

On the other hand, there *is* a fund of knowledge in every student body about the quality of teaching, and in the experimental colleges ways have been found to put it to use in helping to improve the quality of learning as well as of teaching. At Sarah Lawrence, this is done by an elected all-college curriculum committee, which, depending on its membership during a given year, has taken on studies of the work in various sections of the college, analysis of the course offerings, and through interviews with those in the courses has developed reports and recommendations of all kinds which have been of very great use in the work of the faculty curriculum committee with whom the students meet at regular intervals.

The students have also been very useful to individual teachers, since in the Sarah Lawrence teaching program students have considerable individual initiative within each course, with independent study, team research projects, and extensions of the general material used for the whole class into individual projects developed by students under a system of contracts. By this is meant that a student makes a contract with the teacher (this could also be made with a class) to deliver a designated piece of work of a certain kind—a field study, a research paper, a critical essay, an annotated bibliography, a report—by a certain date. In this way, within the course itself there is a constant evaluation, informal and natural, of the teaching and learning, and things which are going wrong, either on the part of the teacher or the student, have a chance to be corrected in the regular flow of the year's work.

In the case of the larger university, very little has been done to apply this concept of evaluation of teaching to the sections of the curriculum in which the students are involved at the time of their involvement. The emphasis has been on the formal organization of student evaluation of teaching in the whole university. As in other cases of students' sharing in educational policy-making, the work is best done at the point where their own education is at stake, rather than in their necessarily becoming legislators of policy for the whole institution. Once the university has been formally organized into students on one side and faculty members on the other, then the problem is one of getting them together again. If the faculty members on their side apply mechanical methods of evaluating students, the students learn to apply similar methods to the faculty.

On the other hand, if the learning and teaching, the students and the faculty, are organized as two sectors of the same enterprise, it becomes natural for students to involve themselves in reporting and recommending to their teachers ideas for change and improvement. These depend not merely on changes the teacher is asked to make in his own teaching style and method, but on changes in the way the students learn, based on their own evaluation of themselves in the role of learners and self-teachers.

This argues for the kind of informal and formal advisory committees of students suggested by the Berkeley Commission on University Governance for work with the departments. Advisory groups of twenty to thirty students would collaborate with a designated member of the department, ideas for special projects and courses could be worked out by the students, and students could be assigned to teachers in the department who shared the particular student's interests. The commission suggests that what might be called a Council of Majors be established, in which selected or elected students would represent the other students in a given field in discussions with the department about educational questions and policies, linking the student advisory committees to the on-going plans of the department itself. In this way, the internal structure of the university and its departments is changed, by bringing the students into close touch with the policy-making while at the same time preserving the opportunity for colleagues of like interests and intellectual ambitions to work together in their disciplines and subject-matter fields. The role of the student is complementary to that of the faculty, not in opposition to it, and the university structure is redesigned from the inside out, rather than from the top down or by outside student force.

18: Students as Teachers

When a university sets out to reform its educational program in direct collaboration with students, the quality of teaching and learning is immediately affected. In the first place, the academic departments have to be much more careful in making appointments to the faculty exclusively on the basis of publication records and academic reputation. Inability to teach, or even disinterest in teaching, then becomes a potential source of embarrassment to the administration and to the departmental chairmen and their advisory committees. Too much concern with academic prestige and research ability, for even a limited period of time, means that soon there are not enough good teachers to go around, not enough scholars who enjoy working with students, or, what is worse for the departmental interest, not enough students to fill the classes and therefore not enough appointments available to sustain the size and position of the department in the university structure.

On the positive side, the academic faculty, when it collaborates with students in the development of courses and educational policy, has the very great advantage of working within its own disciplines with students whose talents and motivation in these fields begin to flourish at a higher level, both in teaching and in learning. Among the cooperating students, a far greater proportion than before becomes interested in working at an even higher level, with intellectual capacities of a broader range because of the experience they have had in their beginning courses and projects. The faculty thus finds itself with a breeding ground for future teaching and research talent and for the development of intellectual interests directly related to their own.

As for policy-making and government in student affairs, a great deal of this can be better arranged by students than by faculty members and administrative officers. The experimental colleges, particularly Antioch, Goddard, and Sarah Lawrence, have given students responsibilities in student affairs which in other colleges are handled entirely by college staff, and have found that not only the policy-making but the administration works in ways which call upon resources in students which would otherwise remain undeveloped. By bringing the students actively into the administration itself, the administrative problems of college life confront the students directly, and refute the idea that anyone who is an administrator belongs to the enemy camp.

The Sarah Lawrence pattern is one in which the Student Council not only has the power of deciding on the rules for the student community, from dormitory hours to chartering organizations, but the responsibility for administering their own rules through a council of vice-presidents of the student houses. In the case of student legislation which in the view of the administration or faculty is unwise or misguided, the opportunity exists for a reconsideration in a joint committee of elected faculty members, elected students, and administration. The joint committee holds the power of ultimate decision in matters of college policy in general. An appeal could of course be made beyond that body to the board of trustees, but to make such an appeal would mean to admit the failure of the very system which brings the students into a position of responsibility for their own college.

In view of the time and energy absorbed by the administration of student affairs by students, it is also necessary to consider that factor in planning a student schedule of education in the college, and in some cases to relieve a student of course work during a given semester or college year, and to pay a stipend for the services rendered to the community. When the educational program is arranged in such a way that the experience of organizing education on behalf of others is a genuine opportunity for the student, he may learn more from that kind of responsibility over a limited period of time than he would in the formal studies which would otherwise occupy him.

This is especially true of those who intend to become teachers or to enter one of the professions where the ability to organize oneself and to develop programs of use to others is a necessary corollary to whatever scholarship and learning one may possess in the field. The experience in personal relationships, in sustaining the delicate lines of connection which flow between persons and groups who are working in voluntary ways to achieve a common end, is a very important one for students in the entire field of the human services and the arts. The student of theater who has not learned to collaborate with others in the work of the theater, and who has not learned what is involved on the practical side in putting a production on the stage, is in the same position as a student who has not learned to do what has to be done when any useful human enterprise involving cooperative effort is set in motion.

[II]

This brings me to another matter basic to the reconstruction of the learning-teaching system, the matter of graduate students and their role in teaching. Their present status as teaching assistants to professors is a function of the lecture system and all its parts, not the result of an examination of how education may best be conducted through the talents which students of all kinds can bring to the teaching system. It is now a truism to say that in most cases in the big universities the graduate students provide one of the few opportunities for personal contact by the undergraduates with the teaching faculty. The rest is a matter of sitting in lectures. The graduate students know this, and are fully aware of the dependence of the present economic and cultural structure of the university on their work in teaching. At many universities they have organized Graduate Student Unions both to advance their economic interests and to influence educational policy. Their ranks contain some of the most intelligent, imaginative, and energetic educators the country has ever seen. The fact that they do not yet possess teaching credentials and higher degrees cannot disguise the fact that they are already functioning as teachers, regardless of faculty status— teachers who are working under wraps by the status they now occupy.

What is true of the graduate schools is true of the whole educational system and the society at large. Everywhere the idea of specified and certified professional and vocational skills, only available for public use after certified institutional training programs, has taken hold of the country's institutional life. It has substituted itself for the idea that anyone who can demonstrate in action the quality of what he knows and what he can do has no need of diplomas and credentials in order to do it. Except in the case of brain surgeons and a limited range of professional talents, the certification is unjustified.

A move away from the pattern of the credential society is essential as the first step toward breaking down the barriers to the full use of all human talent, certified or uncertified. Psychiatric aides, for example, who spend more time with patients than anyone in the mental hospital staff and who have a serious degree of influence on the progress of the patients' recovery, should be given the recognition and responsibility that comes with their function. So should teachers' aides, student assistants in child-care centers, community volunteers, community workers without formal education. Once the obvious fact is recognized that education is an amalgam of influences and not simply a transaction between academic professionals and pupils who appear before them, the way is open for the full use of human resources of all kinds within the schools, the colleges, and the universities.

The students who have organized store-front colleges and street academies have already recognized the ability of ordinary people, without certificates and formal training, both to teach and to learn. Among those recruited by the students as tutors for their projects are high school drop-outs, mothers of children, automobile mechanics, former convicts, college professors. Others at the University of North Carolina and elsewhere have organized "poor people's universities" and in one instance have developed a category of university professor whom they call "poor professors," which, although open to wide misinterpretation, refers to poor people in the community who come to college classes in the humanities and social sciences to talk about social issues and realities from their position in the middle of poverty.

In the case of teachers like David Riesman, in whose undergraduate courses graduate assistants are given an opportunity to collaborate directly both in the teaching and in the educational planning, there is no particular status problem, since Riesman and others like him deal with the assistants as intellectual and teaching colleagues, not as hired hands to carry out tasks for which professors have no time or inclination. But in the system as a whole the graduate assistant, whose maturity of outlook and practical teaching experience qualify him as a full-fledged teacher, finds himself in the absurd situation of acting as a handy man when he should be recognized as a major element in the conduct of university instruction.

There is no need to repeat again the account of how this situation is related to failures of graduate education in general, and the lack of connection between the requirements for the doctoral degree and the preparation of students for teaching assignments in the colleges and universities. What is needed is a conception of teaching and learning which reaches back into the undergraduate student body and considers undergraduates and graduate students as members of one community, capable of teaching each other. There are many juniors and seniors in the colleges and universities whose gifts as teachers and educational leaders are presently ignored, and, were a different attitude to the curriculum and its operation taken by the university, could become a major element in the improvement of undergraduate learning.

I have already referred to the organic unity of undergraduates and graduate students within the civil rights and activist groups, and their intellectual and practical collaboration in educational and political projects without regard to age level or academic status. There is no reason why that kind of collaboration cannot be made a regular part of the teaching system. It requires only the initiative of the faculty to set it in motion, with or without an educational plan for the whole university. A faculty member is free to call upon individual members of his undergraduate classes, both those in the present classes and those whose work in previous classes recommended itself to their teachers, to act as seminar and discussion leaders, tutors, organizers, and aides in educational planning and teaching.

A budget should be provided to allow a teacher or group of teachers to appoint undergraduates with teaching talent who had previously worked within particular courses, with the students invited to reduce their course schedule in a given semester in order to give teaching assistance as aides in a course, with a stipend to match. Freshmen entering the university could be given the advantage of choosing a student adviser from among those appointed to such a student staff; the staff could organize a seminar and tutorial plan by which the freshmen could become involved in the discussion and clarification of the problems of becoming educated at the university. This simply pushes to a larger dimension the informal advising system which already exists among students, but which at present bears the handicap of not being part of a serious effort to give the entering student a chance to find his bearings and to establish a sense of colleagueship with students more advanced than himself in the educational system.

There are many in the ranks of the graduate students who have earned the right to teach students of their own, and who could supply the basic resources for the teaching staff of the freshman and sophomore years, as well as in the upper division. If they were invited to collaborate with the faculty in planning seminars and programs, this could replace the lecture system with one more in keeping with the needs of the undergraduates. Whenever lectures were needed, these could be supplied by calling together a number of the individual seminars into one class for a joint session to be addressed by a lecturer chosen for the particular contribution he could make to the problems under consideration in the seminars. Collaboration among the seminar teachers would be possible, not only in this way, but in many others. Individual students could combine their talents in symposia to be presented to a group of the seminars; outside visitors from the community, the faculty, and the graduate-student roster could also be included.

This would entail a different kind of organization within the graduate divisions themselves. In a given semester, as part of the master of arts or doctoral degree program, a student would spend the whole of his time, with an appropriate stipend, in the work of an undergraduate seminar, with the seminar materials and supervision of undergraduate projects considered as an integral part of the work of the graduate student in developing his own body of knowledge within his chosen field. There is no more effective way of organizing such a body of knowledge of one's own than by teaching it. The rationale for the semester or year of work of a graduate student as teacher is not simply that it would give the future college professor experience in teaching as a necessary component of his preparation, but that it would deepen his scholarship and his intellectual resources by the process of discovering what it was he had learned which was useful to others in the culture.

The rationale could also be extended to the undergraduate curriculum, where, in connection with work in psychology, anthropology, literature, sociology, physics, biology, or mathematics, the students would be asked, as part of their regular work, to volunteer for tutoring assignments with children or with high school students in areas and subjects where help was needed and in which the undergraduate had competence.

When the entire educational system is seen in terms of its interconnections through teaching and learning, not as a series of interlocking social and cultural agencies separated from each other by bureaucratic rules and testing devices, the stream of consciousness which runs from the child to the adolescent to the young adult and beyond then becomes the most vital and important thing about it. Links between one consciousness and another become the crucial matter, not the discontinuities and separations which the institutions make within themselves and among each other. The continuity of experience between the internal life of the school and college and the life of the society becomes a natural educational concept, with broad implications for the union of talents found within the educational institution and the need for these talents for education in the community. The curriculum of the college is then joined to the reality of the society, and through their union the student can learn to locate himself in the wider world and to act upon it. It is this continuity in consciousness which gives the basis for planning the internal life of the university so that at every point the students are linked to others, and education for students becomes the series of influences and experiences through which they teach and are taught.

[III]

How then do we proceed, finally, to accomplish the reforms? Where do we take hold? Who makes the next moves?

It will be clear from what I have been saying up to now that my view is that the moves must be collaborative; they must be made by the faculty, the administration, and the students together. I would add that it does not matter who moves first, as long as the students are centrally involved in what is done. The students can become involved by invitation of the faculty or the administration, by their own initiative, by a new curriculum, by the student's natural attachment to a student organization which is itself involved in educational reform. But in the last analysis, it is the responsibility of the university of which they are a part to find ways of creating the involvement by the structure of the internal life of the college.

The movement in reform can therefore start at any point, without the necessity of another faculty report, by simply taking seriously the proposition already stated that the best place to start a reform movement to improve a student's education is directly in the area of his intellectual life as this is lived at the university— that is, in the courses, on the campus, with his teachers.

The simplest way to set in motion a reform movement which starts in the working areas of the student's intellectual life is to take the educational questions one year at a time, that is, to set a group of interested faculty members and students to work on re-thinking the freshman year, with some relation between their work and that of another group considering how the freshman year develops into the sophomore year. This would be linked to plans for the junior and senior years, with students drawn into the planning from each of the years in view of the recency of their experience and the degree of their talent and interest. In the case of the freshman year, many of the universities have their only connection with the high schools through the admissions office, in the review of transcripts and sometimes interviews with candidates. In some cases, the universities invite high school students to come to the campus for a day's visit, or they show films in the high schools and before community groups of football games or documentaries about the university. In other cases, in connection with some of the new programs for the relatively unprepared entrants, summer sessions are arranged to get the new students ready for entry in the fall.

An extension of the idea of linking each year of education with its preceding one, and the idea of involving students in the university curriculum, would entail the appointment of students, with an

appropriate stipend, not merely to the faculty admissions committee, but to a student admissions staff drawn from a list of students
recommended by the faculty. These students could visit local high
schools, possibly taking a sabbatical leave during the first semester
of the sophomore or junior year; they could visit high school classes,
talk to the students and teachers there, and lead discussions of the
courses and programs presently available to freshman students, and
of other ones which the high school students would like to see organized in view of what they have already learned in high school
and what they would most like to do when they first enter the university.

From the body of material collected by the student-traveller and
reports made to the student-faculty committee on the freshman
year, ideas for patterns of study and programs could be developed
for the entering freshmen, each of whom could be asked to prepare for himself a study plan, or general outline of courses and
their content, to be included among other materials presented as
qualification for admission. Or the applicants could be asked to join
with other students in the high school who were applying for admission, and to organize groups among themselves, on the basis of
common interests, to develop ideas for projects and areas of study
in which they would like to work during their freshman year at the
university.

A program of this kind would have a direct effect in stimulating
some new educational thinking among students and teachers in the
high school about what to do with the junior and senior years aside
from carrying out the obligatory academic exercises necessary to
meet the present admissions requirements. There could emerge
from this an internal curriculum in the high school through which
the students, in order to improve their qualifications for admission
to the university, could work with elementary and junior high
school students as tutors and assistant teachers. Again, the rationale, as in the case of the graduate students, is that the best way
to learn how to organize one's own education is to learn how to
help others with theirs.

This could then serve a double purpose for the university. It
would give to the faculty members who were planning the freshman
year some fresh and interesting material for use in developing the
freshman curriculum. It would help the admissions office to select

the most promising students for admission, not exclusively in terms of their grades, rank in class, and academic credits, but by reference to the level of their intellectual interests and capacities, their talent for self-education, their potential contribution to the student community, their potential ability as teachers, community workers, artists, educational aides, and reformers once they arrived at the university.

The student appointee to the staff of the admissions office and the admissions committee, working with the committee on the freshman year, could review the study plans of high school students, along with the other admissions material from the applicants, some of which would be coming from students in the schools he had visited and whom he would know. From that material the student staff member could present ideas to the committee on the freshman year for various kinds of grouping within fields of study, distributing the freshmen throughout the university in terms of their interests, and organizing the teaching program around them.

One of the assignments for the entering freshmen could be to a seminar of the kind I have already suggested, similar to the exploratory courses taught at Sarah Lawrence by the faculty, to which freshmen are assigned on the basis of the account they have given of their past education and study plans in the admissions materials submitted to the college. The purpose of the exploratory course at Sarah Lawrence is to give a central place in the freshman year to each student, a place where, with whatever help and advice is needed from the teacher of the course, the student can explore the methods and materials for learning in an area of his interest and can raise a variety of questions on topics of concern, ranging from problems in handling the college life to issues of college policy or public affairs.

This kind of seminar provides the common intellectual experience for which the curriculum-makers have been in search, along with a sense of identification with the university, by the directly personal way in which the freshman seminar conducts its business, and the possibility of coming to know intimately and in the setting of a university class other students with similar interests and similar problems. In our experience at Sarah Lawrence, the exploratory course gave to each student a place to begin, a set of intellectual companions, and a central person in the faculty to whom one could go for advice and help on any matter connected with the experience of being in college.

When graduate students and upperclassmen are involved in advising and teaching this kind of freshman seminar, and sophomores and others are involved in the work of the admissions committee and the development of the freshman year, they create a completely new style of educational thinking. They bring to their colleagues in the faculty a wealth of empirical knowledge about students, and educational thinking can proceed on the basis of that knowledge rather than on generalizations about the student as an abstraction. They break down the barriers which separate the academic faculty from the student body, and introduce the idea of the learning-teaching community to replace the concept of the manufactured curriculum taught by hired hands.

They also produce a way of bridging the gap between the administration and the students, by carrying out some of the administrative tasks in cooperation with the administrators. In the case of the student members of the admissions staff, for example, there is no reason why such students should not correspond with high school applicants about their study plans, and prepare mimeographed material which would be useful to the high school student in understanding what would be expected of him when he comes to the university, and what he could expect to find available to him once he arrives there. Entering students can then learn to identify the university with its student body and not simply with its officials and their official pronouncements.

The same kind of approach through student-faculty planning can be taken to the sophomore year, with the returning sophomores asked to prepare preliminary study plans for themselves during the spring of the freshman year. Student members of the student-faculty committee staff could work during the summertime on the collation of the student plans into general outlines of possible courses, projects, and study groups, for use by the faculty in preparing the sophomore course offerings. In the case of the junior and senior years, when most students want to work in a major field, something approximating the student Council of Majors recommended by the Berkeley Commission on University Governance could be organized to work with the departments in making plans for courses in special fields of study.

Liberal allowances of choice could be made for students not yet ready for a full commitment to a specialized field; their programs could include a wider spread of courses, independent study under the supervision of graduate students, or work on a student research team with similar supervision. Not only would this keep the departments in touch with the changing needs of their clientele, but it would give them the benefit of many new ideas for undergraduate course offerings and different forms of organization, while linking their graduate students to the problems of the scholar-teacher.

In this way, from the freshman to the senior year and beyond, a new and sizeable internal network of student teachers and policy-makers would be created on a university-wide scale. There would then be a basis for a far greater cohesion of interest in the student body as a whole and a wealth of opportunity for the undergraduates to combine forces among themselves in creating their own education and in finding close associates and colleagues who shared their interests. Out of that network can come the formal structure of student involvement in basic university policy questions, by elections from the student body, by nominations from both the students and faculty for appointments of students to the faculty bodies, administrative committees, and staff of the university. Through the existence of this internal structure, the primary elements of a true community of learning would have been assembled to carry out the tasks in which it is the business of that community to engage itself.

[IV]

The task of reform in education and society has no end, but only new beginnings. Reform goes on, planned or unplanned, in one way or another way, usually at a pace many years behind the need, by the efforts of those few who cannot be satisfied with what they find, and look for better ways, and by the necessities of historical change which keep pressing upon all institutions and testing their capacity for alteration and survival.

This is the first age in which so many untamed and unmanageable necessities have been pressing all at once, and the first age in which the historical circumstances have combined to produce a younger generation so fully aware of those circumstances. In other times it was possible to say that that is the way things go in the universities. The students enter and leave, the society changes and moves on, the universities stay at the quiet center, giving the mind its due, keeping the ideals of civilization alive.

It is clear that this is no longer a possible attitude, although the necessity for the quiet center continues to exist, and the protection of the ideals of civilization was never more urgent or necessary. The difference now is that the university is already engaged with the necessities and must act to engage itself with them now, on its own terms, without the time to speculate, but only time to confront. The society will not stand still, even to be studied and observed. It insists on acting.

In this situation of the university, once more the students are its greatest allies, and if some of them have declared themselves to be its enemies, let them be met by those in the universities who know and can teach that the real enemy of the university is ignorance, force, and violence, and that the way to overcome these is by knowledge, a passion for justice, and a commitment to truth.

For it is in the ideal of a community of concerned persons who share a common interest in the life of the mind and the quality of human experience that the genius of the university lies. The rest is a matter of how that community can best be constructed by the best efforts of all concerned. There is nobility and strength in the lovely old words "fraternity," "equality," "liberty and justice for all"—and the university is the place where these words can become names for the living experience of those within its environs. Unless the reality of that experience is to be found there, it is unlikely to be found in the larger world. Unless students learn through what they do there that equality is a two-edged sword, that fraternity means giving part of oneself away, that liberty is an affectionate state of mind, and that justice in a democracy is willingness to be faithful in action to agreed-upon principles, all the protest, controversy, radical action, and appeal to the big abstractions of moral enthusiasm will come to nothing but a continual attrition of the very ideals of which the young are in search.

That is why education and the university must both be redefined so that they may become instruments through which the influence of persons on each other may act to secure the elevation of spirit and quality of life which it is the purpose of all education to induce. The university should be a place where students help their teachers to teach them, where teachers help their students to learn, where administrators help both to accomplish what they have come together to do. That is why the role of the students must also be redefined, in order to make clear to them and to all others that students *are* the foundation of the university, that when everything else is taken away, as in fact it can be—the government contracts, the isolated research institutes, the alumni bodies, the services to industry, the travelling faculty, the organization men—what is left are persons working together to learn and to teach.

Learning and teaching in this sense have to do with the totality of human conduct, in which the conduct of the affairs of the mind is by turns political, social, public, private, intellectual, emotional, external, internal, and, in the last analysis, personal. Otherwise conduct has no meaning, the human act is stripped of motivation, empty of content, lacking in truth.

The education of students, therefore, means nothing less than their personal involvement in the conduct of the affairs of the mind. An equality of position in the polity of the community is a necessary condition of their involvement; otherwise they are playing a game the necessity for whose rules they never learn to understand —the commitment to play is never completely made. What the world needs above all is a large and increasing supply of incorruptibles, men and women who have learned to act in the interest of mankind, who are capable of noble action as an outcome of unpremeditated thought, and are capable of clarity of thought as a natural and intuitive result of their experience in thinking and in acting. It is the responsibility of the university so to arrange its affairs that the experience of its students in thinking and acting can teach them what it means to serve mankind and what it means to honor the intellect.

Notes

[CHAPTER 1]

1. According to a Harris poll taken in the spring of 1968.
2. A survey conducted by Danel Yankelovich, Inc., for *Fortune* magazine in its January, 1969 issue estimates a total of 750,000 college students who "now identify with the New Left," and 58 per cent who look at college as a way of improving their economic and social status, with 42 per cent holding sentiments in favor of using their education for making a personal contribution of some kind to society. The survey involved 718 men and women between the ages of 18 and 24, of whom 334 were attending college in October of 1968. My own estimates are based on visits to more than fifty colleges over the past two years in connection with a research study on the education of teachers, and are more subjective than those of the *Fortune* survey, although in general they agree. I would consider the 42 per cent of what the *Fortune* survey calls "fore-runners" to be high, when individual campuses across the country are considered, with the percentage varying from 5 to 10 per cent on same campuses, 30 to 40 per cent on others.
3. Leonard Woolf, *Sowing: An Autobiography of the Years 1880 to 1904.* Harcourt, Brace & World, Inc., New York, 1967.
4. James Perkins, *The University in Transition,* Princeton University Press, Princeton, N. J., 1966, 90 pp., pp. 44–45.

[CHAPTER 2]

1. Quoted by Richard Mowrer, "Unrest in Spain," *The New Leader,* New York, February 13, 1956, p. 14.
2. "The Universal Declaration of Human Rights—Promise and Fulfillment,"

322

Address by General Carlos P. Romulo, Secretary of Foreign Affairs of the Philippines, at the anniversary celebration of the Universal Declaration of Human Rights, United Nations General Assembly, Dec. 9, 1968, 7 pp., mimeographed, p. 7.

3. Quoted by Janet Flanner, writing in *The New Yorker*, July 20, 1968, p. 52. The conversation between Sartre and Cohn-Bendit appears in *"La Revolte Etudiante,"* published by the French newspaper *Le Seuil*.

4. For a full discussion of these and other issues, see *The World as Teacher* by Harold Taylor, New York, Doubleday & Co.; and *The Idea of a World University* by Michael Zweig, edited by Harold Taylor, Carbondale, Illinois, Southern Illinois Press, 1966. The latter book includes a summary of present organizations and institutions, ranging from the World Academy of Arts and Sciences to Universities and the Quest for Peace, which are working toward the conception of a world educational system. The former volume argues the case for the development within the American educational system of a world point of view, reform in the curriculum of teacher preparation, and the extension of existing relations between the United States and the schools and universities of other countries. See especially Chapter 5, "The Cultural Element in Foreign Policy."

[CHAPTER 4]

1. *The Republic and the School: Horace Mann on the Education of Free Men,* Lawrence A. Cremin, editor, Bureau of Publications, Teachers College, Columbia University, New York, 1957, p. 87.

2. Hannah Arendt, *Commitment in an Age of Anxiety,* Northwestern University, Symposium 1962, mimeographed, pp. 18–19.

3. John Dewey, *A Common Faith,* Yale University Press, New Haven, 1934, p. 9.

4. New University Conference Newsletter, May 24, 1968, Chapel House, 5810 Woodlawn Avenue, Chicago, Illinois, vol. I, no. 1, p. 5.

5. Michael Rossman, "Breakthrough at Berkeley: The Anatomy of a Political Style," *The Center Magazine,* Center for the Study of Democratic Institutions, Santa Barbara, Calif., vol. I, no. 4, May, 1968, pp. 41–59.

6. *Op. cit.,* p. 42.

[CHAPTER 5]

1. John Dewey, *Reconstruction in Philosophy,* Beacon Press, Boston, 1957, pp. 154–55.

2. Quoted by Frederick Rudolph in *The American College and University,* Alfred A. Knopf, New York, 1962, 516 pp., p. 178, from William Warren Ferrier, *Origin and Development of the University of California,* Berkeley, 1930, p. 322. The quotation is from a member of the board of regents of the University of California in 1872.

3. See Frederick Rudolph, *op. cit.,* chapter 13, pp. 264–286, and Lawrence

R. Veysey, *The Emergence of the American University,* University of Chicago Press, Chicago and London, 1965, 505 pp. Rudolph and Veysey, using both the standard sources in the history of American education and a fascinating variety of original research have given, between them, a solid basis for understanding the major issues in the development of the American system of higher education. Were these volumes, with the work of Merle Curti, Lawrence Cremin, and a selection of others from the bibliographies the authors provide, to become the content of new courses in the history and philosophy of education, they would revolutionize that section of the liberal arts curriculum now so pitifully served by the educational texts and academic histories.

4. *To Learn Together,* a report from the Committee on Education and the University, New University Conference Newsletter, *op. cit.,* p. 3.
5. Ortega y Gasset, *Mission of the University,* W. W. Norton & Co., Inc., New York (edited and translated by Howard Lee Nostrand), 94 pp., p. 51.
6. Article by James Baldwin, *Mademoiselle,* May 1965, p. 15.

[CHAPTER 6]

1. Christopher Jencks and David Riesman, *The Academic Revolution,* Garden City, N. Y., Doubleday, Inc., 580 pp.
2. *Op. cit.,* p. 510.
3. *Op. cit.,* p. 513.
4. *London Sunday Times,* January 31, 1965.
5. Clark Kerr, *The Uses of the University,* Cambridge, Mass., Harvard University Press, Cambridge, 1963, 140 pp.
6. *Op. cit.,* p. 40.
7. *Op. cit.,* p. 38.
8. Erik H. Erikson, ed., *Youth: Change and Challenge,* New York, Basic Books, chapter "Youth: Fidelity and Diversity," p. 3.
9. *Meet the Press,* vol. 12, June 2, 1968, no. 22, pp. 4, 7.

[CHAPTER 7]

1. *New York Magazine,* Aug. 12, 1968, p. 33.
2. John Kenneth Galbraith, *The Industrial State,* Houghton Mifflin Company, Boston, 1967, 427 pp.
3. The Radical Education Project and its educational results are described in *The World as Teacher,* by Harold Taylor, Doubleday, New York, 1969.
4. Cited by Theodore Roszak, in *The Dissenting Academy,* Pantheon Books, New York, 1967, 304 pp., p. 9, quoted from Frederic Lilge, *The Abuse of Learning: The Failure of the German University,* Macmillan, New York, 1948, pp. 92–93.
5. New University Conference Newsletter, vol. 1, no. 1, p. 58B.
6. Richard Hofstadter, Commencement Address, Columbia University,

June 5, 1968, published in *Phi Delta Kappan,* 8th and Union Streets, Bloomington, Indiana, vol. I., no. 1, p. 15.
7. Clark Kerr, *op. cit.*
8. Richard Hofstadter, *op. cit.,* p. 15.

[CHAPTER 8]

1. *General Education in a Free Society,* Report of the Harvard Committee on the Objectives of Education in a Free Society, Harvard Univ. Press, Cambridge, Mass., 1945, 267 pp.
2. An extended discussion of the philosophy of general education and the philosophy of the Harvard Report is to be found in the *Journal of Philosophy and Phenomenological Research,* The International Phenomenological Society, Univ. of Buffalo, New York, vol. VII, no. 2, Dec., 1946, pp. 287–292; vol. VII, no. 3, March, 1947, pp. 439–452, with articles by Raphael Demos, Sidney Hook, Horace M. Kallen, Claude E. Puffer, and Harold Taylor. Also see "The Philosophical Foundations of General Education," by Harold Taylor, 51st Yearbook of the National Society for the Study of Education, General Education, 5835 Kimbark Ave., Chicago, Ill., 1952, pp. 20–45.
3. *Op. cit.,* p. 51.
4. *Op. cit.,* p. 52.
5. The Muscatine Report in 1965 at the University of California in Berkeley had the benefit of student consultation, empirical research, and philosophical analysis, but both it and the later report of the Commission on University Governance are constricted in their educational usefulness by the character of the internal political system at the university. Recommendations for radical change suffer attrition and modification on their way through the system of policy-making committees and departments. See *The Culture of the University: Governance and Education,* Report of the Study Commission on University Governance, University of California, Berkeley, Jan. 15, 1968.
6. *The New York Times,* news account, Aug. 12, 1968.
7. Hutchins, *The Higher Learning in America,* Yale University Press, New Haven, 1936.

[CHAPTER 9]

1. Daniel Bell, *The Reforming of General Education,* Columbia University Press, New York and London, 1966, 320 pp., p. 210.
2. Quoted by Jane Howard, in *The New Yorker,* Aug. 24, 1968, p. 72.
3. Norman Podhoretz, *Making It,* Random House, New York, 360 pp., pp. 51–52.
4. Pete Hamill, writing in *The Village Voice,* May 16, 1968, p. 3.
5. *Ibid.*
6. *Op. cit.*

7. *Up Against the Ivy Wall, A History of the Columbia Crisis,* by the staff of the *Columbia Spectator,* edited with an introduction by Robert Friedman, Athenaeum, New York City, 1968, 307 pp., pp. 3–4.

8. *Op. cit.,* p. 8.

9. *Op. cit.,* p. 10–11.

10. *Op. cit.,* p. 285.

11. *Op. cit.,* p. 166.

12. *Op. cit.,* p. 145.

13. *Op. cit.,* p. 147.

14. Lionel Trilling, *Beyond Culture,* Viking Press, New York, 1965, pp. ix–xviii, cited by Bell, *op. cit.,* p. 148.

15. *Ibid.*

16. Bernard Berelson and Gary A. Steiner, *Human Behavior: An Inventory of Scientific Findings,* Harcourt, Brace & World, New York, 1964, 664 pp.

17. *Op. cit.,* p. 152.

18. *Op. cit.,* p. 307.

19. *Op. cit.,* p. 308.

[CHAPTER 10]

1. There is now in existence a Union for Research and Experimentation in Higher Education which includes fourteen experimental colleges who cooperate in developing experimental projects and research, with the help of a secretariat and under the over-all administration of Dr. Samuel Baskin. Such efforts in the past have been sporadic and unrelated to the major university movements. Headquarters for the Union are at Antioch College in Yellow Springs, Ohio.

2. Notable exceptions among historians and critics of education in dealing with the progressives are Lawrence Cremin in his broad-gauged study of the progressive movement, *The Transformation of the Schools,* Alfred A. Knopf, New York, 1961, 387 pp.; and V. T. Thayer in *Formative Ideas in American Education,* Dodd, Mead & Co., New York, 1965, 393 pp.; and Frederick Rudolph in the book already referred to, *The American College and University;* the Cremin and Thayer books do not deal specifically with the experimental colleges. Professor Rudolph's account is quite brief.

[CHAPTER 11]

1. Virginia Woolf, *A Room of One's Own,* Harcourt, Brace & World, New York, 1929, p. 123.

2. Quoted from a compilation of Roethke's remarks about teaching and writing by David Wagoner, and published in *The Saturday Review,* June 29, 1968, New York, under the heading "Words for Young Writers, From the Notes of Theodore Roethke," with a note by John Ciardi, p. 14.

3. *The New Yorker,* April 7, 1962, p. 57.

4. For a fuller discussion of the contribution of Peace Corps education and practice, see *The World as Teacher,* by Harold Taylor (*op. cit.*), especially chapter 2, "Colleges for Teachers."

[CHAPTER 12]

1. Quoted by Lawrence R. Veysey, *op. cit.,* p. 107.

[CHAPTER 13]

1. Ortega y Gasset, *Mission of the University,* pp. 36–38. Italics in original.
2. R. D. Laing, *The Politics of Experience,* Pantheon Books, New York, 1967, 138 pp., p. 32.
3. *Op. cit.,* pp. 13, 14.
4. Lawrence R. Veysey, *op. cit.,* p. 302.

[CHAPTER 14]

1. Paul Goodman, *The Community of Scholars,* Random House, New York, 1952, 175 pp., p. 74.

[CHAPTER 15]

1. A full account of the World College experiment and other projects related to the idea is contained in *The Idea of a World University,* by Michael Zweig, and in *The World as Teacher,* by Harold Taylor. The latter book contains a detailed account of present movements in American education which, if strengthened, could develop a major institutional commitment on a national scale for genuine international education.
2. Letter to the *New York Review,* Sept. 26, 1968, from the Columbia Strike Coordinating Committee, p. 78.
3. Through establishing a Center for Educational Reform, financed by a $315,000 foundation grant, the National Student Association has begun to provide a larger degree of coordination within the student reform movement.
4. Quoted by Karen Duncan, in *Proposal for the Expansion of the Community Action Curriculum Project* of the U.S. National Student Association, June 28, 1968, mimeographed.
5. *Op. cit.*
6. *A Brief History* (mimeographed), Southern Student Organizing Committee, P.O. Box 6403, Nashville, Tenn.

[CHAPTER 16]

1. Report of the National Commission on Technology, Automation, and Economic Progress, *Technology and the American Economy,* Washington, D.C. Government Printing Office, Feb., 1966, vol. 1., p. 36.

2. S. 3745, 90th Congress, 2d Sess., introduced in the Senate July 9, 1968, referred to the Committee on Labor and Public Welfare.
3. Letter published in *The New York Review,* Sept. 26, 1968, p. 77.
4. *Ibid.,* p. 34.

[CHAPTER 17]

1. Dr. Marcel L. Goldschmid, of the Department of Psychology at McGill University in Montreal, has organized a course for 300 students in psychology in which the idea of student involvement has been carried out to a remarkable degree. Each student is given the option of working in one of four ways, by discussion, seminar, essay, or learning cell. Since there are no lectures, each group of students has the opportunity to study and work in those ways which seem most congenial to the self-selected groups and to their stage of preparation for independent work and to their level of intellectual and educational maturity.

Index

Rossman, Michael, 62, 64–65
Roszak, Theodore, 121
Russell, Bertrand, 190

ST. JOHN's College (Annapolis),
143
San Francisco State College, Black
Student Union, 110
community action project, 275–
276
Experimental College, 157,
263–271
trustees, 287
Sarah Lawrence College, xi, xii
curriculum, 173–175, 208–210,
305
presidency, 249, 253
student responsibility, 309
students, 34–37
trustees, 274
Savio, Mario, 25
Seelye, Julius H., 230
Society, place of the university in,
14, 51–54, 71, 74, 90, 125,
170, 242–243
Sorbonne, the, and student revolt,
23, 26, 32
Southern Student Organizing
Committee, 277
Spender, Stephen, 70
Spock, Benjamin, 219
State University of New York,
244
in Old Westbury, 245
at Buffalo, 245
Steffens, Lincoln, 204
Student League for Industrial De-
mocracy, 40
Student Non-violent Coordinating
Committee, 37, 276
Student Peace Union, 37
Student Press Association, 278
Students for a Democratic Society,
founding of, 38–46
tactics of, 106, 113, 119, 236

Swarthmore College, 37, 41

TEACHER-STUDENT relationship,
83–85, 178–183, 220–225
Teachers, Inc., 240
Testing and examinations, 173,
213–214
Textbooks, 184–185
Thomas, Norman, 40–41
Trilling, Lionel, 149–160
Trustees, 244, 246–249, 270–274
Tussman, Joseph, 295

UNITED Nations, 120–121
United States Agency for Interna-
tional Development, 42
United States Office of Education,
257, 266
University presidents, role of, 97–
98, 112–113
(*See also* Chapter 14)

VARNADO, Jerry, 110
Veysey, Lawrence, 232
Vietnam War, 37, 107, 114–123
VISTA, 61, 169, 200, 258, 266

WASHINGTON teach-in of 1965,
120
Wayne State University, black stu-
dents at, 110
Wisconsin, University of, ix, 134
Experimental College, 143,
294–295
Wofford, Harris, 245
Women students, 175
Woolf, Leonard, 10
Woolf, Virginia, 183
World College, 259–260
World War II, G.I. Bill, 16
mobilization of colleges, 132
scientists' initiatives, 115

YALE University, 36

ZACHARIAS, Jerrold, 239

About the Author

Harold Taylor became interested in students and their needs while teaching philosophy at the University of Wisconsin from 1939 to 1945. At the age of thirty he accepted the presidency of Sarah Lawrence College. Dr. Taylor's tenure at Sarah Lawrence confirmed his belief that students must be allowed to share responsibility in defining educational goals and discovering the means to achieve them. During the past decade he has extended his commitment to educational reform through study, research, extensive lecturing, and writing. Harold Taylor is author of *Art and the Intellect* (Doubleday, 1960); *Humanities in the School: A Contemporary Symposium* (Citation Press, 1968); and *The World as Teacher* (to be published by Doubleday, spring, 1969).

Dr. Taylor was born in Toronto, Canada, in 1914. He attended the Toronto public schools and in 1935 he completed his B.A. in philosophy and literature at the University of Toronto, followed by an M.A. in 1936. In 1938 he received his Ph.D. in philosophy at the University of London.